Fleeing Toward Scandal

The Secret Lives of a Runaway Kentucky Heiress
and a Nashville Aristocrat and
How They Were Exposed in Texas

Leslie E. Barras

Bon Livres

The Library of Congress has catalogued the paperback edition as follows:

Barras, Leslie E.,
Fleeing Toward Scandal: The Secret Lives of a Runaway Kentucky Heiress and a Nashville Aristocrat and How They Were Exposed in Texas

Library of Congress Control Number: 2024911431
ISBN 979-8-9907472-0-3 (pbk.)
ISBN 979-8-9907472-1-0 (ebk.)

Front: 1920s photos from *Nashville Trust Co. v New York Trust* (1940)

Book formatting: Robert Harrison, Seneca Author Services

CONTENTS

ACKNOWLEDGMENTS

New York Life Insurance Company deserves the first acknowledgement. Its corporate tenacity enabled this story to be documented because of the hordes of lawyers that sparred over Tom Buntin's life insurance benefits. John Seigenthaler's sharp memory of the Palmer story he wrote as a cub reporter for *The Tennessean* richly added to the depth of the "Exposed" chapter.

Duncan Murrell and Adam M. Rosen provided invaluable manuscript evaluations of the initial draft of this book. Laura Jones, former English language-arts educator, penned many precise improvements in syntax. Kathleen Burrows was an insightful reader. Betsy Bennett endured many updates on the status of the book. Margaret Toal, Orange, Texas, journalist and historian, helped me track down details of life in mid-twentieth-century Orange.

Preparation for this book led to in-person research at numerous repositories, where diligent staff responded to my archival needs and questions: in Nashville, Tenn., the Tennessee State Library and Archives; in Russellville, Ky., the Logan Co. Archives and Public Library; in Louisville, Ky., the University of Louisville Archives and Special Collections; in Frankfort, Ky., the Kentucky Historical Society; in Texas, the Heritage House Museum (Orange), Tyrrell Historical Library (Beaumont), and Briscoe Center for American History, University of Texas (Austin); and in Cheyenne, Wyo., the Wyoming State Archives. Zach Johnson, Associate Director of Digital Special Collections, Vanderbilt University Libraries, retrieved and scanned John Seigenthaler's notes on his reporting of the Palmer discovery.

My spouse, Kevin McAdams, was incessantly witty and wise and wonderfully supportive.

PREFACE

Imagine a time when the super-rich were not free to do what they wanted to do in their personal lives; when Kim could not cast-off Kanye, Melinda could not discard Bill, and Ivana could not dump *him*. It wasn't that long ago that this was the case. Regular people could abandon their spouses or have affairs and illegitimate children, while absolutely no one of consequence cared about or paid attention to them. The wealthy social elite were different in that regard, bound tightly by class rules. Although these rules were unwritten, they were as rigid as a whalebone stay in a corset. If the norms were disobeyed, dire consequences followed. Entire families could be branded as social pariahs.

Betty Edwards McCuddy was an independent-minded, unmarried heiress from Russellville, Kentucky. Nashville's Thomas Craighead Buntin was a socially prominent man—and married to someone else with whom he had three sons. The two were southern aristocrats and contemporaries of the fictional children of Grantham hereditary privilege in *Downton Abbey*. Like the British elite, divorce was out of the question. Resolving to make their own destiny, Betty and Tom jettisoned their early-twentieth-century birth and class entitlements for love. After disappearing in 1931, the two surfaced far away from the Upper South as the "Palmers." The couple's lives were financially precarious and grueling ever after.

I met the pair indirectly in the dairy section of the Kroger grocery store in Orange, Texas, in early December 2008. My spouse and I visited southeast Texas—my hometown area—in August 2008 from our home in Louisville, Kentucky. During a bike ride in Orange's downtown historic district, we cycled past a 100-year-old bungalow at the corner of Cypress Avenue and Ninth Street, which was posted "for sale." I was smitten. We made an offer, and it was accepted by the seller, Julia Crews Palmer Miller. The house inspection was scheduled for Friday, September 12, 2008, after we had returned home. Several days before that Friday, we nervously watched from the Bluegrass State as a substantial-looking tropical disturbance formed in the Gulf of Mexico. Julia's realtor called and suggested that we postpone the inspection. We did, also reluctantly cancelling our offer on the house. The following day, Hurricane Ike hurled winds over 100 miles per hour and brought a storm surge of nine feet to 912 W. Cypress Avenue. The house's fate was a question mark for almost a week until we learned that seawater had flowed underneath the pier-and-beam house, and not in it. We resurrected our offer and closed on the purchase in mid-November.

A few weeks later, I saw my mother's friend at the Kroger grocery store in Orange. She asked about the location of our house. When I told her, a look of sheer horror crossed her face: "oh no, that's the Palmer house!" After Hurricane Ike, I was prepared for the worst, sure that someone must have been killed in our charming bungalow. As a lawyer, I was also annoyed by her reaction—my mind immediately wondered if it would be a disclosable condition should we ever sell the place. Instead, in a lowered tone, she said that a "bigamist" couple was discovered there in 1953, putting Orange on the world stage in the worst possible way. *Life* and *Time* magazines had even covered the exposé! I was relieved; it was merely a matter of morals, not murder.

Desultorily, I searched the Internet for the Palmers and found a *Life* photo of their house in the 1953 article. It *could* be our house, but the unruly vegetation in the black-and-white photo obscured most of the dwelling. Of the parts that could be seen, the roof and porch had to have been remodeled in the version we bought. More research revealed that we had not purchased *the* Palmer house. That house was catty-corner to the back of our dwelling and faced Orange Avenue. We had, however, purchased *a* Palmer house. Our house had been owned by David Palmer, the son of Betty McCuddy and Tom Buntin, aka Betty and Tom Palmer.

Like the bungalow we purchased, the Palmer story hooked me. As I dug deeper, the pair's life choices seemed unfathomable. Tom and Betty's love story was authentic and fraught with real-life consequences that were not idyllic. They had fled *toward* scandal, not from it. Their families suppressed the reason for their disappearances in 1931, obviating a scandal at that time. Unknown to the two, Tom's life insurance company searched for them for over twenty years. Their concealed identities were ultimately exposed by John Seigenthaler of Nashville's *The Tennessean*. The young reporter's coverage of the runaway pair was distributed to a shocked worldwide audience and won the 1953 National Headliner Award, a top recognition for journalism of merit in the U.S.

THE FAMILIES

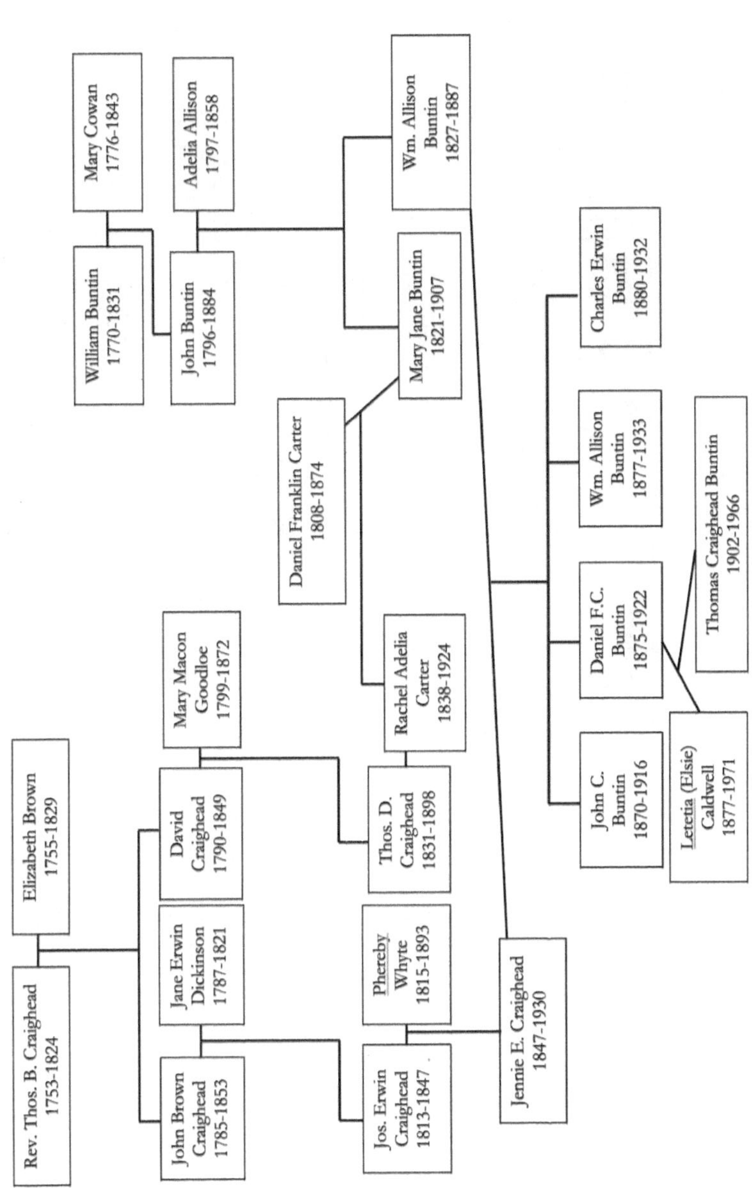

The Edwards Family Tree
(abbreviated)

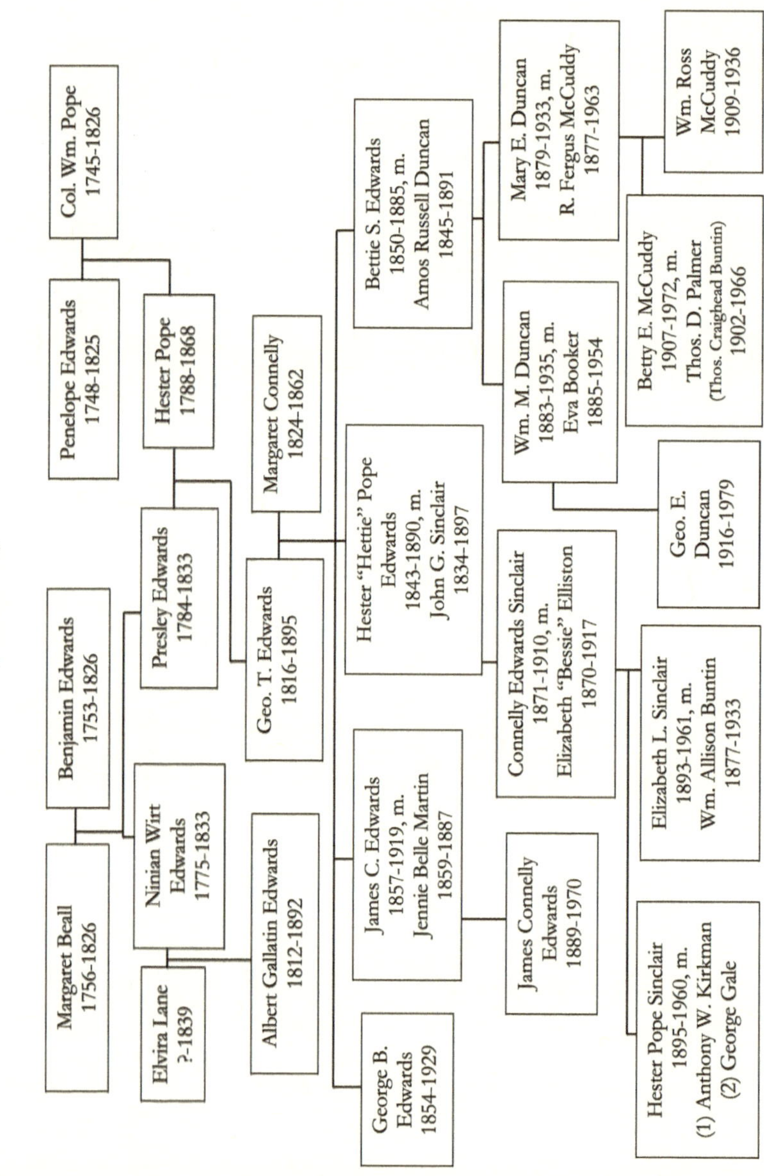

PROLOGUE

SUMMER 1931 AT ROCK REST

By 1925, Nashvillians Tom Buntin and wife Bettie Moore Buntin, both in their twenties, spent summers at Rock Rest in Robertson County with Tom's mother Elsie, widow of Daniel Franklin Carter Buntin. Summer 1931 started out no differently than any other, except that Tom developed the "flu," most likely a euphemism he and his wife used when he was recovering from an alcoholic bender. During these episodes, their three young sons were probably encouraged outdoors to swim in cool, clear creeks, climb majestic oaks, and explore spooky caves.

Robertson County was a favored enclave for wealthy Nashville families because much of the land sits at least two hundred feet higher than the land in humid Nashville and the Cumberland River that flows through the city. In the early twentieth century, summer days averaged seventy degrees, and were seldom "sultry or oppressive," while nights were cool. Before the Civil War, enslaved men quarried the county's abundant limestone and oxen hauled the material away for construction of a series of rock buildings. "Cheek's Stand" stagecoach stop and tavern was one of those properties. Daniel Franklin Carter purchased the site in 1847 and transformed the buildings into "Rock Rest" for his family's summer enjoyment. The setting may not have been the most propitious for Tom Buntin, however, because small stills were found all along the county's numerous creeks. Robertson County's pristine waters helped clandestine distillers produce sour-mash whiskey that was claimed to surpass neighboring Kentucky's bourbons in taste and quality. Regardless of the rivalry, Tom had ready access to both types of distilled spirits, even in the depth of Prohibition.

Summer living among Nashville's elite was relatively informal. Before heading to the countryside, ladies visited the exclusive Grace's Ladies Shop on Sixth Avenue in Nashville for their summer attire. In the summer of 1931, short, sporty, sleeveless frocks were in vogue, made of voile or silky, Liberty Tana Lawn cotton, in florals, stripes, and dot-and-dash patterns. Cool nights brought out shawls of alpaca, a material revived in the Paris couture shows that spring. Men discarded business suits for short-sleeved shirts, striped or plaid, with wide-leg, light-fabric trousers, and straw hats from Davitt's, an esteemed Nashville tailor.

Evenings stayed light till late, so city friends motored up for social events even though the travel was arduous because of the poor, almost impassable, condition of county roads. Bettie and Tom hosted a supper party for Tom's sister May and friends around the time of the summer solstice in 1931. Entertaining was simple in the country. The domestic staff was usually limited to one or two servants, who traveled from the city house with the family. Maids dressed in cotton, white for the morning and black or gray for the evening. Food was served buffet-style because of the reduced number of staff. Candles in candelabras stretched the interior light after late sunsets.

Tom and Bettie may have particularly looked forward to the sojourn from Nashville that summer. City newspapers relentlessly covered how Tom's uncle, Rogers Caldwell, a well-known, high-visibility southern financier, had caused southern investors, bank depositors, and businesses to discombobulate. His recklessness spread ruin and despair, but the man, now convicted for financial crimes, seemed oblivious to the fates of others. He was confident that he would rebound personally. As the weeks progressed, Bettie observed that her husband was highly nervous and excitable. He fretted about how his uncle had disgraced the family and the widespread economic distress he caused. The financial fallout had hurt Tom's insurance business as well.

Thankfully, one incident had been kept out of the newspapers. In a drunken stupor, Tom mistook the house of two elderly sisters back in the city for his mother's house and broke in when he found a locked door, scaring the spinsters out of their wits and landing him in jail briefly. There were possibly other problems that Tom had not shared with his wife. Two years earlier, Bettie hoped that his tendency to worry would be allayed when he purchased two sizeable life insurance policies from New York Life

Insurance Company. The purchase had not eased his mind. A tall man, over six feet, he had become exceedingly thin, weighing under 145 pounds. The young wife may have expected at the outset of their stay at Rock Rest that being away from day-to-day responsibilities for an extended period would improve her husband's mental and physical stability. The reverse seemed to be happening during the three-month period.

City people's summertime in the county ended each year about the time the state fair opened in Nashville. In 1931, Ringling Brothers' and Barnum and Bailey's combined circuses were bringing "fe-e-e-ro-shus" animals and the Wallenda family "high-wire performers" to town, spectacles that appealed to children the age of the Buntin boys. The event would be held September 21 through September 26. The Buntin boys' parents made plans to go the fair's horse show on September 25 with Tom's uncle, William Allison Buntin, and his wife Elizabeth, who summered near Rock Rest. Elizabeth's sister Hester would join them, accompanied by George Gale, a lawyer who owned "Rock Jolly," another summer retreat in Robertson County. Elizabeth and Hester were part of the Edwards family of Russellville, Kentucky, a small town just north of the Robertson County line.

On Thursday, September 24, 1931, Tom left Rock Rest around 8 a.m. to take his distinctive sporty-red LaSalle car to a Nashville garage for repairs. He gave his wife $1.50 when he left, which, as Bettie recalled later, was "all the money she had in the world" to support her children and herself. She never saw her husband in person again and, over two decades later, denied that he was the man in current photos shown to her.

Part One

Tom

New York Life sometimes spends more money in prosecut-
ing a fraudulent claim than it would lose by the payment
of the claim. It does this for the benefit of its other policy
holders and on the principle that the relentless prosecution
of fraud and crime is essential for the maintenance of an
orderly and law-abiding civilization.
> —Lawrence F. Abbott (1930)
> *The story of NYLIC; a history of the origins and
> development of the New York Life Insurance
> Company from 1845 to 1929*

Chapter 1

ELSIE, DAN, AND THEIR SON, TOM

"Lackluster" described Daniel Franklin Carter Buntin's real estate business in the late 1890s, consisting of the sale of modest boarding houses and cottages in Nashville. His family's well-regarded name and social standing ensured that the young man's business fortunes were on a positive trajectory, however. The Buntin name also guaranteed that his social life was active. Although Dan attended dinners, dances, and outings with a few different young women, his path often crossed that of Letetia Caldwell's. She was the only daughter of the president of Cumberland Telephone and Telegraph Company, James, and his wife May. Letetia went by the name of "Elsie."

Elsie and Dan spent Thanksgiving Eve dinner together at Nashville's Hermitage Club in November 1900. Dan then led the 1901 New Year's dance of the Girls' Cotillion Club at the Duncan Hotel with Annie Gettys of Knoxville, a guest of Elsie's. By that time, the couple could be considered an "item," though each still occasionally attended social events with other partners. It is not clear how serious Miss Caldwell and Mr. Buntin were in terms of their future together. Courtship between young women and young men of upper-class southern families in the late 1800s and early 1900s was expected to follow behavioral norms through codes of etiquette. These boundaries and codes were not often stated explicitly in relationships, but they were most certainly recognized.

Coquetry was to be avoided, as was flirting, both of which were likely to lead southern belles to marry "worthless dudes." Falling in love with a "dude" was so ill-advised that wealthy young women were counselled it would be better to "get you a monkey" for the simian was "cheaper and a great deal nicer" and the belle would avoid getting "left about as bad as the Southern Confederacy did at Appomattox." Modesty was prized as one of the few "female graces" that had "captivating powers," which heightened the interest of potential beaus, while deterring them from "rudeness," or, in other words, sexual advances.

Elsie (top) and Dan (bottom), second col. from r., seven months before they married. (Ancestry.com; original source not given.)

A society belle enjoyed an extended engagement to be married, in which she was fêted at elaborate engagement parties. Marriage vows were solemnized in a leading Protestant church, followed by a post-wedding party at which lavish gifts were displayed. These social rites were disrupted when a young woman and her beau were indiscrete before the ceremony, and she became pregnant. In those cases, the event was reported as a "quiet wedding," usually held on a weekday night, and a "surprise" to all, even the couple's closest friends.

Elsie and Dan announced their engagement in April of 1901 during a luncheon held to celebrate another young couple's wedding. The guests' announcement caused a "ripple of surprise and pleasure" among their friends "for the happy secret was unknown, save to the initiated few."

Elsie Caldwell became Mrs. Daniel Franklin Carter Buntin at an *al fresco* marriage ceremony held the evening of Wednesday, June 12, 1901, after a brief formal engagement of two months. The event was held on the lawn of her parents' estate, "Longview." The mansion and land were located along the Franklin Turnpike south of Nashville, which is today Tennessee State Route 6. In the early 1900s, the turnpike was lined with country houses, such as Traveler's Rest, Melrose, and Elmwood. "Silk stocking" road, as the turnpike was called, was favored for year-round living or as a summer place for Nashville's elites, just as Robertson County was to the north of the city.

"No marriage of recent years created more far-reaching social interest," gushed a local newspaper. Of "statuesque loveliness," the twenty-four-year-old bride was gowned in a "superb bridal robe of duchesse satin, veiled with rare rose pointe" and wore diamonds. The jewels were gifted by the groom and his cousin and foster mother, Rachel Carter Craighead, a "lady of fine social standing and abundant means." The landscape was illuminated by "myriads of electric fairy lamps" clustered on the lawn and in trees. A "glowing frame" of electric bulbs in the shapes of hearts and love knots burst forth with light as the pair took their positions in an outdoor chancel. The newlyweds left the following day for a honeymoon in Asheville, North Carolina, and then spent the rest of the summer at Old Point Comfort, Virginia, the South's leading resort at that time.

Later that year, Dan brokered a $110,000 sale of the Castner-Knott department store building on Church Street, representing Nashville's largest real estate transaction in 1901. The deal substantially boosted his portfolio experience. He also had a big idea for downtown Nashville, the city that considered itself the "Athens of the South": a covered area lined with shops, suitable for year-round strolling by fashionable people. Louisville, Nashville's closest cultural rival, had the "Kentucky Trinity"—representing "maiden, equine, and julep"—and a string of municipal parks of exquisite landscapes designed by the Olmsted firm of Brookline, Massachusetts. However, it did not have an arcade, and neither did any other place in the South. It was not an original idea. Arcades of a monumental scale stemmed from the Galleria Vittorio Emanuele II in Milan, Italy, which dictated the structural and aesthetic formula for the world's first large indoor malls: a high, elongated, glassed ceiling spanning the space between two symmetrical buildings with open balconies on the upper levels. Dan visited arcades in Cleveland and Cincinnati to evaluate American versions of the European landmark. John D. Rockefeller's $1 million structure in Cleveland, "one of the most popular business places" in the city, particularly impressed him.

While Dan was occupied with business transactions and plans, his and Elsie's first child was born. Elsie was nearing the end of her pregnancy in early 1902 and limited her social engagements to whist games at the University Club. Thomas Craighead Buntin was not delivered at the City Hospital but at Rachel Carter Craighead's home at 230 Old High St., where the Buntins had moved. There was no announcement in the *Society* section of the local newspapers, as would have been expected for a young couple from prominent families. Nor was a certificate of birth filed in the records of the Office of the Board of Health of Davidson County. Those records documented six other births that day, babies born to the wives of a laborer, painter, teacher, trolley conductor, farmer, and railroad worker. A delayed certificate of birth filed over sixty years later, after Tom Buntin was discovered living under another identity, listed his official birth date as March 16, 1902, a scant few days beyond nine months of the day of his parents' marriage.

As a child, "Master" Tom, as he was referred to in society news, played on his wooden, painted rocking horse in the yard of Rachel Carter Craighead's Old High Street house, either sitting in the leather saddle, reins in hand, or pretend-riding in the attached buggy. The child was always under someone's careful eye. "Servants," every one of which was "originally owned by the Carter family" until emancipation, tended him, along with their children. The first-born could have been called a prince in his luxurious surroundings, indulged with toys and treats, including candy-stuffed Jack Horner pies and desserts of fruit-flavored ices and bonbons. It was assumed that the only knowledge of hardship he would encounter was its definition in Webster's *Common Sense Dictionary*, not the meaning of the word as a lived experience.

"Master" Tom, ca. 1904, Old High Street, Nashville. (The Tennessean.)

Young Tom's world expanded early because his women kinfolk often traveled together, taking him with them when the destinations were domestic, such as Florida beaches or ranches in Wyoming and Texas. When Elsie and Dan went abroad by leisurely steamer travel, Master Tom was left at Longview with the Caldwell family's crew of men—his grandfather James and seven uncles. Otherwise, the boy primarily spent his upbringing in the company of females from the Buntin, Craighead, and Caldwell family lines.

Two of these family lines were doubly related through marriage. In 1859, the tall, striking brunette, Rachel Adelia Carter, only child of stagecoach and banking mogul Daniel Franklin Carter and his wife Mary Jane Buntin, married Thomas David Craighead. Rachel was a solemn young woman. Craighead, on the other hand, was a man of "ready wit and sparkling humor" and "versed in music, the drama and literature," which made him an "ornament and ever-wished-for member at all social affairs." Ten years after the Carter-Craighead marriage, south Louisianan Jennie Erwin Craighead married Nashville's dashing Captain William Allison Buntin (Mary Jane Buntin Carter's brother), even though he was twenty years older than his bride. This marriage established the intersection of the two families. Because of age differences, Jennie was Rachel's cousin through the Craighead line, but Rachel was also Jennie's niece through the Buntin line since Jennie was the sister-in-law of Rachel's parents. Jennie's four sons, including Dan Buntin, were Rachel's first cousins.

To make matters more confusing, in February 1901, years after she became a childless widow, sixty-four-year-old Rachel Carter Craighead petitioned a Davidson County court to adopt twenty-seven-year-old Dan Buntin as her child. Following approval of the petition within the week, the news made the rounds statewide: "lucky young Buntin – another likely young man of Nashville, a great toast in society and an all-round good fellow, has fallen into an easy spot." News articles noted that Dan managed Rachel's estate, "one of the most valuable in the community," following the death of her husband. Dan Buntin also managed the sizeable estate of Rachel's father, who left his only child assets worth $400,000 (almost $11 million today) when he died in 1874. Rachel's adoption of Dan bestowed "all the privileges of a legitimate child" thus providing a clear legal path for inheriting her assets.

After Rachel adopted her first cousin, she was also called his "foster mother." However, Dan's mother, Jennie Craighead Buntin, was still alive. She did not weigh in publicly regarding the adoption and kept continually

Rachel Adelia Carter Craighead and Thomas David Craighead. (The Tennessean.)

Jennie Craighead Buntin. (Annie Gilchrist,
Some Representative Women of Tenn.)

Capt. William Allison Buntin, ca. 1863.
(Tenn. State Library & Archives.)

busy with the numerous women's clubs of which she was a member. Jennie and Rachel may have had an awkward relationship for many reasons. When Jennie's husband, Capt. W.A. Buntin died, Rachel's husband, Thomas Craighead, was named executor of the estate. During probate, the guardian of widowed Jennie's youngest sons sued Craighead for dereliction of duty. Thomas died in May 1898 while the lawsuit was pending, and the case was subsequently settled without resolving the allegations.

By 1901, Dan's financial footing seemed well-established by his two mothers. Despite the toils of transportation over extended areas of land and water and limited telegraph and telephony communication in the early twentieth century, men of means—fathers of little Toms everywhere— pursued business schemes globally. Men in the U.S. needed look no farther to advance their financial ventures than their own continent and the one to the south. Centuries after South America was first plundered by the Iberians, commercial interest plundering resurged in the late nineteenth century in the pursuit of precious gems and minerals, pitch, rubber, and coffee. Young Dan secured permission from the Venezuelan president in the early 1900s to venture down the lower Orinoco River in search of vast quantities of gold. Once there, he purchased an option on land in the Guiana Highlands. He also invested in over 100,000 acres of prime, old-growth forest in British Columbia. The Venezuelan treasure area turned out to be a bust, however, and he gave up on finding gold. He and partner E.R. Tallmadge attempted to profit off the Canadian timber in a quick sell and ended up in court when the purchaser alleged that they had intentionally misrepresented the amount of forest acreage they owned.

For all the setbacks far-afield of Nashville, Dan's dream for a covered shopping mall, the first in the South, was achieved after winning several legal tussles with tenants displaced by demolition of buildings in the way of the Arcade. The $200,000 structure—which still exists between Fourth and Fifth Avenues—was filled with tenants by 1903. Dan served as general manager of the Arcade Company. The Arcade was a wildly popular place where one could buy anything from a "hamburger to a $5,000 diamond." Three years later, Dan left his real estate business to become general manager of the Realty Savings Bank and Trust, where his father-in-law was president. Dan, Elsie, and son Tom (now three years old) stayed in Rachel's house near the state capitol building until September 1907, when they rented a house on the Franklin Turnpike. After a brief period as tenants, they failed to make improvements to the house required by the lease and were adjudged in breach of contract for $4,000 in damages after the owner sued them.

The family of three then moved on to Chicago in 1908, a year after Dan incorporated the Tallmadge-Buntin Land Company there and established an office with E.R. Tallmadge to focus on financing, acquiring, and selling land and water rights in arid Wyoming. Known as "North Town" or the "Near North Side," Chicago's upper-class neighborhood was in a transition period of construction. New buildings were being erected and older ones were being converted into three- or four-story "high-rise," "high-class" apartment homes. These apartments were not flophouses. Nor were they firetraps, most having been constructed after Chicago's devasting Great Fire of 1871. A Lake Shore Drive apartment, on the "Gold Coast," could span twenty-two rooms. A more modest, upscale flat to the west rented from $2,400 to $3,600 per year and included a rear kitchen featuring a range with three boilers (two gas, one charcoal), so that domestic staff never had to cook steaks and fish on the same broiler. Modern innovations were found throughout these upscale flats: "modulating vapor heating," an "abundance of base plugs" for electrical devices, and an artificial refrigeration box that included a "device for freezing small cubes of ice for beverages." The interiors were lavish, with wood parquet floors featuring inlays of pewter or marble and walls and ceilings of oak trimmed with mahogany or plaster and festooned with elaborate murals.

1512 N. Dearborn Pkwy, Chicago. (Google Earth.)

The Buntins secured a rental flat at 1512 Dearborn Parkway, two blocks west of the Lake Michigan shorefront, bringing with them their cook and butler from Nashville. The world's first "Ferris" Wheel was no longer in the city, having been sent to St. Louis for the 1904 World's Fair. Nevertheless, the realm of Tom's childhood experiences included watching steamships dock at Navy Pier, sitting on wooden bleachers to watch Cubs' baseball games at West Side Park, eating the Palmer House Hotel's newly created dessert—a brownie—in the children's dining room, and trotting on a saddle pony at the Rasmussen Riding Academy next to the Buntin's flat. Neighbors included real estate magnate and hotelier Potter Palmer, of the Palmer House Hotel, who lived in a Norman-style Gothic castle that entirely lacked exterior doorknobs. The absence of exterior hardware signaled to the world that doorknobs were superfluous because a servant was always on duty to open the door to visitors. A couple who had recently purchased the residence of Aaron Montgomery Ward, inventor of the mail-order catalogue, were also neighbors.

With Dan away much of the time on Wyoming business, Elsie immersed herself in women's engagements, socially assisted by the entrée and introductions of Elizabeth Buford Evans, formerly of Nashville. Soon, Elsie's reputation spread. She was of a "very old and influential family" of the South and was "thought by many to be the prettiest woman" in Chicago who gave her time to worthy causes, including "destitute crippled children." Elizabeth and her husband, Arthur, lived in the co-joined flat, which is probably how the Buntins found their housing. He was general counsel for Swift and Company, the meat-packing empire headquartered in Chicago, the meat-packing center of the world. His position rendered him legal lord over much of "The Yards," a square-mile-sized congregation of stockyards and packing plants that visitors flocked to see during their visit to Chicago.

Wealthy mothers, like Elsie, may have been preoccupied with women's clubs and lunches, but worried about their children's safety. Living in Chicago multiplied the risks to advantaged girls and boys. The city's population in the early 1900s was about 2.2 million, making it the fifth largest city in the world, while Nashville's population nudged a little over 110,000. Almost at North Town's back door—just to the west of Dearborn Parkway—was an area characterized as "ghettoes" and "slums," comprised of tenement houses inhabited by groups of European immigrants. Within this area, the poorest people in the city were concentrated in "Little Hell." Industrial expansion crept from the Chicago River in the southwest's Near North Side to Sedgewick Street in Little Hell. Fumes exhausted from plants also lent this area the name "Smoky Hollow." North Town and Gold Coast parents were on guard to make sure that their children did not wander. Well before Bruno Hauptmann snatched the Lindbergh baby boy from his parents' home and then presumably bludgeoned the child to death, kidnappings, especially of boys, were not uncommon. Mothers and fathers were vigilant.

The potential for accidents also loomed large. Street and corner cross-ings were mayhem, a tangle of electrified street cars, horses and buggies, and automobiles. Speeding motorized vehicles dominated roads. At one Chicago intersection, Barry and Sheffield avenues, a school-age child was killed at least once a year. Despite the Buntin's diligence, domestic help, and wealth, a traumatic accident *did* happen to their child while they lived in Chicago. Tom fell out of a Pullman car, almost ripping off his left ear. The disfiguration became identity-defining for him for the rest of his life. The almost-severed ear "protruded at a most noticeable angle" and became "very large."

Dan, Elsie, and Tom left their Chicago residence at the end of Septem-ber 1912. The land and water developments in Wyoming that Dan owned with partner E.R. Tallmadge had failed and were sold. The partners split ways. Returning to Tennessee, the Buntins lived very briefly at the Melrose estate and horse farm on the Franklin Turnpike. They then moved back into town in 1913 to a house in the fashionable, new west-end residential section. Another move followed in 1915, a block away, to a five-year-old, stone-veneer, castle-style mansion at 2500 Kensington Place. The multi-story residence of over 6,600 square feet included rooms for sitting, for use in the morning, and for music, and a large ballroom took up the entire third story. In the rear yard, a garage larger than most houses in town included a stable for four horses and carriages, a garage for two automobiles, and servants' quarters for three domestic staff. Master Tom, now age thirteen, and his one-year-old sister May enjoyed generous surroundings.

In June 1917, James and May Caldwell hosted a party at Longview to honor their fifteen-year-old grandson Tom. Though a teen, Tom was tall but had not yet gained his full height. His face was thin, like his mother's, and he had her light eyes. The early summer event was held to celebrate the youth's departure for Culver Military Academy. The academy was an exclusive high school and college preparatory institution and boarding school set on a lushly landscaped campus in Marshall County, Indiana. At the time, the academy was the largest private school in the country, providing military instruction for young men drawn from throughout the U.S. and world. The instructional regime was a rigidly structured program of academics, physical fitness, and military discipline and training, carried out every day from 6 a.m. to 9:30 p.m. In his first year, Tom joined the Black Horse Troop, which was a cavalry squad, and trained in horseback riding, equitation, and drills. Team sports were mandatory, and he joined his squad's football and baseball teams. The following year, he excelled in swimming competitions for the forty-yard backstroke. Tom attended Culver through May 1919, visited at least twice by his mother and once by both parents.

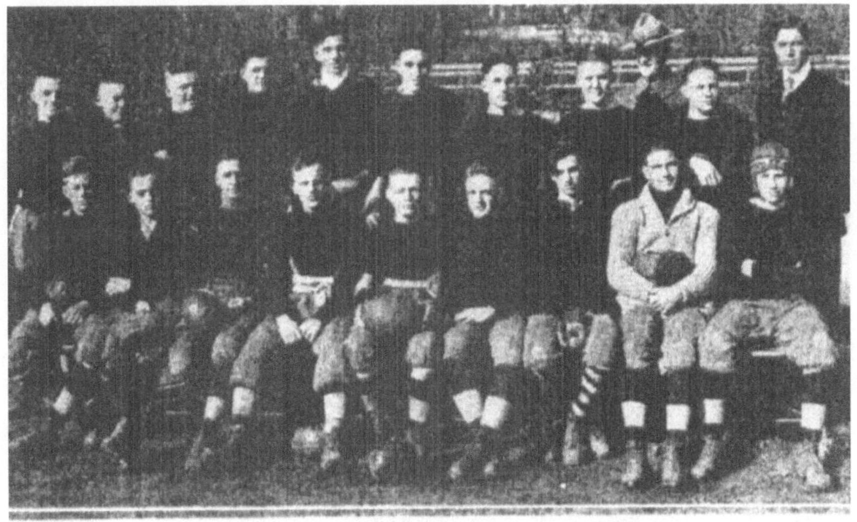

"F" Co. Football Squad

Tom, front row, far left, 1918. (Culver Roll Call Yearbook, 1917.)

When the federal census was taken in January 1920, seventeen-year-old Tom was counted in Laramie, Wyoming, with his family. He then traveled back east to the Cascadilla School in Ithaca, a private tutoring establishment, to prepare for entrance exams for admittance into Cornell University.

Chapter 2

A Father's Legacy

Dan Buntin appeared to be a robust, alert man. In adulthood, he stood six feet tall, and had blue-gray eyes and straight red hair divided by a left-side part and combed back from a high forehead. He was pleasant-looking, round-faced and with a "florid" complexion, and his visage featured a straight nose, dark and full eyebrows, and ears that laid inconspicuously flat against his head. Personality-wise, by all accounts, people liked him. He was regarded as a gentleman who had the "happy faculty of placing anyone at ease" in conversation and "in all things" "actuated by a spirit of determination" that did not know the word "fail." Once, while traveling by train in the West, Dan stood face-to-face with a young and agitated train robber armed with two Smith and Wesson revolvers. The businessman kept his cool and wits and calmed the bandit, ensuring the safety of the other railcar riders.

Jennie and Capt. Buntin's son was in the first generation of southern men after the Civil War who were compelled to a career that was different from that of their fathers. The generations that preceded Dan's stepped into the plantation economy not that long after they stepped off the ships that brought them to the colonies. The planter-fathers' sons, like Dan, would write their own playbook for achieving fortune and power that benefited from the legacy of enslaved labor, while no longer legally able to exploit it themselves. They also calculated how to show manliness in a new commercial and industrial era. Vices were acceptable, particularly gambling on cards or horses. Visits to women at houses of "ill fame" (euphemistically,

DANIEL C. BUNTIN

(John T. Moore, Tenn. the Volunteer State, 1769-1923.)

"disorderly houses") were also tolerated provided that the men were discrete and not overly frequent.

In turn, and for better or worse, Tom would expect to inherit a new type of Buntin financial and social legacy. His father Dan's judgment was considered "splendid" and his action "quick," showing "remarkable executive ability." However, Dan seemed to navigate his way peripatetically in the business world and his choice of partners to help steer his plans for fortune was questionable at times. E.R. Tallmadge was one of those selections. In 1905, three years before he moved to Chicago, Dan associated with E.R., who lived in Chicago, to pursue business opportunities in the West. His new cohort was one of three siblings in the Tallmadge Brothers Immigration Company, which transported midwestern "home seekers" to the Pecos River Valley in the Roswell region of the Territory of New Mexico in the early 1900s. E.R. and his brother C.L. ran into legal problems when some buyers and the federal Interior Department brought suits alleging fraud in the sale of lands. E.R. appears to have then shifted his geographic focus elsewhere.

Buntin, Tallmadge, and a group of easterners formed a syndicate in 1905 to build a railroad from Canyon City in the Texas Panhandle to Eagle Pass, on the Rio Grande River. In anticipation of completing the line, Dan purchased substantial acreage in Panhandle towns along the way, such as Happy, Texas. The proposed line was then to connect with the Mexican International Railroad to allow travel to Mexico City. He and E.R. were each interested in financial opportunities in the western and southwestern U.S. beyond Texas and New Mexico. With Wyoming in mind, Buntin incorporated the Tallmadge-Buntin Land Company in Illinois in 1907 as the western state's population was booming. From 1900 to 1910, residency in the Cowboy State increased by almost fifty-eight percent to almost 146,000 people, while the nation at large grew by twenty-one percent.

Of all of Dan's business ventures, Wyoming development was by far the most ambitious and expensive because it required water rights, irrigation infrastructure, and thousands of acres of land. Sizeable financing had to be secured, so Chicago was a more optimal headquarters for the land-company outfit than was Nashville. Speculation in the West was also one in which Dan was least qualified to succeed without a solid partner and sizeable team of men knowledgeable in finance, engineering, construction, colonizing, project management, and maintenance of water reservoirs, dams, and canals. One well-known example illustrated the need for an experienced team. Dan's slightly older contemporary, William F. Cody ("Buffalo Bill"), invested in one of the first irrigation companies to incorporate after the Carey Act of 1894 gave a million acres of federal land to Wyoming for irrigation projects. The showman's frontier charisma, however, could not stave off the Shoshone Irrigation Company's descent into financial trouble. Cody lost his investment when the irrigation firm filed for bankruptcy.

Dan and E.R. initially focused on the absolute essentials to colonizing western land: securing acreage and precious water rights and carrying out a marketing plan to lure potential investors. Their first purchase was a 60,000-acre cattle ranch in Bosler, Albany County, in the Big Laramie River Valley. They then acquired the Hoge, Haley, and Bath ranches, as well as others. By summer 1908, the Tallmadge-Buntin Land Company was reported to have purchased over 200,000 acres in total. Other developers claimed that potential investors had to be accommodated in a good hotel during their visit, which could cost up to $115,000 to build. Tallmadge-Buntin's marketing did not begin with a good hotel—or even any hotel—at least not at first when the most crucial step was to introduce potential settlers to the land itself, quickly.

Excursion trips were the way to get farmers' boots on the ground, which were all-expenses-paid train travel to the ranches. These travel opportunities were widely advertised in major newspapers in the Midwest, Northeast, and Upper South. Summer, of course, was the best time to showcase the environment and the weather was more hospitable to guests who were lodged overnight in railcars. At first, the tours were comprised of relatively small groups of twenty-five to thirty people, including a few ladies, but soon increased to as many as seventy-five people per trip. At the height of the excursions, the firm's local agent, L.F. Nicodemus, reported that a party of 175 "land seekers" would be hosted after the Independence Day celebration in July 1908.

These trips were said to pay off. After hosting a party of sixty-five, the company reported that at least fifty-six purchased land and "at least some others will buy before the season ends." Many buyers were touted as "invested heavily," such as J.F. Ward of Marianna, Ohio, who was said to have secured 5,000 acres. The water rights associated with a tract of land were sold separately and by far were more costly. A Carey Act acre of land could be bought for fifty cents. The associated liquid assets ranged in cost from $20 to $30 per acre outright or a cash upfront payment of $5 per acre, followed by a $3 per acre payment annually for ten years. By mid-to-late summer 1908, Tallmadge-Buntin claimed total revenue of $500,000 per

"Tallmadge and Buntin Land Company." (Wyomingtalesandtrails.com.)

month representing sales of 500 farms. In January 1909, sales slowed a bit, expected during the harsh winters, but spring sales of ranch acreage picked up. These sales included a transaction described by Tallmadge-Buntin as its largest conveyance to date, to J.H. Falkingham, who purchased 240 acres for $7,200. The recorded deed for 240 acres matched the developer's claim. Just six months earlier, local newspapers published the land company's claim that Mr. Ward of Ohio "secured" 5,000 acres, but there was no published recording of a deed to verify the purchase around that time. No one seemed to notice the divergence between the hype and actual sales.

Large sums of money were expended, but locals thought that Buntin and Tallmadge were backed by "apparently unlimited capital." Excursion expenses were not reported but had to have cost thousands of dollars cumulatively. An initial payment on the James Lake project, designed to irrigate 50,000 acres via a proposed ditch between the Laramie River, James Lake, and Bosler Station, was $15,000. However, the contractors missed their deadline to complete the first segment. Undeterred, Dan and E.R. continued spending. The two acquired the Whitehouse and Palmer ranches in May 1909 consisting of about 9,000 acres at Red Buttes in the Laramie River Valley, followed by purchase of the Hart ranch and Pioneer canal. The total cost of these purchases was estimated to be at least $245,000. A Laramie office was opened for the Lake Hattie irrigation ditch, a million-cubic-yard dirt-moving project that made the James Lake project look miniscule by comparison. Laramie businessmen were enthused that most supplies would be purchased locally, but no one seemed to notice that the 200,000 acres that the company advertised it owned in the summer of 1908 had diminished to 100,000 acres when the Lake Hattie project was announced in the summer of 1909, with no significant land sales recorded.

There were some grumblings among the local populace about the partners E.R. and Dan. Tallmadge-Buntin proposed finishing construction of the Riverton/Wind River irrigation project after a previous company failed to complete the works. Following U.S. Congressional approval of the transfer of responsibility, construction remained stalled. *The Riverton News* questioned the company's *bona fides*, or at least was skeptical. Dan and E.R. circulated positive news about the project. One telegram, sent to the Wyoming State Engineer by a Mr. Rosecrans of Chicago, claimed that Tallmadge had just returned from the East where he contracted with a New York and London syndicate to finance the project. However, as the *News'* editorial staff noted, it was "strange" that the new construction contract was awarded before financing was secured. The newspaper offered to give $25 "for any charitable purpose" in Riverton if the telegram was proven to be true "based on facts" that the land company "means business." The editorial ended by observing that it would be "criminal" to "keep settlers here by sending out false dope" when they had already experienced a "four-year apprenticeship" in the "postponement business."

The Riverton News' criticisms were prescient. The same year, in 1910, Tallmadge-Buntin sold its entire land business in the Laramie River Valley. Of the initial acquisition of either 100,000 acres or 200,000 acres—the accurate number was never clear—the partners conveyed their remaining land to the Wyoming Land and Credit Company. The Riverton/Wind River irrigation project under construction on 400,000 acres of Carey Act land was sold almost contemporaneously to the Wyoming Land Board. By 1912, the partners transferred the entire stock of the James Lake Irrigation Company to a committee authorized to look out for the interests of Carey Act bondholders. E.R. returned to Chicago to market land in the Great Plains.

During this same period, the Buntins moved from their Chicago apart-ment back to Nashville, but they did not forswear Wyoming. Dan, Elsie, and Tom spent the summers of 1912 and 1913 in Laramie, when Tom was age eleven and twelve, respectively. Dan also began to whittle down his personal holdings of Wyoming land by September 1913. He contracted to sell some of his Albany County acreage but reneged when oil drilling started in the vicinity. Ultimately, the spurned buyer acquired the property when it was sold at auction for his delinquent tax payments. Following daughter May Winston's birth in February 1914, Dan announced that he was once again doing business in the Laramie plains. His approach was as optimistic as it had been at Tallmadge-Buntin. He advertised that he was willing to rent his own land to prospective settlers at rates much lower than they would pay in the East. Gus Palmer of the Palmer ranch subsequently remarked to the local newspapers, however, that Buntin was having little success renting property.

Dan's last large venture in the state occurred in 1917 when he purchased the Laramie Water Company, which had plans to develop thousands of acres between the Big and Little Laramie Rivers by constructing sizeable dams. The transaction, reported as in the "seven figures," was bankrolled by his father-in-law, James Caldwell, who joined the board of directors. Caldwell discovered that the company had a "heap" of debt and he was asked to furnish a "heap" of money, which he did. He continued to give money to the outfit to "keep it afloat." Newspapers reported that Buntin's plans to quickly colonize the Laramie River Valley would "no doubt be widely advertised" and that it is "probable that a large number of people will take up farms there." By spring 1918, the middle-aged entrepreneur sold the water company to an Illinois land developer.

Although Dan had declared Wyoming as his place of residence, he made only two business trips to Laramie each year after the land company folded. One occurred in mid-winter and the other occurred during the summer, when Elsie, Tom, and May joined him. In early April 1919, however, he left Nashville to take care of "exceptionally urgent business" in the Cowboy State. Business kept him in Wyoming for several months in 1920 as well, leading to his and Elsie's decision to winter in the state that year. Tom had elected to start his freshman year of college in September 1920 at the University of Wyoming in Laramie, rather than Cornell, and tried to be available to help his dad when he could. However, an unspecified health problem of Dan's required that he and Elsie return to Nashville in October 1920. Local doctors advised him to go to a lower altitude to improve his health and that he "pay no attention to business" over the winter and observe "complete rest." Dan could afford to take the advice thanks to a hefty financial cushion of $20,000 in annual income from a trust that his still-living cousin and foster mother Rachel Carter Craighead established in his favor.

In early 1921, the Buntins left Baltimore upon the newly built "floating palace," the *S.S. Hawkeye State* steamship, bound for Hawaii via the Panama Canal. On their return voyage from the islands, the couple disembarked in San Francisco to travel to Laramie to see Tom for a few days before returning to Nashville for springtime. During their Wyoming visit, the *Laramie Boomerang* noted that the Buntins would be unable to spend summer 1921 locally, as they typically did, because of Dan's health. The newspaper noted that the businessman was "seemingly recovered from his indisposition," however. In his absence, Dan's land projects would be handled by men in his firm who, according to the optimistic editors, would undoubtedly bring "many new people" to Albany County. The entrepreneur never returned to Wyoming.

On a cold Wednesday, January 18, 1922, Dan walked into a bedroom of the family's Nashville house at 2500 Kensington Place a little after 1 p.m. and shot himself through the heart.

When a physician arrived thirty minutes later, he was dead. The forty-seven-year-old left behind Elsie (age forty-four), Tom (age twenty), and May (age eight). Funeral services were held at the home the following Saturday, after Tom arrived from college. Dan was buried that same day at the grounds of the Carter family mausoleum in Nashville's Mount Olivet Cemetery. The burial place included Daniel Franklin Carter and his wife Mary Jane Buntin Carter and Thomas D. Craighead, Rachel's husband.

In shock, people sought a reason for Dan's demise. A popular conception in Nashville and Chicago was that Dan was a successful businessman. The Wyoming ventures, like his gold prospects in South America, had not panned out the way he expected, however. Suicide was not uncommon in Dan's family. Joseph Erwin, his second great-grandfather on his mother Jennie's side, owned vast sugar and cotton plantations in Iberville Parish along the Mississippi River south of Baton Rouge. The planter was constantly in an "embarrassing condition" financially, however. In 1829, his body was found at his daughter's plantation in Ascension Parish with his head stuck in a drainage barrel. One newspaper characterized Erwin's suicide as a case of "wet death, dry feet."

During Dan's time, businessmen were prone to self-destruction when they thought their minds were deteriorating. A contemporary of his, a well-known author and newspaperman in Chicago, traveled to New Orleans by train to procure laudanum then went directly to Biloxi where he ingested the poison and died in a hotel. At the age of forty, he felt his brain no longer "worked right" and was repulsed that his friends might refer to him as a "dead one." Sometimes, suicides of members of prominent families were not reported locally. Two years after Dan and Elsie married, Elsie's brother William was reported to have "accidentally" shot himself "through the body" seriously damaging his left lung. People "supposed" the event happened when he was cleaning a pistol. He died at Longview when he was twenty-one, in 1908. The method of his death was not published locally. In other parts of Tennessee his death was reported as a suicide, along with the observation that his mind was "unbalanced."

In Dan's case, an underlying condition was not noted on his death certificate. The newspapers obliquely wrote that he had suffered an "incurable malady." The Tennessee Supreme Court later observed in a published opinion that "he had, or thought he had, a disease which would render him imbecile and make of him a nuisance to his family." A Nashville physician on the medical staff at Vanderbilt University concluded that Dan may have had "paresis," a "softening of the brain" that was sometimes "feared to be the type associated with syphilis." The condition typically led to serious mental disease.

Elsie and Nashville's First Savings Bank and Trust, as co-executors, opened probate in Albany County, Wyoming, in August 1922, followed by the filing of his Wyoming will in Nashville for probate there. Dan specifically instructed in his will that his "larger debts, including mortgages, collateral notes, etc.," not be paid with "such rapidity" that his estate would be "sacrificed." The probate petitions listed his assets as having a "probable" value of $218,000 ($4.05 million today). Almost one-third of that amount was bills receivable, which might or might not be collectible, and a little over half of the value of his assets was in land that appeared to be mortgaged. After the filings, litigation entangled Elsie and her children for years. Several business claims were filed. A Chicago man asserted a claim to $14,500. Two Texans sought to recover real estate in the Texas Panhandle town of Happy, where E.R. and Dan had first ventured to make money. The Fourth and First National Bank, James Caldwell's bank, secured a court order requiring a public-auction sale of two lots near Vanderbilt University to pay monies that his son-in-law Dan owed on the land.

Another set of claims that arose within Dan's will probate period were associated with Rachel Carter Craighead's death in 1924 and came from within the extended family. Rachel's assets were a key source of wealth for Dan and Elsie, and a probable source of wealth for the Buntin's two children after their parents died. Rachel had, of course, assumed that she would die before Dan, her adopted son and legal heir. Before her death, Rachel passed on many of her assets through trusts and gifts, such as the 700 acres in Robertson County (the Rock Rest property) that was conveyed to Dan and Elsie. Rachel died without a will, however, leaving a confused fate for some assets. Family member May Meriwether contested whether Tom and May could inherit their father's share of Rachel's estate, since Dan predeceased Rachel. The Tennessee Supreme Court resolved the matter in Tom and May's favor in December 1925. Ida Flynn Williams, who had been informally adopted by Rachel as a young girl, launched a different attack on Tom and May's inheritance. The adoptee claimed that "Miss Puss," as she affectionately called Rachel, left valuable Public Square property in downtown Nashville to her in a letter. She won her claim.

Attorneys were hired to defend the claims against Tom and May as defendants but also to protect their interests as plaintiffs. They sued their Aunt

Elizabeth, the widow of their Uncle John (Dan's brother), now remarried as Mrs. Elizabeth Plummer. Elizabeth claimed that she owned a valuable commercial parcel on North College Street (including a dry goods store) that Rachel put in trust for she and John in 1912. Tom and May asserted ownership through Dan's inheritance from Rachel. The siblings' attorneys advised that the complicated case would take years to resolve, and the outcome might not be favorable.

Rather than leave his son a firmly established business and financial legacy, Dan's self-destruction rendered Tom an emotional wreck. The suicide "preyed" on Tom's mind "a great deal." He acknowledged that Dan had experienced "financial reverses," which he believed were not a cause for suicide. The specter of mental illness was another matter, which Tom openly justified as a reason to extinguish one's own life. Disturbingly, the young man feared and dreaded that he had inherited his father's "curse of one of the social diseases" and would himself develop a serious mental disorder. This fear became an omnipresent, destabilizing influence in his life.

Chapter 3

Mr. and Mrs. Thomas Craighead Buntin

Two years before his father's death, Tom began his freshman year of college in September 1920, not at Cornell University as expected, but at the University of Wyoming in Laramie, a familiar place. The Prairie League prevailed over the Ivy League. It was a huge leap—some would have said a step down—intellectually and career-wise. The western university's student newspaper was proud of faculty and alumni's service during World War I and decried Cornell as a "pretentious" institution that had not given as much to the country. At the same time, the Laramie campus's lack of a master plan and a "landscape gardening" design, hallmarks of Ivy League universities, bothered student leaders.

Tom jumped into student life with both feet, elected as president of the freshman class, serving as editor of *The Wyo Yearbook*, and joining Alpha Tau Omega fraternity (a military fraternal order). He was also chosen as an alternate for one of the two men's intercollegiate debate teams his very first semester. The debate season in the 1920 to 1921 school year was a "lamentable failure in forensics," but the freshman debates were commended for being "interesting and instructive" and "exceptionally well attended." He signed up for the infantry unit of the campus ROTC as a second lieutenant, a rank that reflected his previous military training at Culver. The unit helped form the first rifle team on campus, of which Tom was a member. Male students sacrificed some of their "beauty sleep" to report to the shooting range in the early morning hours.

Of all of Tom's collegial activities his freshman year, the most important occurred when he met pretty Bettie Gould Moore. Bettie entered the University of Wyoming in the fall of 1920, the same semester as Tom. Their class was small, at about 180 students, so they probably crossed paths often, particularly through their participation in the debate teams. Her childhood was marked by tragedy and financial struggle. Rev. John Moore, a Congregational Church preacher, suffered a brutal railcar accident in 1907 while hopping off the Douglas, Wyoming, depot platform onto a passing train. He fell between the cars and was run over but survived initially. Four-year-old Bettie sat by his side in the hospital. After a double amputation of his legs, the minister died. The not-so-benevolent Ministers Casualty Union subsequently refused to pay widow Louella Gould Moore's claim for $5,000 in death benefits because of the young churchman's questionable judgment in jumping from a platform to board his train. She was then forced to move herself and her two young daughters to Cheyenne to find work. Louella rebounded, becoming head librarian at Cheyenne's magnificent Carnegie Library, a position she held for the rest of her life.

Tom was a popular student and considered a "handsome, affable young man," known for his raccoon coat and expensive Packard touring car. When the *Wyo*'s staff argued, tongue in cheek, for alternate, less rigorous educational programs on campus, he was recommended as the dice instructor, with the curriculum including the "importance of fading, how to coax the cubes, the knuckle on a blanket, and the odd and hard points." He was also gently ribbed for waiting until the end of February to don "goloshes," well after everyone else started to wear theirs "in great gobs of frequency" during the rainy, sleeting, snowy, frigid Wyoming winters.

The young man may have been teetering toward "playboy" status as early as that time. A "playboy" was a derisive label for a man who had money to freely spend, most often unearned income from an affluent family. However, Tom was not yet of an age to fully exhibit a playboy's life, which was comprised of multiple marriages and divorces, shady deals, breach-of-marriage-promise lawsuits, process-server avoidance, and the unexplained falls of lovers and friends from balconies. Nevertheless, at that point, his path to that life was outlined because another key characteristic of a playboy was—in the slang of the Jazz Era—being splifficated.

Bettie seems to have been a stabilizing influence, as she was steady and reserved. Her moment to shine was as a Thalian—when she was on stage. The campus drama club performed comedic as well as non-comedic plays and the young actress was particularly well-reviewed in her dramatic roles.

Bettie and Tom, sophomore year, 1921-1922. (Wyo Yearbook, 1921.)

Tom, 1st row, far left, rifle team. (Ibid.)

In one such part, she played Blanche de Malétroit in "The Lesser Evil," a stage adaptation of a Robert Louis Stevenson novella. Beautiful Blanche, unmarried and *enceinte*, is sequestered in her uncle's medieval chateau in France, where, one day, he urges her to don her bridal dress quickly for the marriage ceremony. She does so only to find that the man presented her at the altar is not the man she expected, given her condition. In real life, Bettie's boyfriend, Tom, would similarly turn out not to be the man the young actress expected. This was a lesson learned after, not before, their marriage.

Dan and Elsie met Tom's new girl when they visited on their way back from a Hawaiian cruise in the spring of 1921. They liked her. In mid-June, Tom attended ROTC summer training at Camp Lewis on the Pacific Coast in Washington State, where he placed well in competitive rifle shooting. He and his university cohorts then went on a sightseeing excursion to Mt. Rainier, Tacoma, Seattle, American Lake, and Vancouver. Returning to school, he motored to Cheyenne in early August to attend the Frontier Days celebration, probably joining Bettie there. Frontier Days was an annual riotous celebration of the West. Events included men's and women's pony races, steer roping, fancy shooting, bucking contests, and wolf roping. Cowgirl Lorena Tricky, a tiny woman, was a crowd favorite that summer. During the relay race, she daringly hopped from one galloping horse to another, and then topped off her performance by winning the ladies' saddle bronc competition. Tom likely met Bettie's mother, Louella, during his visit.

Following Dan's demise in January 1922, the tragic deaths of their fathers must have particularly bonded the dating collegiates. In an abrupt announcement and, "to the surprise of their many friends," the two young people married mid-morning on Thursday, September 28, 1922, at the Episcopal Cathedral in Laramie. No one in either of their families attended. Elsie and May had just returned to Nashville after a summer stay at the Palmer ranch. Elsie, however, approved of the marriage, commenting that "if she was my own daughter, I couldn't have any more affection for her." Congratulatory announcements for the "exceptionally well known and very popular" couple predicted that both were expected to obtain their bachelor's degrees in May 1924.

The couple gave every indication that they would complete their studies and graduate. A week after marrying, Bettie was elected secretary of the Associated Students of the University of Wyoming, the student government organization, which, at that time, included few females. The same week, Tom was named to a student planning committee to welcome the University's new president, a Pennsylvanian. A western greeting was held, including a staged capture of the astonished man and his wife by a posse of "cowboys" (students on horseback) as they drove into town in their automobile, followed by the couple's transport into Laramie in a real stagecoach.

Nashville society clamored to see the couple. The newlyweds obliged shortly after Thanksgiving 1922. Bettie was introduced to Tom's Buntin, Caldwell, and Carter families during a social whirlwind. The bride's debut occurred the day after she and Tom arrived following a long trip from Laramie. May and James Caldwell hosted three hundred family members and friends at Longview for a tea dance the afternoon of December 8. As a child and teen, Bettie Gould Moore had likely spent many hours in Cheyenne's public palace—the Carnegie Library where her mother worked—amidst a splendid interior featuring mosaic-tile hearths surrounded by Mexican onyx, marble drinking fountains, and bronze statuary. However, the interior setting did not rival that of the Caldwell's private palace. The Franklin Turnpike estate was first known as "Leafy Lot" for its magnificent forest, then became "Hood's Waste" during the Civil War when the routed Confederate

General John Bell Hood's troops clearcut the old-growth trees for firewood in the freezing winter. May and James transformed the abandoned house into the monumental, twenty-two-room "Longview," illuminated by fourteen crystal chandeliers and light fixtures, cooled by fifteen windows that ran from ceiling to floor on the first floor, and heated by eleven fireplaces.

Bettie stood with Tom and his grandparents in the mansion's drawing room, surrounded by chrysanthemums and white roses, to greet guests. Her choice of attire—a pale green velvet gown—was favorably received by the attending women. Sixteen Caldwell and Buntin matrons, as well as Elsie's best friends, assisted with tea in the large dining room, lit by a two-tiered glass chandelier from Italy. The refreshment table was decorated with a massive centerpiece of yellow chrysanthemums and American Beauty roses. Dancing followed in the Great

(The Tennessean. Digital photo restoration by Bill Roughen, Lexington, Ky.)

Hall where flowers sent by well-wishers complemented plants from the "extravagant glass solarium" onsite.

Nashville's main newspaper featured "Mrs. Thomas Craighead Buntin" in a large portrait splashed across the *Society* page of the Christmas edition. The close-up image was probably taken at the Longview party held shortly after Tom and Bettie's arrival in Nashville. In the image, Bettie was seated, holding an arrangement of roses and baby's breath. Her look into the camera was direct, unsmiling, and sultry. Her short, dark hair was cropped in flapper style and the velvet dress featured a low, scooped neckline and peek-a-boo shoulders with edges trimmed in either brocade or beads. In all, the westerner presented a sophisticated look to the southern ladies of Nashville. No one could whisper that Tom had married a cowgirl from the wild, wild West.

The couple returned to Wyoming in January for their spring semester in 1923 and moved into the Palmer ranch. Bettie had been pregnant for a month. Elsie and May made their usual sojourn to the west that summer, greeting the birth of Daniel Franklin Carter Buntin in August of 1923, a month before the start of his parents' senior year of college. Elsie wanted to help financially, so she began to give Tom $200 per month after her first grandson's birth.

Despite college graduation on the horizon, it seemed increasingly likely that his family would draw Tom back to Nashville. He spent several months in Chicago with Elsie toward the end of 1923. Bettie realized that mother and son were "very good friends," with never a misunderstanding between them, and that he greatly comforted Elsie. The young couple permanently abandoned their senior year studies and degrees, quietly moving to Nashville in late 1923 or early 1924. Tom secured a realtor license and joined the Buntin and Company real estate firm headed by his uncle, Charles ("Charley") Buntin. It must have been disconcerting for the young mother, however, when her mother-in-law asked the family of three to stay in the house where Dan died two years earlier. They moved not only into Elsie's house, but the very room in which Dan committed suicide, with the bullet hole still in the wall.

Elsie needed Tom's help to sort out the legal and practical issues associated with Dan's and Rachel's deaths, consisting of complicated property ownership in several states and litigated claims. There were even "dead letters" to chase down: unclaimed and undeliverable correspondence to Dan that branch offices of the federal postal service's Dead Letter Office listed in newspapers around the country. If not claimed, the letters were sent to paper-pulping mills. Despite these unpleasant and time-consuming matters, the young Buntin couple quickly assimilated into Nashville's "smart set," immersed in family events, entertaining at the Kensington Place home, attending society weddings, and enjoying travel. Attractive Bettie Buntin's fashion choices were often noticed in society news, and she became a club woman, joining the society and historic preservation organizations of which the Caldwell and Buntin women were members, such as the Ladies Battlefield Park Association. She helped raise funds for various causes, including Nashville's new Home for Crippled Children, and sold newspapers on the corner of Broadway and Sixteenth Avenue downtown as a fundraising ploy for the Junior League.

The young parents' family was completed in Nashville with the births of Thomas Craighead Buntin Jr. in August 1925 and Rogers Clark Caldwell Buntin in July 1927. A portrait of the mother and Rogers appeared in the *Society* section of *The Tennessean* when her last child was about six months old. The baby favored his father, with apostrophe eyebrows and protruding ears and his mother appeared very somber, in plain dress, and with short, wavy hair and heavily darkened eyebrows and eyeliner. The image was quite a contrast from her portrait when she arrived in Nashville five years earlier as the sultry and fêted Mrs. Buntin.

Troubles had appeared in the marriage. Her husband seemed extremely fragile. Rogers was accidentally put into a tub of scalding water by his nurse and blistered all over, requiring a hospital stay and then a lengthy healing period at home. Rather than comforting the child, his father was "very disturbed" about the incident and "went to pieces," not going near him. It was clear that Tom had no "stomach for hardships."

Bettie also observed that her husband's drinking worsened after they married. She did everything she could think of to help him overcome his "habit," as she called his alcoholism,

(*The Tennessean.*)

to no avail. Divorce, generally viewed as disgraceful in the South, was out of the question. The proceedings were expensive, usually allowing only women of means to file and be successful, and Bettie had no money of her own. Dissolution of marriage was also a legal creature of state legislatures, comprised of men who required sufficient cause to break the union between a couple. Fault was tricky—cruel treatment could be alleged but the paperwork and court hearings were public. The safest allegation of fault in a respectable woman's petition was her husband's failure to be a "responsible family member." By no means was any divorce assured since the court had discretion to deny the petition, and judges disfavored breaking up a family, especially when children were involved. Bettie had no reason to believe that Tom would end their marriage and probably did not even consider that possibility because men rarely filed petitions for divorce. Under no circumstance could a man or woman decide the institution of marriage was no longer for her or him, or that they wanted out because they had found a more suitable partner in life than the one to which they were married—that choice was taboo for the wealthy.

Tom's time in the Buntin and Company real estate office was limited, whether because of his performance or a problem in his relationship with his Uncle Charley is unknown. Around 1926, James Caldwell appointed his grandson to manage his insurance company, James E. Caldwell and Sons. One of Tom's friends, John Dougherty, worked in the insurance office and he and his new boss shared a mutual interest in cars, and drinking. Dougherty observed that when Tom was depressed, he would sit in his office doing nothing. After work one day in 1927 or 1928, they drank in the office until Tom was "drunk and staggering." He told his subordinate that "I might as well kill myself," and pulled out a gun from the safe in the stamp drawer. Dougherty demanded that Tom hand it over. His boss complied but then spoke of Dan's suicide, saying that he believed "his daddy" went to heaven, "if there is such a place."

Tom's salary was $300 per month by the end of the 1920s and he still received $200 per month from Elsie that she started giving him after her grandson Daniel's birth. Altogether, it was a sizeable monthly income for the time, which Elsie also supplemented with a variable "allowance" from monies she received from Rachel's estate. Tom also had the promise of considerable assets from interests in Rachel's estate, though they were tangled legally. Yet, Bettie acknowledged when questioned years later that she and Tom "didn't have a home of our own, we lived with his mother, and she turned Rock Rest over to him to manage for her and we spent the summers there." The young Buntin's dependence seemed to confirm what some friends thought—that Bettie's husband could not make it economically or emotionally without being propped up by his family. Later, when questioned under oath, Laurence Howard, an attorney, bluntly assessed him as a "man that had never stood on his own feet at all. He had never gotten a job except by some family pressure." Based on his observations of his friend at work and around town, Howard concluded that Buntin could never earn a living on his own.

The Caldwells and Buntins instilled in their children a deep duty to family. Tom defined in a singular way, when viewed retrospectively, how he would carry out his duty. At the close of the nineteenth century, New York Life, one of the largest life insurance companies in the world, somberly advertised that the "doctrine of duty" required that men ensure "immortal" financial security for their families by buying a policy. By the 1920s, the company proclaimed that life insurance was an entitlement of a man's beneficiaries. His wife gave up her right to "earn an independent income" to care for his home and their children and the children "have a right" to be raised well and educated. While the marketing angle varied over the decades, a key concept of the advertiser's business model did not: lucrative premiums.

When he was twenty-two (the age at which he married), Tom took out his first New York Life policy in the amount of $3,000. In 1929, following the births of all three sons, he purchased two policies totaling $50,000 (about $930,000

New York Life Home Office, 1928. (National Museum of American History, Smithsonian.)

in current dollars), for an annual premium of $1,128. Local field agents of New York Life's Inspection Department made "delicate," though "not prying," inquiries into an applicant's social, moral, and financial standing for proposed high-value policies like his. The company assured applicants that the investigation was not intrusive. Applicants were rated for risk based on physical build and condition, race, personal and family history, habits, location of residence, and occupation. A substandard score did not necessarily prevent an applicant from being enrolled, but his life's monetary value was reduced in the policy, to the detriment of the man's beneficiaries.

In his April 1929 application for life insurance, Tom listed his current and five-year past employment as insurance and real estate. He declared that he had stopped taking "aerial flights" and did not imbibe in any habit-forming drugs, such as morphine or cocaine. His medical history description was limited to traces of albumin in his urine in 1917, pneumonia in 1920, and, in 1927, an appendectomy and a fractured left clavicle. Other than claiming he no longer flew airplanes, the most untruthful part of Tom's submittal was his response to the use of alcohol. He identified himself as an "occasional" social drinker, and claimed he had not drunk beer, wine, spirits, or other intoxicants to excess in the past five years.

Dr. John Burch, the Nashville physician who had watched over the healing of baby Rogers when he was burned, was also childhood friends with Tom and saw him as a patient. He noticed that Tom would go on "sprees," starting in 1927 or 1928, drinking for several days, then sobering up for a while before the next drinking bout. Dr. Burch's treatment consisted of keeping him in bed and giving him the usual sedatives to control his "nerves." Formaldehyde was the most effective drug, in his opinion. Once, when Tom needed surgery, he was first admitted to the hospital for about a week to get him "sober enough to operate." Burch, as friend, would haul Tom out of jail after he and his "running mates" got into trouble; these incidents never made it into the local newspapers. Tom frequented Merten's Turkish Baths, where men took medical baths, alcohol rubs, electric treatments, Swedish massage, and hot fomentations, but Burch never brought him there.

Contemporaneous with the purchase of the policies, Tom established a trust with the Nashville Trust Company, where his grandfather James Caldwell was president. The purpose of the account was to invest and manage life insurance proceeds that would be distributed after Tom died, a specter that seemed far off for a twenty-seven-year-old man. The trust agreement instructed the trustee to pay net income from the invested proceeds to Bettie and provided that, after her death, the proceeds be held in equal shares for the three Buntin sons and distributed when they turned twenty-five. Tom later extended the distribution age for his sons to thirty-five. Life insurance was a prudent step to provide for his family, but the policies served as a sad and scary refrain when he was depressed. Following issuance of the policies, Tom began to tell his wife that she and the three boys would be better off without him—with him dead—and when they had the insurance money.

The Buntins, ca. 1929. L. to r.: Daniel Franklin Carter, Thomas Craighead Jr., Rogers Clark Caldwell, and their mother. (Find-a-Grave.com; original source not given.)

Tom Buntin, 1929. (Buntin Case 1.)

Chapter 4

Tom's Denouement and Disappearance

During the summer of 1930, Bettie Buntin awoke in the middle of the night, not sure at first what had interrupted her sleep. She then realized her husband was standing in the middle of the bedroom, holding a gun pointed at his head. She did not say anything to him for fear of what might happen but stepped behind him and tried to take the gun away. It fired as she did so, but neither was hurt, and Tom began to cry when she removed the weapon from his hand. His wife crept out in the back yard during the night and hid the gun "somewhere back of the house" at Rock Rest.

Bettie undoubtedly reasoned that Tom's troubles primarily stemmed from his uncle, Rogers Caldwell. Caldwell's financial imbroglios were splashed across the newspapers in front-page, above-the-fold stories, not just in Nashville but across the South and nation. The young Buntin had an "extremely sensitive" and prideful disposition according to his grandfather James Caldwell. The elder observed that his grandson Tom was extraordinarily disturbed by the family's financial scandals even though Tom was not involved whatsoever. The senior Caldwell himself was part of the coverage, implicated in Rogers's machinations.

Compounding Tom's unsteady emotional state, he lost his paternal grandmother in 1930. Jennie Craighead Buntin died at age eighty-three at her son Charley's house on Lebanon Pike. Her other son, lawyer William Allison, completed the medical certificate of death, an official state record, writing that "I have no idea of cause except that she was very old. The cause was probably related to heart or brain." She left her grandson Tom money to buy a "solid silver coffee service," and her granddaughter May money to buy a "handsome bracelet," each bequest as a "token of affection."

First manifested in 1930 and continuing into 1931, Tom's behavior seemed more erratic to friends, not just to his immediate family. During one of the last mental-health exams Dr. Burch conducted on Tom, the physician classified the young man as "being of a good disposition, gloomy in temperament, and a 'four-plus' worrier and fretter." Running buddies thought he was "addicted" to reading Russian novelists and fixated on their weird "suicide theories." He also seemed determined to show them the bullet-hole remnant of his father's demise at the Kensington Place home. His drinking brought on "boogers," as Tom called them, or "notions" in his head. Dr. Burch thought they were simply "queer ideas" in which he fantasized of escaping the "encircling gloom" surrounding him by retracing his father Dan's journey to South America and traveling up the Orinoco River in Venezuela.

Laurence Howard represented a liability insurance company that sold policies through the James E. Caldwell and Sons firm and considered Tom a friend as well as a professional cohort. He also observed that Tom's "bad habit" was getting worse over time, often landing him in jail. Howard, as his lawyer, would see that Tom was too drunk to go home so he would leave him overnight in lockup until the next morning or afternoon.

Tom and Laurence Howard, far left, 1925. (The Tennessean.)

James Caldwell was a notorious supporter of temperance and Prohibition, stating publicly that "prominent business institutions" would not "employ men addicted to drink." Rogers Caldwell claimed he had given up whiskey. The senior Caldwell's grandson's known condition must have substantially concerned and vexed the old man but there is no indication he ever intervened.

The drinking worsened in the summer of 1931, when Tom became a "four-plus" drinker, the heaviest of alcoholism according to his doctor. There seemed to be something else going on besides his uncle's troubles to cause Tom such distress. Dr. Burch wanted to see him two-to-three times per week, but his patient's stay at Rock Rest stretched the appointments to twice per month. In June 1931, his wife and boys were at Rock Rest and Tom returned to Nashville briefly. During his stay, Tom broke into the house of two unmarried sisters in their sixties during the middle of the afternoon. Drunk, and thinking it was his mother's house on Kensington Place, he first knocked on the door and tried to get in. When no one answered, he broke the door's glass and reached through to unlock it. He then walked into a bedroom, shed his clothes, and went to sleep. The terrified women fled, one running upstairs and the other bolting outside.

Tom was arrested and spent the night in jail, though his wife claimed to their inner circle that he was not charged with breaking-in and larceny. The event never made the Nashville newspapers. Tom called Howard the next morning and the attorney arranged for his friend to pay a fine in City Court for public drunkenness. Howard then contacted Clare Britton, who was a friend of his and the Buntins, and was also a nephew of the women. Britton arranged for the women and Tom to talk together, which resolved the matter by Tom having the door fixed and paying them $75. In return, he secured a written release from all civil liability.

Tom's ills continued. Dr. Burch got a call that his patient had driven off the road and his car was stuck in a gully in the yard of Rogers Caldwell's brother-in-law Goulding Trousdale. The physician continued to monitor the young man, seeing him for the last time at Elsie's house around the time the 1931 state fair opened. Buntin was "pretty blue" and drank during the entire twelve hours of Burch's visit. Consequences of the break-in returned shortly as well. When the two women's brother heard about the incident, he decided the settlement was too low and sent the intruder a "rough," "rather nasty letter" that Tom turned over to Howard.

In the early morning of Wednesday, September 23, 1931, Tom visited Elsie at the Kensington Place house. She had not spent much time at Rock Rest that summer while Tom and his family were there, so he came by regularly. That morning, she gave him the $200 stipend. Even though he returned to Rock Rest late that night, around 10:30 p.m., Bettie did not believe he had been drinking—or at least it was not noticeable to her. The following morning, her husband left Rock Rest early, telling Bettie he was taking the car to Nashville for repairs. Instead, he was in Howard's office by mid-morning and the two then visited Assistant District Attorney Harry Nichol about the threatening letter. Nichol assured Tom that there was "nothing in the world" to the brother's demand and he had no recourse. Tom seemed satisfied and asked Howard what he owed him. They settled on a Coca Cola together and then went their separate ways.

When Tom failed to return from the car repair trip to Nashville that night, September 24, Bettie was concerned but she did not report his absence to anyone in the family. Nothing to upset their family relationship had occurred that summer, she rationalized, so perhaps he was out of sorts for a bit, in his usual style. With the help of their sons' nursemaid, the young wife looked through Tom's belongings on Friday, September 25, and found his suits, suitcase, toiletries, and watch in place. She was certain that he did not have a second stash of clothing, because he never left clothes at the Hermitage Club in Nashville, as some patrons did. That afternoon, Bettie informed Tom's uncle, William Allison Buntin, of his nephew's failure to return from Nashville and then called her mother-in-law. Elsie was already on the alert because Tom had not visited in two days. Each woman asked trusted friends to "look around" discretely to see if Tom could be found, but there was no immediate luck.

Bettie weighed her options regarding telling others. George Gale, a childhood friend of her husband who summered at Rock Jolly nearby, had invited her and Tom to the horse show at the State Fair that Friday night. About 6 p.m., she called Gale, to tell him that Tom had not come home and asked whether she could come alone. Gale then called another friend to attend and the six, including Bettie, William Allison and Elizabeth, and her sister Hester, went on with their plans.

On Saturday, September 26, the letter arrived at William Allison and Elizabeth's summer home. He brought Bettie to their house to read it. As a reflection on crimes of that time, she may have expected a ransom note but this communication was far more distressing. The typewritten envelope was postmarked St. Louis, Missouri, dated the day before, Friday, September 25, 1931. Inside was a single sheet of typed text that appeared as follows, except for Tom's handwritten signature:

> I, Thomas C. Buntin, being of sound mind, do
> make this my last will, revoking all other wills
> which i may have made. i leave all of my property
> of every kind to Elizabeth Buntin.
> I also leave all interest I now have in the
> Craighead estate, and all interest I may hereafter
> have, to my wife, Elizabeth Buntin.
> I leave all interest in my life insurance policies to the Nashville
> Trust Company for the benefit of my children.
> Signed at St. Louis, Mo., this 25th day of September, 1931.
> (Signed) Thos. C. Buntin

Elsie called her son William Allison Saturday night around 9 p.m. and he read the communication over the phone to her. She was frightened and alarmed, fearing that the contents "showed plainly that something terrible had happened." On Sunday morning, she called her father, asking him to come over because she feared that Tom had committed suicide. When her father James Caldwell arrived, he carried an original of an identical will that he received in the mail, typed, postmarked St. Louis, and signed by Tom in his handwriting.

Bettie had a lot to think about, but she was also thinking very clearly. After "Yankee" soldiers destroyed the second Rock Rest house on the day of Christmas 1863, Rachel Carter Craighead rebuilt a Victorian-style farmhouse decades later, with lots of wood for framing, gingerbread trim, siding, and a porch. Rock Rest's third iteration lacked fireproof limestone-rock masonry, and a safe. The important piece of paper had to be stored in a secure area, so Bettie asked William Allison to bring the will he received to George Gale for safekeeping at Gale's Nashville law office.

William Allison walked into the lawyer's office Monday morning, September 28, and brusquely threw an envelope down on the desk, instructing Gale to "look here." Gale examined the envelope and its contents carefully. He thought the paper was written in a very awkward way, reflecting a layman's attempt to write an instrument in legal style. He also observed that it was probably written on an old typewriter, or that Tom did not know how to type, because the capitalization of "I" was uneven. Substantively, two items struck him. First, Tom did not say in the first paragraph "to my *wife* Elizabeth Buntin." Second, the Craighead estate was in litigation over property on North College Street and Tom knew he was not likely to win he and his sister's suit against their aunt Elizabeth Buntin Plummer. Gale was not asked to do anything about the will or Tom's disappearance, however, his only role being to safeguard the document. He stored it in a locked steel filing cabinet in his office.

Gale assumed that James Caldwell would safeguard the will he received in the mail, which Caldwell claimed he did by entrusting the document with the Nashville Trust Company. Tom had a checking account at his grandfather's bank, the Fourth and First National Bank, but there were no recent transactions that suggested suspicious activity. The old man then called on Sidney Souers, a vice president of the Missouri State Life Insurance Company in St. Louis, a firm that Caldwell's son Rogers had controlled, and scammed. The senior Caldwell had served on the board of directors of Missouri State Life until the previous December 1930. During Rogers's heyday, Souers often dined at Longview when he was in town. The St. Louis man also knew Tom generally from encounters in Caldwell's insurance office. Caldwell explained the letter, postmarked St. Louis, and asked the businessman to make discrete inquiries to see if Tom was in town.

Souers thought of Tom as a "gentleman" and a "fellow who would rather go to a fairly decent hotel, rather than the gutters," so he searched the places where he thought he would find him. In all, he called about ten to twelve hotels. Though Caldwell had not said what he thought Tom might be doing in St. Louis, Souers assumed that Caldwell thought his grandson might be "tooted somewhere" in town. In the end, he called "even the lower grade ones, The American and York," since Missouri State Life's parent company, American General Life, ran several hotels and Souers knew "fairly well the custom of these drunks." The search yielded no information. He assumed that the senior Caldwell wanted the inquiries kept quiet, so he did not check with the local police or the morgue.

New York Life was notified about Tom's disappearance and the family's fear, immediately expressed by his mother, that he had committed suicide. Local representatives, who reported to the Death Loss Division, interviewed Elsie first, in January 1932. Paul Johns, District Inspector in New York Life's Atlanta regional office, was then assigned the case around March 1932, about six months after the disappearance. An experienced investigator, he graduated from Vanderbilt University in 1924, so he knew Nashville well. He was tasked to report directly to the insurance company's

Law Department in the Home Office about the status of the investigation and any findings.

Disappearances of policy holders were a small part of the company's investigative work. In the Atlanta office, there were fewer than ten cases per year in the 1930s, and investigatory tactics, whether carried out by private investigators or the police, were not sophisticated. Frenchman Alphonse Bertillon had devised a technique to describe individuals—primarily, men who were criminal suspects—in a consistent, organized way based on a suite of physical measurements. His system could also be used at times to identify individuals who had disappeared but were then found. However, there was insufficient physical data about Tom to make a complete evaluation for a Bertillon index card, which relied on measurements of the length of the head, middle finger, left foot, little finger and forearm, the circumference of the head, and eye color.

Further, at that time, dactyloscopy, popularly known as "fingerprinting" identification, was rare for non-criminals, and the FBI almost always declined to initiate its own investigation of missing persons in the absence of fingerprints. The most fruitful query would have been to check with agencies responsible for unclaimed bodies/deaths, vital statistics, or passports, but New York Life did not do so for unknown reasons.

On May 23, 1932, W. W. McNeilly, a vice president of Nashville Trust, sent the insurance company formal notice that Buntin had disappeared and that the trust company might have a valid claim for the insurance proceeds in the future. New York Life only asked for a photo of the insured in return. Upon receipt, an alarm should have sounded but apparently did not. The trust company sent a copy of the photo from Tom's private pilot's license application to the U.S. Department of Commerce, Aeronautics Branch, the federal agency that first issued civil aeronautical licenses beginning in the late 1920s. One of Bertillon's lasting contributions to forensics was the *portrait parlé*, also known as a "mug shot." The pilot's license application photo was a clear, full-frontal mug shot of Tom, in which his mangled left ear was on display. If the insurance company had inquired about the date of the full application—and there is no indication that it did—investigators would have realized that the May 12, 1929, pilot's license application was dated one month after Tom's April 12, 1929, application to New York Life, in which he stated that he no longer took "aerial flights."

Tom's $50,000 policies dwarfed the average policy amount of $3,000 issued by New York Life and other insurers in the 1930s. However, Paul Johns did not interview Tom's wife until March 1936, at the Kensington Place house. Bettie gave him Tom's pilot's license that included his signature and the mug-shot photo. When asked if there was anything distinctive of his that was missing, she described an unusual ring that he wore: a dark green stone speckled with little red spots, engraved with a crest and boar's head. The setting ran across the face as a band, instead of orientation along the long way of the finger. She told Johns that she did not believe her husband was dead. She said he had talked about going into the fruit business in South America.

New York Life was one of the first insurance companies to cover deaths by suicide, as early as 1850. Sane or insane policy holders were covered under a "self-destruction" clause so long as the deceased had not been drunk or had taken opium. By the early twentieth century, actuarial data showed that New York Life's clients rarely died by suicide. These deaths comprised 3.4 percent of all covered deaths, occurred after the policy had been in effect from five to ten years, and were primarily committed by men who worked as merchants or were employed by merchants. New York Life was loath to accept that Tom's disappearance was circumstantial evidence of suicide because he did not meet these actuarial characteristics. He had also been investigated for insurability, including moral character, when he applied. The company's Medical Board and Classification Committee had even approved his fitness for the policies because of their substantial death-benefit value.

Following the company's preliminary investigation in the early 1930s, the case was placed on a "survey basis," which meant that "casual inquiries" were made from time to time in the places originally searched by the Buntins. New York Life's management always kept "one eye on the money" spent during an investigation. Rewards were out of the question since company policy prohibited offering money for information leading to the discovery of a missing policyholder.

Chapter 5

NASHVILLE TRUST COMPANY V. NEW YORK LIFE

At age twenty-eight, Bettie Buntin was a young woman when Tom disappeared in 1931, leaving her with three young sons. She did not have her own money and continued to live with her mother-in-law for twelve years, until 1943. The Great Depression raged in the years following Tom's disappearance and Bettie, like other once-moneyed widowed or single women, needed income. At her request, the auto dealer took back Tom's luxury LaSalle and Bettie sold his second car for $100. In 1935, she took a job as a saleswoman in the children's section of a large department store downtown. A few years later, she moved to sales at the Town and Country Shop, a small, exclusive ladies ready-wear shop that was initially started by two society women who needed income. The owners then employed other society women of distressed means.

As the years passed, she may have thought of her mother Louella who was also widowed young, at age thirty-three, and never remarried. Bettie was an educated, attractive woman. As "Mrs. Buntin," she kept active in clubs, social events, family holidays and dinners, traveling, and summers at Rock Rest. She was almost always in the company of Elsie or the Caldwells or went out by herself, unaccompanied by a male. If she thought of re-marrying while in her late twenties or early thirties, Tennessee's "Enoch Arden" marriage laws—which are still on the books—provided an option to avoid potential bigamy in case Tom was still alive. These laws were enacted in many states as a way "to meet intelligently" the situation in which one spouse has been absent for some time and the other spouse remarries, thinking that the first spouse is dead, though that turns out later not to be the case.

The informal name for these marriage laws ("Enoch Arden") was inspired by a mid-nineteenth-century poem by Alfred Tennyson. In the composition, an English woman remarried after Enoch, her sailor husband, went missing at sea for over a decade. The impoverished wife had given up all hope for his return. By a twist of fate, the mariner was marooned on an island but was then rescued and returned to his village. There, he found his loved one in a new life, married to a mutual (and wealthy) childhood friend. Heartbroken, he never disclosed his presence to her because of her secure financial standing. Enoch died a sad and lonely man.

In Tennessee, two Enoch Arden legal options were available. First, a spouse could marry a second time without getting the first marriage dissolved legally if the first spouse had been absent for two years and there was a "well-founded" rumor (though subsequently shown to be false) that the first spouse had died. If the absented spouse later reappeared, he (or she) could, within a year, ask a court for a divorce or to restore conjugal rights. This option was risky in that it placed the legal rights in favor of Enoch Arden, the long-lost spouse. The second option gave Bettie a favorable legal position and no discretion on the part of a court. The law stated that a second marriage could not be "contracted" before dissolution of the first, but provided that the first marriage "shall be regarded as dissolved" if either party had been absent for at least five years and the absentee spouse was not known to the other to be living. She had told the insurance company that she did not believe that Tom committed suicide, which undercut using this legal option.

There was also the matter of Tom's sizeable insurance policies. They did not prohibit a payout if she remarried but it would have been wise to take no chances. In case of a dispute, the company would surely argue that a remarriage, especially if the second husband was wealthy, showed she did not need the money. The terms of the policies required "due proof" of the insured's death, of which there was, to date, no direct evidence. The general rule of law then, as it is now, is that a person is presumed to be dead if he or she has not been heard from for seven years by those who would normally have heard from the person if he or she was alive. Tom failed to return to Rock Rest on September 24, 1931, making the seven-year presumptive-death date September 24, 1938. New York Life's calculation for payout may have been to pay for a $3,000 policy. However, with this case, the company owed at least the $50,000 value of Tom's policies, independent of interest, penalties, and court costs if the case was litigated.

Thus, the insurance company doubled down in its investigation in 1937, a year before the presumptive-death date. The company's surety on the policies was Laurence Howard of the law firm Bailey and Howard in Nashville, the lawyer who claimed Tom as an intimate friend. Howard oversaw a renewed and expanded nationwide search in mid-March 1937. Letters were sent to police departments in twenty-five cities, including Cincinnati, New York City, New Orleans, Miami, Washington, D.C., Denver, St. Louis, Philadelphia, Boston, Laramie, San Francisco, and Los Angeles. Information was sought on the whereabouts of Thomas Craighead Buntin, a "decided blond, almost straw colored with just a touch of red coloring," blue eyes, and an abnormal protruding left ear, depicted in the pilot's license photo that was enclosed in each letter. Howard's secretary even checked with the "Sing Sing" prison in New York. There was no trace of Tom anywhere.

A legal dance between the trust company and insurance company began in the fall of 1938, carried out through letters. The correspondence culminated in the Nashville Trust Company's submittal of Bettie Buntin's affidavit and completed proof-of-death forms in mid-December 1938. New York Life responded quickly, refusing to pay, and asserting that "the evidence which we have points to a voluntary disappearance and not to death." By that point, New York Life had spent about $2,000 to $2,500 trying to find Buntin, an extraordinary sum compared to its usual cost of an investigation.

In February 1939, *Nashville Trust Company v. New York Life Insurance Company* (the "Buntin Case 1") was filed in the Second Circuit Court of Davidson County, located in the county seat of Nashville. The plaintiff sought to recover proceeds under two policies issued on April 12, 1929, to Thomas Craighead Buntin, for a total amount, including interest, of $63,608.29. The trust company's case was based on the inference that Tom had committed suicide. He had been in a "highly nervous and excitable condition" before he disappeared that was "aggravated and strengthened by the financial difficulties" wrought by the Great Depression. The presumed deceased had a "very unusual appearance" because of a childhood accident in which his left ear was severely cut, leaving it noticeably protruded. In other words, a body had not been found, but, if it had been found in some state of intactness, the ear would have enabled his identification.

New York Life's lawyers filed an answer on May 22, 1939, to dismiss the case, mostly arguing against the claim of suicide because a suicide note and a body were never found. At a hearing on June 17, 1939, Judge Albert Bramlett ("A.B.") Neil rejected the insurance company's argument to dismiss the case on the pleadings, which would have prevented a jury from considering the evidence. Following a year of pretrial discovery, the trial was held before Judge Neil and twelve male jurors over five days in June 1940. The courtroom was packed with reporters and curious onlookers. The plaintiff trust company's strategy was to show that it was reasonable to infer that Tom's absence was based on suicide. The defendant insurance company's strategy was to convince the trier of fact that Tom disappeared of his own accord, for reasons that would come out during the trial.

Curiously, the primary evidence in the case—the two originals of Tom's will—had vanished. William Allison Buntin gave the original will he received in the mail in September 1931 to George Gale, at Gale's office in Nashville. Gale had moved to Washington, DC, from 1935 to 1938 as an attorney with the federal Reconstruction Finance Corporation. In 1938, when Laurence Howard was retained by New York Life to represent the company in the dispute over Tom's policies, he visited Gale in the nation's capital to request his file on Tom, including the original will.

Gale stated that he left the file in his office at the law firm in Nashville, so he wrote his secretary there and asked her to give Howard the entire file. He well-remembered the physical characteristics of the file. It was in a "stiff cardboard" folder eight inches by twenty or twenty-four inches, with a tabbed label at the top on which was typed "Mrs. Thomas Buntin." Miss Roach, his secretary, wrote back that she could not find the file, although she found "many other" Buntin files in the filing cabinet. A search through the firm's archived materials turned up nothing.

During the trial, Nashville Trust also failed to produce the original document entrusted to the company by James Caldwell, who was the trust company's president at the time. Caldwell claimed that he delivered to Nashville Trust the original version of Tom's will that he received in the mail shortly after his grandson's disappearance. He recalled that he made a trip to the offices within two to three days of receiving the will in 1931 and that he never saw it again. However, he never said to whom he entrusted the document, and no one ever asked him in sworn testimony to whom he gave it to. During cross-examination by Albert Stockell, another New York Life lawyer, Charles Nelson, President of Nashville Trust, testified that he had never seen the original that Caldwell claimed he delivered. Nelson could not explain why the trust company had failed to safeguard critical evidence.

To compensate for the missing originals of the most key document in the trial, the trust company put George Gale on the witness stand to recollect the contents of the original will that William Allison Buntin received. The document that Tom supposedly mailed from St. Louis is from the contents of an exhibit to Gale's testimony and is based entirely on the lawyer's recall after nine years, including incorrect capitalizations and incomplete punctuation. Further, the exhibit is titled "Will" though Gale admitted on the stand he could not completely remember whether the document had a title. There was "no doubt" in his mind it was a will, however. Astonishingly, the judge allowed what amounted to a hearsay substitute for the missing documents—crucial evidence in the trial.

On Monday afternoon, June 10, 1940, the trust company called Bettie Buntin to the stand. Dr. John Burch had observed that the Buntin's relationship was "all right" and that Bettie was the type of wife that did not nag at Tom or worry him, but instead tried in every way to help him. She testified that she loved her husband and that that there were no signs to indicate that he had any other feeling for her except that of "deep affection." Other than his

Exhibit 1 to testimony of George Gale.

"WILL

"I, Thomas C. Buntin, being of sound mind, do make this my last will, revoking all other wills which I may have made. I leave all of my property of every kind to Elizabeth Buntin.

I also leave all interest I now have in the Craighead estate, and all interest I may hereafter have, to my wife, Elizabeth Buntin.

I leave all interest in my life insurance policies to the Nashville Trust Company for the benefit of my children.

Signed at St.Louis, Mo., this 25th day of September, 1931.

(Signed) Thos. C. Buntin "

(Buntin Case 1.)

drinking, there was nothing to "interrupt the pleasantness and sweetness" of their marriage, including Tom's devotion to and pride in his sons. She agreed, however, that he was always living "up on the heights or down in the bottom," a "vicious circle."

On cross-examination, Stockell inquired on behalf of New York Life whether it was true that Tom wanted to farm in South America, but she replied, "no," and that his father had not had a ranch there, as rumored. And "no," he was not still flying airplanes. She stated that he had given up piloting the last two to three years they were together, a curious answer since Bettie knew that Tom secured a pilot's license in 1929. She had even given the license to New York Life's investigator Paul Johns. Stockell posed a final question: was Tom an unintelligent man? "No sir." "Rather a smart man, wasn't he?" "Yes," she replied, "with the exception of his drinking; he wasn't smart about that."

John Dougherty, who had worked in the insurance office under Tom, testified that he was with him on Monday and Tuesday the week of his disappearance. They drank together all day on those two days, and Tom was "blue and melancholy." Buntin called him to meet at noon on Wednesday, the day before he disappeared. Though Dougherty felt Tom was "very peculiar" in that he did not "want anybody to know very much about his business," he declined the offer to meet even though it was clear that his friend had a matter to discuss.

Three days into the trial, Stockell's cross-examination of Dougherty gave the first glimpse into the insurance company's theory of Tom's motive for disappearance. Laurence Howard first heard the speculation from New York Life's in-house attorneys in "casual conversations" during the initial phases of the case. Charles Anstett, New York Life's Superintendent of Inspections, was deposed in May 1940, a month before the trial started but his deposition had not yet been made public. During the interrogation, he confirmed that there was a probability that Buntin had a relationship with a woman who disappeared contemporaneously with him and that they might be together somewhere. The insurance company's attorney had to tread carefully in his cross-examination. Crimes could be inferred against Tom—if he were indeed alive—depending on the answers to the questions. At that time, a married or unmarried man who wooed a woman (not his wife) into intimate relations could be found guilty of "felonious seduction," carrying a penalty of up to five years in jail. Bigamy, the act of being married to two people simultaneously, was also a felony offense.

Stockell posed the question to Dougherty: "There is a young lady that worked here in the office by the name of Miss Betty McCuddy; did you know her?" "Yes sir. She left the insurance company about a year before Tom left." Dougherty was then asked to describe what she looked like. The witness did his best to denigrate her physical appearance, calling her "not very neat," "heavy set," and not attractive "by a long shot." When handed a photo of a sweet-faced young woman, with bobbed hair and one kiss curl over her forehead, he agreed that it was her, claiming that the photographer had been "mighty good" and did her "good justice." Stockell inquired whether James Caldwell complained about her. The witness hedged and claimed he did not know, but that she was working there when he (Dougherty) left the firm. He estimated she was making about $150 per month, a "good salary."

Nashville Trust's lawyer pressed Howard Van Arsdell of the insurance office to describe Miss McCuddy's appearance, in an obvious attempt to negate the inference that Tom may have been attracted to her. The co-worker complied. She was "very untidy," let her clothes get in a "terrible condition," and neglected to keep her hair and fingernails "nice." He even ventured that the young woman "always looked like her neck was dirty." Left unsaid was that Van Arsdell and his wife were friends of Tom and Bettie's and the two couples socialized together, so his relationship with the matter was more complex than just that of an employee. His and Dougherty's testimony left the impression that no man would have been attracted to the office worker—or at least no self-respecting man on the jury who considered himself an effective arbiter of who was and was not a "dish."

New York Life clumsily attempted to remedy the impressions. On cross examination, Van Arsdell was asked whether it was possible that she might be suitable for romance with an alcoholic man and he conceded that she might because there was no "accounting for the tastes" of such men. The query provoked sparring by each side's lawyers regarding whether liquor drinkers had "delightful" taste in the opposite sex or not—perhaps influenced by their own experiences. The judge finally halted the exchange, though noting that it was a "matter of argument" whether imbibers had good taste in women. It was not clear who had bested the other regarding taste in women, but New York Life prevailed in the exchange in one sense. The strongest evidence was physical, and the photograph depicted a decidedly good-looking female. Years later, Van Arsdell would admit to a news reporter that Miss McCuddy was, after all, a "very attractive girl."

James Caldwell, age eighty-six, was called as one of Nashville Trust's final witnesses. Following AT&T's acquisition of Cumberland Telephone and Telegraph, he was named president of the Fourth and First National Bank. His hair had thinned and turned white, but a full moustache and beard lent a continued vitality. He was a sharp businessman who brooked no nonsense, hardened by surviving many vicious battles. After becoming president of Cumberland early in his career, the company's treasurer accused him of defrauding the company of $10,000. Through Caldwell's keen powers of observation, he turned the tables and proved that the claimant was herself the defrauder through precise cutting-and-pasting of false numbers in the paper ledger. He then incessantly fought Cumberland's cutthroat competitors from destroying phone poles. AT&T's president Theodore Vail threatened Caldwell financial ruin if the non-deferential Caldwell stayed at his company after its acquisition by AT&T. Caldwell left on his own terms and with his money intact.

A southern elite was on the stand, a man who "never let anyone forget" that he was a "dignified aristocrat," even as his life ebbed. He testified about his insurance business, its business misfortunes (for which he claimed Tom was not responsible), Tom's sensitive nature, and the love and affection his grandson had for his wife and three boys. During Stockell's cross-examination on behalf of New York Life, the elderly man refused to answer whether he recalled a woman named Miss McCuddy. Nashville Trust's lawyer then redirected questions to Caldwell, noting that his opposing counsel "seems to know a lot about your business. His firm represented Fourth and First Bank, didn't it?" "Yes," the elder Caldwell replied, and "they put in the most unconscionable fee I ever looked at." Rebuked, Stockell declined to further question Caldwell on behalf of the insurance company.

The Tennessean's coverage of the trial that day was headlined "Jury Hears Buntin May Be Alive; Woman's Name Enters into Case." The location of the article, which had no reporter byline, was curious. The salacious news did not appear on the front page where it would reach a wide and curious audience. Instead, it was tucked away in an obscure interior page filled with advertisements, church-event announcements, and obituaries. It is possible that the Buntin and/or Caldwell families influenced the story's placement because of the information that came out in open court that day. The deposition of New York Life's Superintendent of Inspections had been read into the record. In the transcript, he acknowledged during cross-examination that the insurance company had obtained a picture of a young woman known as "Miss Betty McCuddy." The clear implication of the questioning—and the news coverage—was that Miss McCuddy was integral to Tom Buntin's disappearance. Who was Betty McCuddy of Russellville, Kentucky?

Part Two

BETTY

Chapter 6

Betty Edwards McCuddy

"Dead" titled the story in the *Herald-Ledger*'s November 20, 1903, edition of Russellville's newspaper. George Duncan McCuddy, the baby boy of Mr. and Mrs. Robert Ferguson McCuddy, "died rather suddenly last night" at four days old. Sorrows continued. Three years later to almost the exact day, a second son, "bright-eyed, cherry-faced" Robert Ferguson McCuddy Jr., "fell asleep in Jesus" at noon at his parents' home. He was ten months old. At a time in their marriage when most young parents would have barely thought of their own interment, the McCuddys had buried two babies in Maple Grove Cemetery in the south-central Kentucky town.

The tragedies could not have been imagined when the young couple, so full of promise, were married in the summer of 1902. Mary Edwards Duncan, "one of the most beautiful girls of Russellville," abruptly wed Robert Ferguson ("Fergus") McCuddy in the Episcopalian rectory in town on a mid-summer afternoon. The two forewent the "very fashionable wedding" that was expected following their long courtship and the social standing of their families.

Mary's family tree, particularly through her mother, Bettie Edwards Duncan, was branched with intellectuals, including men with an acumen for law and finance. Her maternal great-grandfather, Presley Edwards, settled in Logan County (where Russellville is county seat) around 1800. He married his first cousin, Hester Pope, known for her "superior cultivation" and "uncommon conversational powers." Her parents were Penelope Edwards and William Pope. Pope, along with five other appointees, laid out the town of Louisville in Jefferson County in the late eighteenth century. Mary's remote cousin Albert Gallatin Edwards befriended Abraham Lincoln. After a lengthy career as assistant secretary of the U.S. Treasury, Edwards founded a stock and bond brokerage firm in St. Louis in the late 1880s called A.G. Edwards and Son.

Fergus's paternal family first settled in Logan County in 1829, when Isaac Boswell McCuddy and wife Mildred Malina Bohannon, his great-grandparents, moved from Woodford County, Kentucky. Isaac began farming with thirty acres of "excelent corn," purchased for $4.50 per acre, and some "fatning hoggs." They bought the Robert and Frances Guinn Baylor house and property called "Flint Ridge"—reportedly haunted by Mrs. Baylor—which encompassed 800 acres of land south of Russellville. In 1895, Fergus graduated from Bethel College, a "thorough institution" in Russellville. The Baptist school advertised that its location was in an unsurpassed "moral and religious" setting, especially since there no saloons nearby to afford "attractions of vice." His senior class, whose class colors were pink and lavender, was small, only ten males. It was sizeable enough, however, to ensure that the baseball and football programs had complete teams. Fergus was senior-class secretary, a member of the literary society, associate editor of the newsletter, and an officer in the athletic club. He was tall, with dark, full hair parted in the middle, and dark, prominent brows.

Following graduation, Fergus taught school for a few years. George B. Edwards then hired him as a teller at the Deposit Bank in 1897, the same year that Mary graduated with a bachelor's degree from Logan Female College. Whether this is where he first met the banker or whether Mary's uncle was inclined to hire him, possibly because he was a suitor of his niece at that time, is unknown. Fergus's employment announcement noted that he was "spoken of in the highest terms by those who know him." What is clear is that Mary and Fergus were a pair by August 1901. That month, they hosted the "greatest social event of the summer," with an orchestra and party favors, for friends of Mary's visiting from Philadelphia. Fergus had been promoted to the bank's cashier (chief operating officer) position.

At the time of their second son's death in November 1906, Mary was expecting another child. Betty Edwards McCuddy was born at home on June 27, 1907. The joyous news was not announced in the local newspapers or in the Louisville or Nashville newspapers. The absence of public announcements was perhaps attributed to her parents' experience with the births, then losses, of their first two babies. In 1908, when Betty was

BETHEL COLLEGE.

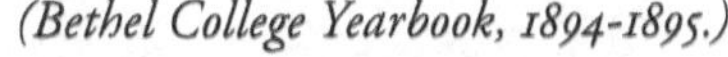

Ca. 1885. (Library Research Collections, Western Kentucky Univ.)

(Bethel College Yearbook, 1894-1895.)

Fergus McCuddy, senior year. (Bethel College Yearbook, 1894-1895.)

one year old, the family moved to "Mockingbird Hill," last owned by her mother's Uncle George B. Edwards. The property was originally known as "The Oaks" or "Oakhill" for its treed allée terminating in a circular carriage drive in front of the house. The Greek Revival-style mansion was constructed between 1837 and 1850 on an expansive yard in the southeast part of town and was occupied by the U.S. Army during the Civil War. Today, the house sits at the end of Boxwood Drive.

Early atlases commended Russellville as "one of the prettiest, best watered, and healthiest villages" in Kentucky. Mockingbird Hill had a superb vantagepoint of these environs because the house sits high on a

Mockingbird Hill. (Photo by author.)

hill and is largely defined visually by numerous windows. From the front (north-facing) and west windows, almost all of town could have been viewed, though trees would have obscured most of the one-story businesses and houses in the early twentieth century. The steeples of First Baptist, First Presbyterian, and Trinity Episcopal would have been noticed first above the greenery. Dominating the skyline, however, would have been the Queen Anne-style turrets of the family house of C.W. Courts at Ninth and Main streets. The cupola of the new 1904 county courthouse would have been partially visible, with clocks on each side and a weathervane on top. Curious, Russian-looking double-onion domes squatting on the roof would have been evident. The Logan County Jail and the outlines of City Park at Old Courthouse Square would also have been partially visible. Black Bottom, the African American community to the northeast, would not have been visible, its small shotgun and single-pen houses shielded by trees. Immediately to the west, the central bell tower of the Logan Female College would have loomed large when the Victorian-era damask drapery was pushed aside to peer out the windows.

Well-to-do Christian families of the time placed their bibles on a sitting-parlor table. Conspicuous to visitors, the white-leather cover for the "book of hope" was a new hue in the bible-making business, which had made only black-leather covers until the early 1900s. The town's gentility, including the McCuddys and Edwards, worshipped at those soaring-steepled Christian churches visible from Mockingbird Hill. Russellville and Logan County were in a violent and lawless period, however. In Betty's first year of age, white mobs raided the county jail to lynch rapists or brawlers, and Ku Klux Klan-mimicking night riders associated with the dark tobacco planters' association torched tobacco warehouses downtown. It is likely that Fergus and Mary could see the flames from their house. Six months later, four Black Bottom men accused of being "troublemakers" were arrested on minor charges and then hauled from the jail and lynched in the hanging tree, a cedar just south of town.

Baby Betty would have been kept far away from those troubles, and the conflicts would not have directly affected her parents. Fergus advanced at Deposit Bank, becoming a vice president by January 1907, and was elected to the Russellville Board of Councilmen that same year. However, his and Mary's personal joys, followed by tragedies, continued. Son William Ross ("Bill") was born in June 1909. Daughter Margaret Connelly was born in September 1912 but died at six years of age of diabetes, after a six-month bout of influenza.

Little is publicly known about the personality and character of the McCuddy's only daughter when she was a child. However, based on the traits that people identified in her as a young woman, Betty was independent, intelligent, and determined from toddlerhood on. While in elementary school, she was active in Russellville's Musical Art Club and had an inquisitive mind, often mailing in answers to children's puzzles in the newspapers and winning contests.

The Edwards and McCuddy families' expectations and social status dictated private, girls' boarding-school education for intermediate and senior high school and college preparation. Betty was enrolled in Nazareth Academy near Bardstown, Kentucky, by the time she was twelve, in 1919, and stayed through May 1923. Situated in the gentle rolling topography of Nelson County in the bluegrass region, the academy was quite rural and less developed in the early 1920s, even less so than Logan County. Nazareth, one of the oldest private educational institutions in Kentucky and the South, was founded in 1814 by the Catholic Sisters of Charity and renowned for a "disposition toward conservative innovations." Students came from well-heeled families who, like the McCuddys, were not necessarily Catholic, and were drawn from across the South, including Kentucky, Tennessee, Alabama, and Louisiana. Although Nazareth was on a line of the Louisville & Nashville ("L&N") Railroad, the 129 miles between Russellville and the school was the farthest Betty had been from her hometown, and over twice the distance to Nashville.

In the fall of 1923 following graduation from Nazareth, Betty enrolled as a boarding student her senior year of high school in the exclusive Ward-Belmont School for Young Women in a more familiar setting, Nashville. She attended for the 1923 to 1924 term. Her limited stay may have precluded active involvement in school organizations, in which the other girls had participated for four years, or she simply may not have been a joiner. She was a member of one social club, called the Del Vers, however. Ward-Belmont was much larger than Nazareth, attended by almost 600 young women from across the nation, many participating in one of twenty-three state clubs on campus. The thirty-acre school, including the antebellum Belmont mansion, was located on the grounds of the former estate of Adelicia Hayes Franklin Acklen Cheatham. Adelicia was a multiple-time widow and the wealthiest woman in Tennessee following the sale of her first husband's Louisiana estates after he died. The largest of those properties was the Angola plantation and its enslaved workers, subsequently notorious as a brutal state prison.

Girls could pursue a variety of academic courses at Ward-Belmont leading to a high school education or a two-year junior college diploma, including liberal arts, fine arts, home economics, physical education and playground supervision, and business (stenography, typewriting, and book-keeping). The latter was offered to prepare young women to manage the "business affairs" of their domestic households and, less frequently, to "fill positions of executive responsibility" or manage their own estates. *Careers for Women*, a contemporary publication of the Intercollegiate Vocational Guidance Association, described 160 occupations "open to women" in order to educate "every girl who has felt that her choice of career is limited to nursing, teaching and stenography." Some options were clearly directed to exceptional females who had exceptional opportunities and fortitude—such as careers in opera, bond sales, optometry, surgery, architecture, and corporate law. Others were outright puzzling even for those times, not to mention penury-inducing: beekeeping, poultry-keeping, genealogy, and professional storytelling. Some careers were assumed to be "beyond the capabilities of the gentler sex." They were nonetheless carried out ably by

Betty, lower left, Ward-Belmont, 1923-1924. (Milestones Yearbook, 1924.)

women in the mid-1920s, as some business publication editors begrudgingly admitted: law, stock brokerage, civil engineering, cotton brokerage, industrial plant management, iron and steel sales, and welding.

The possibilities of women's careers were promoted. In reality, curriculum

Ward-Belmont Senior Hall, 1924. (Ibid.)

was limited during the 1920s, even in private female schools. A practical girl, Betty ultimately chose, or was directed into, stenography, which is the writing technique called "shorthand." In this process, the stenographer writes shorthand symbols on paper from oral dictation given by another person, and then the stenographer transcribes the shorthand to a typed communication on hard-copy paper. By the time Betty entered high school, Gregg shorthand was the standard system in the country. This skill would prove invaluable as her life progressed.

She returned to Russellville to live with her parents after graduating from Ward-Belmont. During the summer and fall of 1924, the young woman traveled back and forth to Nashville with friends. She read incessantly, liked to quote the author Rudyard Kipling in her letters, and was not particularly outgoing, though she enjoyed a "good joke" and had a "jocular side." She was considered "intelligent," "strongly independent," and a "steady" young woman. The small-town residents especially noted that she did not have "beaus," nor did she seem interested in boyfriends.

Chapter 7

Betty's Great-Uncle - George B. Edwards

Tragedy seemed to afflict the Edwards of Russellville, a family whose "cup of sorrow and grief" was continually "overflowing" from premature deaths. Betty's mother Mary lost two babies and one child to illness by the time she was forty. Her siblings George and Hester died a year apart, in 1903 and 1904. He succumbed to a gunshot wound in a hunting accident. Hester shot herself in the heart following her beloved brother's death and was found with the pistol still in her hand. Their parents died young, as did their aunts and uncles, except for George Benjamin Edwards.

George B. Edwards was a large man whose big shoulders and financial resources carried his family. He took on financial responsibility for his young nieces (including Mary Edwards Duncan) and nephews (including Nashville lawyer J. Connelly Edwards) following his siblings' deaths. He then deployed his resources for his great-nieces and great-nephews. George B. had graduated from Yale University with a finance degree (where, during his last two years, he roomed with another large man, William Howard Taft). He then earned a law degree from the University of Virginia. As a young man, Edwards returned to Russellville and initially represented the L&N Railroad in regional matters. There was a surfeit of lawyers in town, at least seventeen "good" ones. Finding consistently well-paying clients would require sharp elbows—deployed in southern gentlemanly fashion— and possibly not that much financial remuneration over a career. In his mid-forties, the bachelor was rumored to be President Grover Cleveland's choice for appointment as the Minister to Hawaii, but his substantial family ties prevailed. He stayed in southwest-central Kentucky.

The lawyer made a financially sound decision to pivot to banking, eventually becoming Russellville's first millionaire. He became president of Deposit Bank in 1891, and then purchased the bank, renaming it the Southern Deposit Bank. By 1906, it was the largest bank in Logan County, one "sound as a dollar." The local newspaper lauded the "conservatism, safety, and soundness" of the experienced and capable young men in charge and noted there were "no dummies" on its board of directors. The institution also featured the only burglar-proof safe in the region. The door to the double-decker storage area of the safe was held shut with screws that withstood dynamite blasts. Enhanced security was an artifact of a successful heist of Deposit Bank's predecessor bank in 1868 by a gun-toting, "reckless firing" gang of men. Their take was said to have ranged from $9,000 to $19,000, a wide divergence but an astonishing amount of money. The masterminds of the heist, brothers Jesse and Frank James, hid nearby but did not participate because of injuries from previous thieving.

Banker Edwards' physical heft and the large ring he wore on his thumb left an indelible impression. Townspeople appreciated his approachability and his willingness to freely offer investment advice. Once, he told an elementary-school-age girl that he passed on the street to buy Standard Oil of Kentucky stock if she ever came into any money. Taft and he kept in touch, sharing anecdotes and advice for years, even after the Cincinnatian became U.S. president and then chief justice of the U.S. Supreme Court. Taft sentimentally called Edwards an "old fat carcass" in their personal correspondence. To others, Edwards was the "best of fellows" and the "ablest man in southwestern Kentucky," despite his "Bourbon Democracy." George B., in turn, called his friend "Bill."

By 1924, his siblings' children had begun to pass away. Four nieces and nephews were left. There were six great-nieces and great-nephews, including Mary's two children Betty and Bill (both unmarried minors), Elizabeth Sinclair Buntin (married to William Allison Buntin of Nashville), her sister Hester, and George Edwards Duncan. Edwards' assets were valued at around $1 million in 1924 ($18.4 million in current dollars). He experienced bouts of an unspecified serious illness over the years, which confined him to home at times and led him to travel south for his health at other times. Still, he seems to have enjoyed a vigorous and busy work and personal life.

He waited until October 1924, when he was seventy years old, to tackle the complex issue of his will.

First, George B. designated Fidelity and Columbia Trust Company ("Fidelity Trust") in Louisville, Kentucky, as executor and trustee. He then bequeathed his nephews and nieces $30,000 each, including Mary Edwards Duncan McCuddy and J. Connelly Edwards. Mary's gift provided that, following her death, the trustee could, in its discretion, pay her two children Betty and Bill interest from the trust until they reached the age of thirty, at which time the trustee could pay each one-fourth of the principal. When each child turned forty, the trustee could pay the remaining amount of the principal of the trust, one-half to each. The most significant part of this gift provided that, if either Betty or Bill died before receiving their final distribution, their one-half share of principal would convey to their surviving child or children (if any) and if either sibling died without their own children, their share would convey to the other sibling if she or he were living. Following Betty McCuddy's disappearance, this clause became litigious.

In addition to the specific monetary bequests, Edwards addressed his residuary estate, which consists of the assets left after deducting payment of the deceased's debts; funeral expenses; estate taxes; and costs, fees, and expenses of probate administration and setting up the trusts established in a will. The value is not known at the time a will is made, but it can be sizeable. Edwards' residuary estate turned out to be substantial, more so than what he directly left his nieces and nephews by making $30,000 gifts to each. His will divided the residuary estate into equal parts, held in trust to pay for the support and maintenance of niece Mary McCuddy (and her two children) and his three nephews.

Edwards subsequently re-dictated portions of his will to his house-keeper/typist Martha seventeen times, tinkering with gifts to non-family members but not substantially changing the initial bequests to his extended family members. The last codicil was executed in May 1929. On October 24 and 25, 1929, the New York Stock Exchange experienced a "dramatic collapse," the news of which took a few days to reach the general public in southwest-central Kentucky. Edwards would have been informed of the Great Crash almost immediately, however, as a banker who was still heavily invested in stocks. In mid-November 1929, George and Martha traveled to Louisville for a "slight operation" he needed, after which they intended to return to Russellville. While recovering in Louisville he became ill and was admitted to St. Joseph Infirmary, where he died on December 15 at seventy-five years of age. The cause of death was listed as "acute dilation of the heart" with "chronic myocarditis" as a contributing cause. His big heart simply gave out. He was buried in Maple Grove Cemetery in Russellville, his gravesite marked with a simple, in-ground headstone in the Edwards' family plot.

Chapter 8

BELKNAP HARDWARE, LOUISVILLE

After graduating from Ward-Belmont in May 1924, Betty was ready to move into the world as an adult. Stenographer skills were not highly sought in the small town of Russellville, and, in any event, she was probably eager to expand her vistas in a large city. Nashville was a logical choice because of family and social ties there. A trip back to see her parents in Russellville took less than half a day by bus.

She stayed in Russellville for about a year, working on other plans for her life. At Ward-Belmont, she wore a page-boy bob, popularized by actress Louise Brooks, and no makeup. Following graduation, she had her straight, dark hair, parted down the middle, cut in an even more boyish bob, with a provocative and prominent kiss curl. Her kiss curl was a single, thick strand of hair, in a backwards "C," boldly covering her forehead and reaching between a widely spaced and slim set of darkened eyebrows. Some women wore numerous kiss curls, though it was rumored that the number of curls equaled the number of men that had kissed them. For that reason, or reasons imposed by the school, most bobs at Ward-Belmont were page bobs or wavy bobs without the forelocks. Now that she was preparing to be out on her own, Betty wore one kiss curl. With the bob and makeup, the effect was assertive and forward-looking.

Betty chose Louisville as the place to start her work career, even though she had not spent much time there. The city's population slightly exceeded 155,000, larger than Nashville, whose population was about 120,000 in 1924. Her great-uncle, George B. Edwards, who was in his seventies when

Betty McCuddy, ca. 1924. (Buntin Case 1.)

she graduated, knew Louisville and its business community well. With his likely help and other proper referrals, in 1925, she rented Apartment 34 in the prestigious eight-story Weissinger-Gaulbert building at 300-310 Broadway, on the southwest corner adjoining Third Street. Securing a place there depended on reputation and connections. Weissinger-Gaulbert was one of the first apartment blocks to be built in the city of Louisville, in 1903.

In high demand, it was advertised as one of the most modern apartment houses in the city with a fireproof brick exterior and modern conveniences. Furnished flats rented for $85 per month. A typical unit in the main building was about 600 to 650 square feet total, with one bedroom and one bath.

Weissinger-Gaulbert Apts., ca. 1904. (Modern Sanitation magazine.)

A bay window extended from the living room, allowing natural light to filter into the small space. If the numerous smokestacks associated with the stockyards and breweries were at a lull, the steeples of the German Catholic churches in Butchertown could be seen to the east from the front (north) and east apartments. Although the exterior architecture of the apartment building reflected the Victorian era, the interior design would have rejected the overcrowded, fussiness of Betty's parents' home furnishings in favor of the modern style, consisting of simple, nonperiod furniture in each room.

The apartments comprised a main building (where she was located) and associated annex, and a Third Street annex, which together occupied a prominent place on Broadway. The essentials were close by, including Julius Strauss's grocery store on the ground-level floor of her building and the Wilderness Road Book Shop on the ground level of the new Brown Hotel across Broadway. Opened by iconoclasts Henrietta Bingham and Edie Callahan, the bookstore was considered a book lover's place and stayed open until 10 p.m. for hotel guests and after-hours shopping by locals. Broadway and the blocks between Third and Fourth Streets were heavily used, making the apartments noisy, but there was a shaded, central courtyard in the complex, alleviating some of the bustle of cars and the trolley. The refuge was ideal for reading books at leisure.

300 block of Broadway looking west, 1926. The Brown Hotel is on the right. (Metropolitan Sewer District Collection, Archives & Special Collections, Univ. of Louisville.)

The young woman began her first job in stenography at Belknap Hardware and Manufacturing during mid-to-late 1925, most likely with her great-uncle's help. One of George B. Edwards' classmates at Yale was the son of the founder of Belknap and the banker undoubtedly knew the current president, William Heyburn. By the early 1920s, Belknap's office on the northeast corner of Second and Washington streets was exploding at the seams. A new twelve-story office building was completed at 111 E. Main St. in 1923 where the beloved Galt House hotel formerly stood on the shores of the Ohio River. The company's advertisements could then claim that, with over 1.6 million square feet of floor space, it was the "largest single unit hardware plant in the world."

Befitting a modern young woman, Betty's new workspace epitomized the modern business office, reflecting Frederick Winslow Taylor's principles of scientific management. An "automatic telephone system" for calls within the building reduced time spent by 1,400 employees wastefully moving back and forth to communicate in person. Centralized coat rooms, which encouraged mingling and socializing before work, were abolished, replaced by locker rooms on each floor, close to worker spaces. Wood furniture was discarded—it cracked, peeled, came apart at the joints, warped, burned in fires, and required polishing. Steel furniture had none of these problems.

Office noise was reduced by installing heavy linoleum to cover the floors. The interior walls and pillars were painted white to rid work areas of dark, unlit spaces and light globes were "scientifically placed" to promote optimum workspace conditions. The cafeteria was sized to serve up to 600 employees at a time and there was a dance floor on the tenth level of the building, presumably for after-hours recreation.

Appropriate business attire for a stenographer was a slim-fitting, tailored suit of tweed in gray, with silk braid slightly darker, and a lined short coat, correct for the office and yet *chic* for lunch. A Margaret Rorke hat, washable suede gloves, and dressy oxford pumps trimmed in alligator completed the outfit. Betty's daily commute to work by walking or trolley could have taken her north along Third Street to Belknap but jogging over a block to the west took her to Fourth Street. A major north-south commercial corridor and promenade, one could find almost anything needed in life there, plus frivolities. Beauty parlors, dressmakers, ladies' ready-to-wear shops, grocers, florists, tobacco-product sellers, Turkish baths, rathskellers, restaurants, confectioners, haberdashers, shoe stores, milliners, stamp-collecting shops, cutlery establishments, and every kind of professional office were housed along the street, from Broadway on the south to the Ohio River on the north.

On her way to work, the most interesting shops would have been on the west (opposite) side of Fourth Street, but almost impossible to see due to trolley traffic, the multitude of Model Ts darting in and out, and the crush of people on the sidewalk. On her right on South Fourth Street, after Broadway was crossed, the Wilderness Road Book Shop advertised a new novel published in the spring of 1925: *The Great Gatsby* by F. Scott Fitzgerald. Slightly beyond the bookstore, the Kentucky Theater was a favored place to view movies because of its recently installed "Arctic New Air" cooling system, a first in the city. A few months after Betty arrived, the theater featured Gloria Swanson's latest photoplay, *The Untamed Lady*, a silent drama in which a sensible young man rescues an heiress from ruining her life due to her willful and wayward ways. The "super thriller" *Phantom of the Opera* silent movie was scheduled to follow.

After crossing Chestnut Street heading north, most of the 500 block of Fourth Street was consumed on the east side by the massive U.S. Customs House and Post Office (the location of the sizeable federal Prohibition Enforcement Office) and the City Library. North of Walnut Street, the Starks Building housed a multitude of medical and legal offices, but Busath's Candy Shop next door was more enticing, especially its hand-wrapped

Original Modjeska Caramels. Closer to the river, the chain-giant S.S. Kresge had two stores on the east side: one a five-and-ten-cent store and the other, just a few doors down, a twenty-five-cent-to-one-dollar store. After arriving at Main Street, Betty would have walked right (east) towards Belknap Hardware.

Looking southeast at the intersection of Fourth St. and Walnut St., 1929. (Historiclouisville. weebly.com.)

As she approached the massive brown-brick building, delivery carts and trucks were lined up along the employee entrance. On any given day, the regiment included over a dozen carts each powered by a pair of mules or oxen, a half-dozen trolley cars, and another half-dozen enclosed, motorized trucks. In the lobby, an assortment of hardware products, including drill bits, punches, and chisels, was artfully displayed in the pattern of the bald eagle on the Great Seal of the U.S. Once inside, the volume of space was staggering. The editor of *Hardware Dealers Magazine* said the space made him feel like "a mole on a mountain. It's so big it takes your breath away. Just imagine neat desks with busy people at every one of them parked row on row over a space big enough to stage a baseball game. I never saw so many typewriters, adding machines, telephones and billing machines at one time in my life."

A business the size of Belknap handled tens of thousands of pieces of mail and internal documents each month, including pamphlets, inquiries, orders, invoices, shipping documents, trade periodicals, newspapers, research requests, and marketing follow up. The flow of paper back and forth demanded the division of responsibilities to avoid chaos and disorganization and to meet schedules. Duties were rigidly defined for the army of librarians, clerks (billing, filing, shipping), correspondents, stenographers (stenos), typists, and memory clerks (responsible for the tickler system of files to remind managers of daily deadlines).

Of all the paper handled, outgoing letters represented the "most complicated, intricate and exacting instrument" of any business. Thousands of letters went out on Belknap stationery each year, dictated to a steno in person or through a recording machine and then typed, carefully folded, and placed in a crisp business envelope before sending to the mail room. Letter preparation was assigned to different skill levels of steno staff, often noted by a hierarchy of color coding for internal distribution and filing. "Lemon" girls worked on the most important papers, such as contracts, high-value sale transactions, and major claims and adjustments. "Pink" girls worked on medium-value letters. "Green" letters were of the lowest value and

Belknap Hardware entrance, 1929. (Caulfield & Shook Collection, Archives & Special Collections, Univ. of Louisville.)

not often kept in the permanent filing system. Their content could run the gamut of clerical topics, inquiry letters about products that were not classified as a sales letter, and goodwill ("feel good") letters aimed at prospective, current, or former customers.

Betty likely started as a green-letter steno. Regardless of a letter's placement in the hierarchy of business importance, all stenos were expected to contribute to perfectly transcribed letters issued on Belknap's letterhead. Upon hiring, each employee was given "House Rules and Regulations for Guidance of House Employees." The "General Conduct" rules prohibited spitting on the floor, using a cuspidor, or brushing one's hair on the open floor. None of these were of concern to her. However, the strictures also required that a work error be reported to a department manager, with the possibility that the offending employee would be expected to pay part, if not all, of any loss associated with their mistake.

In steno work, especially the lowliest like hers, this threat was unsettling. A letter's content was the responsibility of the man dictating it, who was urged to use language that was "live and vital." However, green letters were often dictated by the newest male employees, at the lowest level of the organization. Inexperienced correspondents seldom planned their thoughts in advance, resulting in a string of half-formed or misplaced sentences that the steno had to finish or reorganize on the typed page. "Sloppy" letters were not tolerated by Belknap, including those that used "mistreated" words. For a quick and eager learner like Betty, inartful dictation was stressful but provided important experience early in her career. Her shorthand required focus, speed, and accuracy.

Heading south on Fourth Street to her apartment after work was more interesting as a pedestrian or a passenger. The signature product in the display case of the Bon-Ton Cloak and Suit shop in the 300 block of North Fourth was its own "Black-Bottom" ladies' shoe, made from the "blackest of black velvet with underlays of satin and touches of rattlesnake on tongue and bow," offered in "spike heels only." After crossing Walnut Street, the Seelbach Hotel, at 500 S. Fourth, was on the right. The elegant building was a much-older competitor of the Brown Hotel, and renowned throughout the world. Her great-uncle often stayed there when in town, as did F. Scott Fitzgerald. The author took inspiration from the setting and the Grand Ballroom in staging Tom and Daisy's wedding in *The Great Gatsby*. Like most locals, Betty would have known that Al Capone frequented the hotel. The gangster played cards there in private nooks and crannies, and carried out his bootlegging and racketeering business just a stone's throw from the federal government's Prohibition Enforcement Office.

Seelbach Hotel, 500 S. Fourth St., 1928. (Library of Congress.)

Besten and Langan's shop, also in the 500 block of South Fourth Street, may have held mild interest. The bridal outfit in the storefront window featured a modern, simple waisted and slightly flared wedding dress, which ended above the ankles. The effect was weighed down with an oppressive-looking traditional headdress and lacy train three times the dress length, taking up two entire display windows. The Nu-Bone Corset Shop, just a few doors down, was pivoting its inventory from Victorian-era dress corsets that her mother had worn, which clinched waists and hid the months in which ladies were *enceinte*, to surgical wear and abdominal support. Betty may have had her bobbed cut styled at La Poudre Pouf (the "Powder Puff") Beauty and Marcelle Shoppe closer to Broadway, which specialized in the popular boyish shingle cuts. Marcel waves were out of the question for Betty, however, not because they required heated curling irons that singed scalps if the stylist was clumsy, but the effect was more *froufrou* than the serious young woman would have tolerated.

Chapter 9

NASHVILLE BECKONS

Women who entered the workforce in the early twentieth century, whether by choice, like Betty, or by financial necessity, had detractors: wives of businessmen. Mrs. Benedetto Allegretti, wife of a millionaire candy manufacturer in Chicago, learned that "the girl in the downtown office is a constant menace to the wife in the home. She is a Love Pirate." Mrs. Allegretti could commentate authentically because her husband's office *bon bon* was a "pretty, young Scotch girl." His jilted wife concluded that office women had a "disturbing influence on the American home" and shattered the "gray respectability" of domestic tranquility. Most suspicious were stenographers and secretaries, who had frequent interaction with businessmen, all day long, each day of the workweek. A business "girl" was invited to rebut Mrs. Allegretti's diatribe in the same issue of the Chicago newspaper. The young woman agreed that men were "polygamous by nature," but were "trained and educated into monogamy and kept there chiefly by the law, backed by a large and very practical penitentiary." She shared her own workplace rules: never go to lunch with the boss, keep a distance from his wife (particularly on the phone), and, ultimately, leave the job if you fall in love with him.

The South's love pirates could deliver a double whammy in the workplace. A Vermont visitor to the lower Mississippi River valley was gob-smacked by southern women, finding them racy and supremely confident. In contrast, Atlantic belles were distressing to watch in a crowded room, gathering in huddled clumps together and looking out "despairingly" for someone to approach them. He marveled that a southern woman "dashes through the crowd as she would through a river mounted on horseback … throwing dandies aside as a ship does the billows." "Nothing impedes her."

Louisville offered remunerative work and interesting social and cultural diversions that were different than those found in Nashville. Belknap was an extremely large and successful company with a global marketplace, but Betty was an infinitesimally minute cog in a fast-paced work environment and corporate bureaucracy. She stayed at the hardware company for about three years. In 1928, acting on the urging of her friend Lucy Hardy, she moved to Nashville. The two young women grew up together in Russellville, and Lucy worked in the office of James E. Caldwell and Sons insurance company, which had an opening. It was a small office in a familiar setting. Betty was hired as a stenographer initially, but was promoted to executive secretary, answering directly to the office manager, Tom Buntin.

In Russellville, some women regarded Betty McCuddy as "mannish" with her short, bobbed hair—even though that was the fashion of the time—and non-lithe figure. Mrs. Byrne Evans, the publisher and editor of Russellville's *News-Democrat* newspaper, who knew practically everyone in town, concluded that Betty did not care about clothes or her personal appearance. In the late 1920s, Betty was at an age when most young women would have stocked their hope chests with trousseau: linens, sheets, tablecloths, napkins, towels, blankets, a kimono, chemises, slips, stockings, hats, and dresses. There is no indication that she put much emphasis or interest into such customs, however. She was an heiress but was most certainly not a southern belle, except for her determination and confidence.

The young woman settled into Nashville, living in Lulie Meriwether's boarding house southwest of downtown, near Centennial Park. In 1929, the year following Betty's arrival in the city, Lulie moved to a home at 2513 Kensington Place, and her young boarder followed. The house was across the corner from the castle mansion where Tom Buntin, her boss, lived with his family. Despite what the women in Russellville thought about her clothing interests, the saleswomen at the upscale Grace's Ladies Shop knew her as "Miss Betty," where she spent about $300 to $450 per year during the Great Depression ($5,600 to $8,400 annually in current dollars).

With one exception, businessmen who encountered Miss McCuddy in a personal or professional setting were favorably impressed. Nashville attorney, J. Connelly Edwards, her mother's first cousin, found Betty "very intelligent, very intellectual." He got along well with her and appreciated her independence as a woman who would not stand for anyone interfering in her business "at all." Attorney Laurence Howard had a "very pleasant casual acquaintance" with Betty when he encountered her in the Caldwell insurance office. The one exception was James Caldwell. He was unhappy with the young woman from Russellville, though she was related to the Buntins, his daughter Elsie's married family. The young woman's mother was Mary Edwards Duncan McCuddy, whose cousin, Elizabeth Sinclair, had married William Allison Buntin, Elsie's brother-in-law. By reputation, Miss McCuddy was a responsible and competent worker, but when the senior Caldwell dropped into his insurance company office, he probably noticed his grandson, Tom Buntin, often chatting animatedly with her.

Caldwell boasted that his grandson was the best manager the business ever had and that, as a manager, he earned his $300 monthly salary. The elderly man knew that Tom had his weaknesses but considered his grandson a solid family man with a gentle, pretty wife and three boys Tom was "crazy" about. Nevertheless, office gossip—as well as talk in town in the society circles—undoubtedly reached him suggesting that the relationship between Tom and Betty might be more than supervisor-subordinate. Later, a knowledgeable witness refused to answer under oath whether Caldwell edged out Betty, but it seems likely that he helped the process in the summer of 1930. The official story, also true, is that the insurance company was in financial trouble during the lead-up to the Great Depression. As a result, Tom Buntin had to let staff go, including Miss McCuddy, an action that he must have deeply regretted.

Part Three

BETTY AND TOM

Chapter 10

Rendezvous and Betty's Disappearance

Betty returned to Russellville in July 1930 to live with her parents while determining her next steps. She had some income. After George B. Edwards' death in December 1929, Fidelity Trust began distributing funds from his residuary estate to Fergus for Betty and her brother Bill's financial support. The young woman's circle of friends in Russellville had always been small and had diminished even further. About a year before she left Nashville, she was maid of honor in the wedding of her closest friend, Lucille Lannin, but Lucille L. Tatum then moved to Chattanooga with her husband. Lucy Hardy was retained at the Caldwell insurance office despite Betty and other staff members' termination during the beginning of the economic downturn. Harold Fuqua still lived in Russellville, working as a bus driver for the Bowling Green-Hopkinsville Bus Company on the Russellville-Springfield-Nashville route. He was a male friend but not a romantic interest. Betty tended to stay in at night. When she did go out during the day, she often borrowed one of her parents' cars to drive around town or to Bowling Green, with Fuqua as a frequent companion.

The young woman was restless and wanted to work, but Russellville was a small town of about 3,000 people, and the businesses and government offices seldom had openings for stenos. She nonetheless remained, biding her time, presumably looking for a job. Her favorite past-times kept her busy for only so long: reading, knitting (including crafting her own dresses), and playing bridge as part of the Russellville-Auburn Bridge Club. Brother Bill enlisted in the U.S. Navy in 1927 and visited Russellville shortly after graduating from the Naval Academy in Annapolis in June 1931. The hometown stop was during travel to the West, where he was assigned as an ensign on the battleship *USS Arkansas*. His trip home surely marked a high spot for Betty in that early summer. He had matured into a handsome young man of twenty-two, tall with wavy dark hair, dark eyes, and dark eyebrows. The resemblance to his sister, especially around the eyes, was noticeable. "Mac," his nickname at the naval academy, was outgoing and friendly, often teased that his only weakness was "feminine company and conversation."

Kentucky and the rest of the country were deep into the Prohibition era in 1931. Before Prohibition, the private sector invested heavily in bourbon production in the Bluegrass State and paid approximately $1 million annually in state tax revenues derived from the production and sale of distilled spirits. Notwithstanding, Kentucky was one of the first states to ratify the Eighteenth Amendment to the U.S. Constitution, which banned the manufacture, sale, and transportation of "intoxicating liquors." By January 16, 1920, enough states had ratified the amendment for Prohibition to become the law of the nation.

When a driver parked at the Russellville City Park in the Old Courthouse Square, a city ordinance required that the car's front end face the curb under penalty of a $5 to $10 fine per violation. The ordinance was not as quixotic as it seemed: the law foiled quick getaways associated with backed-in parking. State patrol officer Isaiah DeShazer did not enforce the local law, but he and a partner sometimes frequented City Park while on duty to scout for potential bootleggers. At event times, thousands of people might assemble there for political speeches, Confederate memorials, ice-cream socials, live music, or Ku Klux Klan rallies. During weekdays, the site was usually quiet. In the fall of 1930 through the spring of 1931, he noticed a young woman several times, usually once a week, though sometimes more often. She would meet a tall, thin young man, walk with him to a bench in the middle of the park, and talk under the trees.

Officer DeShazer recognized the woman, whom he estimated as about twenty-two or twenty-three, as Betty McCuddy. He had known her and her family his entire life because her dad was a local bank officer and she and her brother were active in town life as children and then as young adults. He did not know the man he observed but never considered their meetings as suspicious or that they were in any relationship other than as acquaintances. He considered her a "fine young lady" of "virtue and chastity, above reproach." He also saw the two walking in town at other times and observed her getting into a car with the man. He asked a co-officer on patrol about the identity of the man and was told he went by the last name "Buntin" and lived in Nashville.

Harold Fuqua drove the bus between Russellville and Springfield, Tennessee, several times a week. If a passenger's destination was Nashville, she or he changed buses in Springfield. Betty often boarded in Russellville and then exited in Springfield where Fuqua would see Tom Buntin meet her. Fuqua also knew that the couple met in several places, because Betty would tell him so during their auto rides.

The fastest way to drive from Russellville to Nashville at that time was to take the Kentucky Route 100 road from the east side of town, swing southeast past the hamlet of Corinth, then head into Franklin. At Franklin's main street, the road intersected with U.S. Hwy. 31W, which was then a straight shot south to Nashville. John Thomas ("J.T.") Shugart and his brother ran a general merchandise store on Route 100 at Middleton, about equidistant between Russellville and Franklin, just over the Logan County line, in Simpson County. The site was a choice location for a store because five roads came together there. Still, in the early 1930s, there was seldom traffic other than during the mornings when farmers went to and from work and fieldhands came in to grab a sandwich at lunch.

Shugart had plenty of time to watch comings and goings from his perch in the store and the land around was relatively flat so he could see clearly in all directions. In late summer 1931, he began noticing a young woman driving a dark, expensive-looking car, which he thought was a coupe, coming from the direction of Russellville about three or four times during

KY Rte. 100 at Middleton, at the five roads where Shugart's Grocery was located. (Photos by author.)

the week. She would usually pass by two days in a row, then skip two days. The time of day was usually the same: she headed to Franklin about 1 p.m., give or take ten minutes. He did not always see her return, but when he did, it was about 5 p.m. After tallying about nine-to-twelve trips over a three-week period, the storekeeper suspected that she might be driving a bootlegging car, so he reported the sightings to his close friend, J. Harb Milliken, the night chief of police in Franklin.

Milliken, in turn, told Simpson County Sheriff Ed Bogan, who had heard a similar story from Arthur Edwards, a U.S. Post Office Department rural mail carrier on the Franklin route. Edwards also owned and operated the Sunrise Grocery and filling station on Kentucky Route 79 (now KY 383), the blacktop road from Franklin to Springfield, Tennessee. His house was about fifty feet from the store. He usually finished delivering mail by mid-morning, depending on when the train arrived, and then worked in his store in the afternoon. During August 1931, he spotted a young woman in a black luxury car, a sedan he thought (which had a profile quite different than a coupe), driving by about two or three times per week. She never looked toward the store when she passed, heading south.

The mailman was busy with local and transient customers during the two years he owned the store, from 1930 till 1932. It was the only filling station on the Franklin-to-Springfield road, so he sold lots of gasoline as well as sodas since harder liquids were off limits. He remembered a tall, thin man—he thought with black eyes and black hair—who stopped by about three times during the same period that he saw the woman. The man asked for a beer the first time and bought a Coca Cola when Edwards told him he could not sell beer. His customer spent a few minutes in the store with the soft drink and then left. It was the same routine twice, but one time the man was in the store when the woman drove by, and the storekeeper noticed that he "seemed to get in a right smart hurry then to leave himself."

Heading north on former KY Rte. 79, approaching the locust tree thicket. Sunrise Grocery was farther north, on the right. (Photo by author.)

A little over a mile south of Edwards' grocery store, on the right (on the west side of the road), was a large locust-tree thicket interrupting the rows of tobacco and grazing fields for dairy cows. The thicket was so dense and full of thorns that Edwards could not hunt rabbits there without tearing his clothes and cutting himself. Only once did Edwards see the young woman park her car along the road, at the thicket, and leave it there. He saw her meet the tall, thin man, who drove a red roadster, but he had not come into Sunrise Grocery that afternoon. When Edwards reported the sightings, Sheriff Bogan demanded to know, "Where the hell is she going?" Edwards, who was no fan of the lawman and thought he was a "wicked sort of fellow," replied, "Search me, I don't know." He shied away from making any definitive identifications by name. Edwards may have had an idea who the woman was, at least, because he later said in sworn testimony that he had feared of slandering "someone."

The sheriff thought about T. Bush Taylor's farm, which was on the opposite side of the locust-tree thicket (on the east side of Route 79) and had a clear view of the road from the house. A gravel road (today, Charlie Butts Road) bordered the farm and led off the main road to the east about one-hundred yards from the thicket, heading down to a swampy area along Neely Branch stream, then on to Sch-

Charlie Butts Rd., the gravel road that led in 1931 to Milligan Swamp. (Ibid.)

weizer, an enclave of German families. At Schweizer, if a driver turned right, heading south, he or she reached Orlinda, Robertson County, Tennessee, in about five miles. Taylor confirmed to the sheriff that he saw a black-haired, black-eyed woman and a man wearing a hat—"nice-looking people"—meet about six or seven times that summer. They would pull their cars to the side of Route 79 and the woman would get into the man's car, a "sport model, sportily painted."

Once, when the farmer was on his horse in his tobacco field, they drove toward him, going north, but then turned right on the gravel road to Schweizer and, he assumed, headed down to the swamp or Orlinda. He

Taylor's farm field (in 1931) on the east side of the locust tree thicket. (Ibid.)

never saw them return but noticed that the cars were gone a few hours later when he returned home after finishing his work in the fields. Taylor thought they were bootlegging whiskey, either selling or picking up illicit liquor at the swamp or picking up booze in Orlinda. Before Prohibition, Robertson County was celebrated for its sour-mash whiskeys. Tobacco had since surpassed liquor production, but there was a legacy of small-batch stills, reportedly spaced as close as "every 100 yards" along streams. The farmer paid no further attention to what they were doing until he was questioned by Simpson County law enforcement.

Sheriff Bogan asked J.T. Shugart, the Middleton store owner, to keep watch and tip him off the next time he saw the woman drive by. Shortly after Labor Day, around September 10, 1931, Shugart called the lawman. The sheriff, his son J. Robert (a deputy sheriff), and Franklin police chief Milliken headed out. Not seeing her on Route 100, they headed to Franklin and took Route 79 to the southwest, where they saw the woman driving a 1925 Packard. They followed her about a mile and a half to Curtis Meador's farm near Sulphur Spring. As they crested a hill, they saw her car stopped ahead in their lane. She was in her car talking to a man in a red coupe with the canvas top down. The men thought his car was Cadillac's luxury brand LaSalle.

The two vehicles faced opposite directions and were blocking both lanes of the road. The man, whose car was facing them, spotted the sheriff's car and tried to back up to let them pass. Sheriff Bogan thought he was trying to get away, even though the choice of a LaSalle (and a Packard) would have been distinctively flashy for bootlegging. To stop him, the sheriff drove up slowly and hooked his vehicle's metal bumper onto the front metal bumper of the man's car. The senior Bogan jumped out of the car with a gun in his hand, but when his son approached both vehicles, the junior Bogan recognized Tom Buntin, with whom he had hunted in Kentucky and Tennessee. Buntin exclaimed, "Mr. Ed, don't do that," and the sheriff, laughing, said, "Why Tom, is that you?" The two talked briefly and the sheriff turned to his son and indicated that it was "all right," that the woman was "Tom's girl."

They had some difficulty getting the two cars unhooked, which gave the law enforcement men a chance to take stock. Deputy Sheriff Bogan recognized the woman as Betty McCuddy, who was from a family of "good people up in Russellville and a girl of good reputation." Milliken also knew her because his daughter and Betty briefly attended school together in Bowling Green and Betty had visited their home in Franklin. She kept quiet during the incident, and no one questioned her. After Tom's car was free, each of the three cars drove off.

The encounter was shared with Shugart, Taylor, and a few others and it was the last time the storekeepers and farmers saw the two together. Sheriff Bogan, however, informed farmer Taylor within the following two months that Tom Buntin disappeared from Nashville about two weeks after the encounter. None of the law enforcement officers mentioned the meetings to Betty's father, but he learned of them from Coleman Taylor, a Russellville attorney. Fergus subsequently claimed that he never proved the rendezvous to be true to his own satisfaction at the time.

J.H. Woods tended a U.S. Department of Commerce intermediate airfield on the south side of Russellville. It was little more than a landing strip but featured a beacon with a rotating light because the airfield's main purpose was for emergency stops during mail flights on the route between Chicago and Atlanta. Seldom did Woods, or his son who sometimes joined him there, see any air traffic. When he did, he remembered the circumstances. On Thursday, November 5, 1931, a young woman drove up to the airfield and stayed in the car. Not long after, a small, private airplane—a distinctive red color—appeared on the horizon and Woods watched as it landed on the strip he tended. When the couple checked in with Mr. Woods to leave, he told the man who piloted the red airplane that he would have to register as a pilot before taking off. The man resisted, saying that he did not have to register because it was a private plane. Woods knew the federal Aeronautics Branch regulations well, which required that "visiting pilots" register their name and pilot's license number, when they expected to leave, and how many passengers would be on board at departure. He argued back that he would notify "Washington" if the man refused to register.

At that point, the couple left together in the car she drove to the airstrip. When they returned after about an hour, the man registered, but then left her and departed in the plane, circling the field and heading toward Nashville. Curiously, when interviewed by a reporter over twenty years later, Woods could not recall the man's name, but knew the rest of the details of the encounter. Whether the event really happened or not is unknown. However, Tom's securing of a pilot's license exactly one month after his life insurance application in 1929 suggests careful planning at a time when he was deep into his relationship with Betty.

Though Woods experienced an important memory lapse regarding the pilot in the airport encounter, Fergus McCuddy remembered "very distinctly" the following day, Friday, November 6. It was the day that his twenty-four-year-old daughter Betty "left" Russellville. He did not use the word "disappeared." She came into Southern Deposit Bank, where he was vice president, around mid-morning and asked him how much money she had in her account. She told him she was going to Grace's Ladies Shop in Nashville to pay on her bill. Her last purchase was made in the month of May, and she owed a balance of $148.50. She wrote a check for $50 in the bank lobby, leaving around $8 in her account. Betty then casually told her father "goodbye," "so-long," or, as Fergus later remembered, "something like that" and left to catch the 11 a.m. bus from Russellville to Nashville.

She bought a round-trip bus ticket and sat near Harold Fuqua, the driver, during the trip so they could talk. They had met in Bowling Green the day before—though it is unclear whether it was before or after the airfield meeting that Woods reported much later—at which time she told him she was going to Nashville the next day for a short visit. As he was driving the bus that following day, November 6, he noticed she had "only a small bag," which was consistent with her story about the trip being brief. Betty had to change buses in Springfield, so he walked with her to the bus headed for Nashville, where she said good-bye and that she would see him later.

Betty's parents were not concerned about their daughter's departure because she was an experienced traveler to Nashville. She visited friends there often or visited family, mostly her second cousin Elizabeth Sinclair Buntin and her husband William Allison Buntin (Tom Buntin's uncle). If she stayed overnight, the young woman usually roomed at Lulie Meriwether's, who ran the boarding house where she lived when she worked for the Caldwell insurance firm. Nothing had seemed amiss in the McCuddy family that summer and fall of 1931. Mary played bridge with friends often, including a summer card game in the coolness of Dunbar Cave to the southwest of Russellville, near Clarksville, Tennessee. She and Fergus recognized that their daughter was restless and neither hesitated to loan either of their cars when she wanted to go out.

The morning of November 6, Betty told her mother that she would return on November 13 on the late afternoon bus. She left the boarding house's phone number. When Betty failed to return on November 13, Mary called Lulie and learned that Betty had never been there at all over the past week. Her parents were stymied. They considered their relationship with her, and she with the rest of the family, as "cordial, pleasant," and "affectionate."

Fergus acknowledged that she was "very independent," "would not stand for any restraint" on her, and "thought her business was her business." He felt that Betty did not lie to him or her mother, but that she also did not tell them anything she did not want to tell them and did not consider her parents as confidants.

He found that the $50 check to Grace's had been paid and returned to the bank around November 9 or 10. Through inquiries, probably from George Trammell (the store manager and Grace's husband), Fergus found that there was still a balance that had not been paid, about $98.50. He then started a discrete investigation on his own that lasted about seven-to-ten days, but he did not contact the police, newspapers, or radio stations. Betty was an adult and "unusually intelligent," according to her father. Fergus reasoned that if she had gone away intentionally, it was her right to do so and that he, even as a father, "did not have any right to put police on her trail." Plus, local police had their hands full with non-indulgent matters: desperate parents stealing food to feed their children during the hard times, jurisdictional spats with federal Prohibition agents, and Prohibition-related murders by organized crime gangs.

In his search, Fergus called Betty's friends in town, in Louisville, and other places, as well as Ward-Belmont and Nazareth Academy. He asked a friend, Pat Ryan, to find out if she had gone into a Catholic convent or another religious institution and he and a former Logan County sheriff, Morton Barclay, traveled together to Nashville to investigate matters. Fergus informed Fidelity Trust in Louisville of her disappearance, but there is no indication that he checked his daughter's bank account in Nashville.

Fergus then enlisted the help of his wife Mary's first cousin, J. Connelly Edwards, to search for information in Nashville. Given that family was involved, and the matter needed to be handled quietly, he called the young attorney at home on a Saturday evening about a week after Betty left. Fergus went to Nashville the next day and, at his suggestion, the two men visited with a former Russellville resident, Mrs. Tom Frazier. The woman knew Betty well and her sister had worked with Betty at the Caldwell insurance agency. Fergus told Mrs. Frazier about his daughter's disappearance and that he feared she was dead. Following the meeting, J. Connelly and Fergus talked briefly about the other interviews the lawyer would carry out and Fergus then returned to Russellville.

J. Connelly went back to the Frazier house after Fergus left. Earlier in the evening, and out of earshot of Betty's father, Mrs. Frazier quietly asked him to return later that night. When he arrived by himself, she stated that there were "some things" that she wanted him to know but had not wanted to say in front of Mr. McCuddy. Betty had been "running around" with Tom Buntin. The woman was surprised that Edwards had not heard this information, saying that it was "common talk" around town in private circles.

Edwards did not initially discuss the news with Fergus, but his subsequent investigation was more focused than it otherwise would have been. He turned up several facts during the following month. Betty arrived in Nashville by bus as she told her parents, but then took a Yellow Taxi to Union Station on Broad Street around 2 to 2:30 p.m. During the ride, she asked the driver when L&N's Pan-American ("Pan Am") train left. Since the northbound train departed two hours earlier, he assumed she meant the southbound train, to New Orleans. That train, he said, left at 5 p.m. When they arrived at the station, Betty paid him. She then asked him to carry her luggage, now expanded to include a large suitcase and two bags, to the parcel room where she collected her checked luggage tickets. Edwards was convinced that she then took the Pan Am train south.

Shortly after Betty failed to return from Nashville, Fergus learned that Tom Buntin had been missing for over a month. He had met Tom "on two or three occasions" and thought him "a man of business ability and unusual intelligence" who was perhaps "busted" by the tough economic times and "owed more than he could pay." The banker claimed he did not know the Buntin family, but nevertheless considered them "highly extravagant, rich people." In one example of their profligacy, Dan and Elsie Buntin took a Hawaiian cruise in 1921 on a steamer that featured $2,900 suites. Despite his disclaimer, Fergus well-knew Mary's first cousin once removed, Elizabeth Sinclair Buntin, who visited Mary and he just two weeks before Tom disappeared. When Elizabeth returned home to Nashville, daughter Betty went with her, and it was only a few days later that William Allison Buntin received Tom's will in the mail. Despite the close relationship between Mary and Elizabeth (and Elizabeth's sister Hester, who sometimes traveled with Tom's mother Elsie Buntin), Betty's father later claimed that he was not aware of the efforts taken by the Buntin family to locate Tom.

Fergus did not want to publicize his daughter's disappearance or seek law enforcement's help. Even though he told Mrs. Frazier that he thought his daughter was dead, deep down he knew it was possible that she was with Tom Buntin somewhere. That the disappearances of the two might not be coincidental had been discussed between he and J. Connelly a few weeks after the lawyer ended his investigation in Nashville. They also evaluated whether to expand their search by broadcasting a message over the airwaves of the two Nashville radio stations to try to reach Betty and ask her to come home. The men "agreed that if she had gone off with this Buntin man under the conditions as they seemed to be, such an appeal would have no effect, and, balancing all things together," they decided not to do it.

Ultimately, Fergus and Mary became convinced that their daughter "disappeared of her own will and accord" and, resignedly, stopped looking.

Chapter 11

Brownsville, Texas

"City Briefs" were tucked away in a corner of an interior page of *The Brownsville Herald* on Monday, September 28, 1931. International travelers arriving or leaving by plane for Mexico City and the Panama Canal Zone that day were highlighted first. Domestic travelers were also identified, at the very bottom of the column, including the fact that "Thomas D. Palmer of Louisville, Kentucky, is in the city." Mr. Palmer's mode of travel—plane, train, or automobile—was not mentioned. Tom Buntin had journeyed five days from Nashville, so he likely arrived in south Texas on the St. Louis, Brownsville, and Mexican Railroad. The line came in from the northeast along Eleventh Street, a comfortable walk to paved Elizabeth Street, a main road in town.

Six weeks later, Elizabeth McClinton Palmer traveled by rail from Nashville, changing trains in New Orleans, and arriving around November 11, 1931, a similar five-day journey. Her arrival was not noted in the newspaper. Betty had fewer emotional ties to leave in her birthplace than Tom did in his. She also had a more certain financial legacy from her great-uncle's estate than Tom appears to have had from his family because of complicated interests associated with Rachel Carter Craighead's estate. With another type of woman, he could have had a life-long affair, maintained a semblance of a contented married life, financially leaned on his mother's benevolence, and avoided an expensive and scandalous divorce proceeding. Betty would never have countenanced the option of an affair, so the love-locked pair had to escape to be united authentically, though each

92

left different tallies of loss and foregone opportunities. It was a risky action and an overwhelmingly optimistic one, especially during the tumultuous economic conditions of the early 1930s.

New York Life's absence in Texas most certainly drove the couple's decision to flee there. By the early 1900s, the insurance behemoth had 208 branch offices in metropolitan areas of the U.S. and Canada and foreign operations in South America and Europe. The business network did not extend to the Lone Star State, however, because of the Robertson Act of 1907. The statute required out-of-state life insurance companies to reinvest seventy-five percent of the legal reserves required on Texas policies in Texas securities (government bonds, real estate mortgages, or bank stock). State legislators' motive was two-fold: to prevent the flow of "good money" out-of-state, particularly to northeastern states, such as New York, and to increase local revenues from taxes collected on the reinvested funds. Faced with these compulsory investments, twenty-two companies, including New York Life, withdrew from doing business in Texas. Critics noted at the time that "Texas lost more than did New York Life from a business standpoint."

During the Buntin Case 1 trial, New York Life's Superintendent of Inspection acknowledged that it was "exceedingly difficult to locate anyone that doesn't want to be located" because changing one's name was easy. At that time, Social Security did not exist so there were no unique identifying numbers that followed a person across state boundaries. Driver's licenses were not required in Kentucky, Tennessee, or Texas. Fingerprinting and passports were exceedingly rare and births were unevenly recorded across the country. There was little need for adept forgery—most people's word was taken at face value and did not require supporting documents for verification. Pilots were an exception, requiring federally issued licenses because use of the skies was burgeoning and becoming unsafe, especially after the barnstormers arrived.

For these reasons, Thomas David Palmer and Elizabeth McClinton Palmer probably did not have any paper documentation showing a history of their assumed last name (which was her "married" name). It is also possible that they chose that surname for an association with a place or places rather than a person. Tom perhaps fondly recalled visiting the Palmer House Hotel in Chicago as a child. The Buntin's ranch in Wyoming was known as the "Palmer ranch" for the family that sold to them, and Tom spent many summers there as a young child and youth, and then lived there when he attended the University of Wyoming. Betty Palmer claimed she was born in the Deep South. Coincidentally, a black woman named Elizabeth McClinton from the Deep South lived in Louisville at the same time as Betty, working as a domestic servant and laundress. It is possible that she was a laundress or maid for residents of the Weissinger-Gaulbert apartments during Betty's Belknap years.

The couple chose a place so completely different from their familiar homes and landscapes of the Upper South, it must have seemed like a foreign land. In many ways, it was, historically, and at the time of their arrival. The Lower Rio Grande Valley's cultural identity was, and remains, overwhelmingly Latino. The 1850 U.S. Census identified Brownville's population as 8,541, of which two-thirds were individuals born in Mexico. By the early 1930s, the Latino population was still large and remained at the bottom of a rigid social-class system that was racial and corresponded to socioeconomic standing. The Mexican peasant class and *mestizos* (mixed-race individuals of indigenous Indian and European parentage) worked the ranchlands and agricultural fields and performed other manual labor.

Brownsville's boundaries are largely defined by the Rio Grande River, which twists around to the south and west of town in a vast delta featuring sandy-loam soils that are highly alkaline. The "Valley" is this delta. In the coupling of fertile soils and an outstanding growing season of 320 days per year, a prosperous commercial agricultural industry thrived. The most eponymous product, the giant Ruby Red grapefruit, was successfully produced only a couple of years before the Palmers arrived. Dan Buntin's early-1900s investment lands in the Texas Panhandle, nine hundred miles to the north, were being stripped away by 1931 during the Dust Bowl's decimation of drought-desiccated soils. His son's new life was in a fecund setting, supporting cultivation of citrus and diverse vegetables: tomatoes, carrots, cucumbers, cauliflower, eggplant, peppers, snap beans, green peas, lettuce, sorghum, and cotton. Snowbirds were enticed by the "finest all-year-round climate in the world." Omitted from glowing promotional ads were serious issues, such as flood control and tick eradication. Vicious salt-water mosquitoes plagued the coastal marshes and low-lying areas, necessitating months of manual labor to dig drainage ditches and reduce the risk of malaria.

By 1930, the "Magic Valley" was home to almost 200,000 people. An aerial view of Brownsville in 1931 shows a well-developed central business district of mostly one-to-three story buildings. Winter sojourners expected a "barren, sunbaked town of adobe buildings" and were surprised to find homes of wood or brick, grassy lawns bordered with flowers, and palm trees lining the streets. Still, the city was relatively isolated from the rest of the country geographically and far from the mainstream news. San Antonio, the closest large U.S. city, lay 300 miles to the north.

(Briscoe Center for Am. History, Univ. of Texas at Austin.)

Finding jobs was essential, but initially difficult for the Palmers, people with no local family and, seemingly, no history and no money during the Great Depression. Tom immediately began working in the Valley's agricultural fields with Mexican and *mestizo* laborers, picking beans for seventy-five cents per day. His physician in Nashville had opined that the tall, exceedingly thin patient became "excessively fatigued" when he tried to play tennis and most certainly could never do any kind of manual labor because he would "play out in ten minutes." Yet, Tom Palmer worked in the excruciating heat and humidity and blazing sun for hours each day to survive financially.

The young couple rented a fully furnished efficiency unit, utilities paid, at the recently built Nel-Roy Apartments at 701 E. St. Charles St., just a few blocks northwest of downtown and the Cameron County Courthouse. The brick apartment building had a central façade mildly resembling the front of the famed Alamo mission in San Antonio. Each apartment in the "new, exclusive, ultra-modern" complex featured ceiling fans (but not air conditioning), gas cooking, hot water, electrical refrigeration, a dinette, and "overstuffed" living room furniture in a "tasteful selection." Rent for a two-person apartment ranged from $25 to $65 per month. Their neighbors were also transplants—from Missouri, Nebraska, Iowa, Ohio, West Virginia, and Kentucky. Notwithstanding the challenging economic times throughout the country, most of the other apartment dwellers had secured well-paying jobs in accounting, government service, aviation, manufacturing, and railroad work. Tom barely scraped together $20 per month in manual-labor wages, not enough to pay rent. Soon, the newly arrived couple sold the expensive clothes they brought just to have money to eat.

The Palmer's honeymoon of sorts was in a strange, unfamiliar land and a substantially different culture, where tuberculosis and fevers still raged. They had no formal engagement period and no more than a two-year clandestine courtship. Whatever intimate information a couple was encouraged to share in the premarital relationship, which began after their engagement was announced and celebrated formally, was already in the open between the two: Tom's alcoholism, his depression, his "nervous troubles," his marriage and fatherhood, and the wealth each abandoned. Bringing Palmer children into the world may have been discussed for a time when they were settled and secure in their future, but they knew the implications. Any children of theirs would not know their grandparents, aunts, uncles, first or second cousins, or removed cousins.

Tennessee's Enoch Arden laws may have been unfamiliar to Tom and Betty, but most people knew of the seven-year presumption-of-death period. Tom could be presumed dead legally in September 1938. Any children born before Bettie Buntin secured a court decree adjudging Tom dead, after which the Palmers could marry, would be illegitimate. Illegitimate children were disfavored by society and state legislatures at that time. Unless birth certificates were falsified, a newborn's legal status was public information in counties where births were recorded. In Texas during the 1930s and 1940s, "natural" (that is, illegitimate) children did not have the right to inherit from their father. They could inherit from their mother, but not her lineal relatives, such as her parents, or her collateral relatives, such as uncles and aunts, including great-uncles like George B. Edwards.

Marriage, legal or illegal, would have been risky in any event. In most states in the 1930s, a premarital blood test was required by law to curb the spread of syphilis in adults but also in newborn babies, because congenital syphilis was "fairly common" at the time. The two would have tried to avoid life events that involved physical documentation of their identities. Only Tom had a recent photo that was a federal record—the mug shot taken when he applied for a pilot's license in 1929—but the evidence was buried at the U.S. Department of Commerce in the nation's capital in layers of branch, division, and section records. Texas required a premarital blood test from the fiancé, but not the fiancée. Though indicating only blood type, the test nonetheless created a shred of evidence, which was a shred of worry that would have added to the couple's many worries. State law recognized common-law marriages, in which a couple agreed to live together as wife and husband, but this arrangement was also legally out of bounds while Tom's first marriage was still recognized under the law.

Tom was married for nine years when he left Nashville and had seen a wife through three pregnancies, though he would not have had any involvement in baby care whatsoever. Betty had no experience in these life events at all, and no mother, sisters, aunts, or cousins in which to confide or consult. Contraceptives were a rarity in the 1930s. The federal Comstock Act of 1873, which prohibited the use of the federal postal service to transmit information about contraception, was still in effect. The American Medical Association had not yet taken a stand on birth control. However, the Lower Rio Grande Valley was heavily Catholic. Pope Pius XI's 1930 encyclical on "chaste wedlock" proclaimed that any use of matrimony to "deliberately frustrate" its "natural power to generate life" was an "offense against the law of God" and an "intrinsically evil" act. Neither Betty nor Tom were Catholic. Nevertheless, the pope's pronouncement would have propelled doctors to promote "natural" family planning—not prohibited by the Church—which was the practice of "normal relations" but "continence during a certain period in the menstrual cycle" if children were not wanted.

The couple's first child, Elizabeth Ann, arrived at Mercy Hospital on September 3, 1932. Betty conceived in less than a month after joining Tom in Brownsville, interrupting any plans she may have had to find work to help in their subsistence. The baby's parents had barely had time to adjust to each other as a couple, much less their unfamiliar environment, when the baby was born. She was identified in her birth certificate as the legitimate child of Elizabeth McClinton, age twenty-four, born in Jefferson County, Alabama, and a homemaker, and Thomas David Palmer, age twenty-seven, born in Huntington, Tennessee. Tom's occupation was now listed as real estate sales, which probably helped them manage to stay at the Nel-Roy apartments.

Mary McCuddy did not live long after her daughter went missing. In January 1933, just a few months after the birth of her first grandchild in Brownsville (a granddaughter she would never know of or see), she became extremely ill with the flu and pneumonia. Fergus arranged for radio broadcasts extensively throughout the nation asking his daughter to "come home" because her mother was not expected to recover. Mary lingered for a few more days following the broadcasts. Her obituary included "a daughter, Miss Betty Edwards McCuddy," as a presumed surviving family member. The fifty-three-year-old mother was buried in the Maple Grove Cemetery next to the graves of three of her five children. No word was received in response to the radio pleas, but during the interment, a small plane flew over the cemetery, swooped low, circled, and then flew away. Attendees who knew that Tom Buntin had been an "ardent" private pilot speculated that he brought Betty back to pay respects to her mother. It would have been quite a feat of money and logistics for the couple to have made the trip, especially with a four-month-old baby at home.

The first two years in Brownsville must have been especially terrifying and difficult for the Palmers. Daughter Jane was born in January 1934, when her older sister was nine months old. A few months before Jane's birth, two devastating hurricanes slammed into the Valley about a month apart. The first, in August 1933, was the strongest to hit the area in fifty years. Vast tracts of ruined citrus crops were buried to quell the stench of rotting fruit and suppress flies. The other hurricane, in September, was not as strong but still caused extensive wind and water damage. A double punch of stagnant water that did not retreat for days invited a plague of mosquitoes. Public-health agencies inoculated residents to prevent a typhoid epidemic. In a massive effort to control mosquitoes, kerosene and crude oil were sprayed on pools of water. At night, stacks of debris were doused with crude oil and lit to create enough smoke to keep insects away from homes. Valley air was unhealthy and stifling, requiring that windows be closed in homes, most of which were not air conditioned.

Son David Preston was born in February 1936. Betty's brother, Bill, was killed just three months later. The accident was sadly consonant with the Edwards family's premature losses and the McCuddy family's joys, followed by tragedies. The twenty-six-year-old lieutenant was observing torpedo practice of the submarine *USS* S-25 to which he was assigned. About two miles from Kalaeloa, anglicized as Barbers Point (near Pearl Harbor), the two-seater Corsair observation plane crashed into the Pacific Ocean. The reason was never identified. His and the pilot's bodies were never found, only Bill's notebook. Son Robert Ferguson McCuddy ("Robin," Betty's nephew), by wife Doris Waller, was a little over three weeks old. Hearing no word from his daughter following widely disseminated news of the accident, Fergus gave up all hope that she was still alive.

Despite the Palmer's economic hardships, more babies arrived in stair-step fashion: Margaret Ross in June 1937, William Duncan in September 1938, and Mary Ellen in October 1941. With each birth, there were no christening gowns and caps of the finest cotton destined to be heirloom outfits. No birth announcements or christening celebrations appeared in the *Society* column of the newspaper. Betty would have sewn or knitted the tiny day dresses and nighties for their early months. She would also have likely sewn the recommended quantity of three- or four-dozen twenty-inch by twenty-inch diapers of birds-eye cotton or flannelette and a dozen clothes protectors of quilted pads and oilcloth. Domestic servants would have performed most maternal tasks for Betty McCuddy as a married woman. Betty Palmer washed soiled diapers, an elaborate and tedious process of disinfection in a diaper pail and then boiling the cloth on the stove before hanging yards of diapers outside to dry on a clothesline. She had to retrieve the pasteurized milk delivered daily for "artificial feeding" of her babies through a bottle as soon as the bottles were delivered outside the door to prevent the dairy liquids from spoiling in the Valley's hot morning sun.

As each baby progressed in age, there was abundant citrus and other fruit and green vegetables for healthful vitamins and the climate was ideal for fresh air, outdoor play, and sun baths. Over three decades earlier, Elsie had reasons to fear for her child Tom Buntin's physical safety during a rash of kidnappings across the nation, which was one worry that escaped moneyless Tom Palmer. Nevertheless, childhood disease was cause for apprehension. Whooping cough, measles, dysentery, tuberculosis, diphtheria, yellow fever, typhoid fever, and malaria lurked in Brownsville. The highly contagious poliovirus, which particularly jeopardized children under the age of five, was concerning because a vaccine had not been developed in the 1930s and 1940s.

Over the years, the Palmers built their life with their family in south Texas. Tom left, or was encouraged to leave, his real estate job and went into the auto business, working as a mechanic or salesman at auto lots. The couple rented a newly built house at 1017 W. St. Francis St. in the developing West Brownsville Addition after Jane was born, which was northwest of downtown. Although the location was much farther away from their work, the house was a little over 1,100 square feet in size and included an outdoor porch and a fenced yard to corral the children. The extra space was needed following the births of David and Margaret. Tom often interacted with Mrs. Lilliam Kemmy at City Hall when the family's utilities were cut off for delinquent bills. Though dealing with unpleasant matters, she found him a "very courteous gentleman, obviously a man with an excellent education" but in a "seedy condition" financially. Friends described their financial condition the entire time they lived in Brownsville as "always very poor." At some point, Betty took a court reporting position for extra money.

The family downsized their living space and yard by May 1938, possibly for financial reasons. They moved to a rented, furnished apartment at 1417 Lincoln St. in Victoria Heights, followed in a few months by Duncan's birth. Betty and Tom's fifth child contracted polio, leaving him with a permanent mobility disability requiring the use of crutches. His parents arranged for care in a Corpus Christi clinic for a period, requiring weekly visits 160 miles up the Texas Gulf Coast. When the resources for therapy ran out, Betty worked tirelessly with Duncan to keep his muscles working and prevent atrophy of his legs. Almost thirty years earlier, his paternal grandmother Elsie had raised funds for "destitute crippled children" in Chicago but was unaware of her own grandchild's impaired condition and financial needs.

September 24, 1938, marked the seventh anniversary of Tom Buntin's disappearance, about three weeks following Duncan's birth. Nashville Trust Company filed the Buntin Case 1 lawsuit in February 1939, seeking his insurance proceeds and a legal declaration of death. On June 13, 1940, the jury returned a verdict in favor of the trust company in the amount of $53,588.76, which represented the values of the two policies plus interest. Judge A.B. Neil denied New York Life's request for a new trial, stating that "I am of the opinion, after full consideration of all the evidence, that this man died before the expiration of the policies ... We must also consider the fact in these modern days it is well-nigh impossible for anybody to escape. A fugitive from justice, making every effort to escape, mighty few of them ever are not apprehended after such a search was made in this case."

New York Life appealed to the Tennessee Court of Appeals in Nashville in October 1940, and, for the first time, claimed that Tom had defrauded the company. Nashville Trust responded that the circumstances of Buntin's family (that his Uncle Rogers was a convicted felon and Dan Buntin had committed suicide) and the financial troubles of the James E. Caldwell and Sons insurance agency made it reasonable for the jury to presume death by suicide of Tom, a person of "weak moral fiber." The trust company further asserted that it was "unnecessary" for Buntin to "leave the comfort and security of his home to live on his own resources with Miss Betty

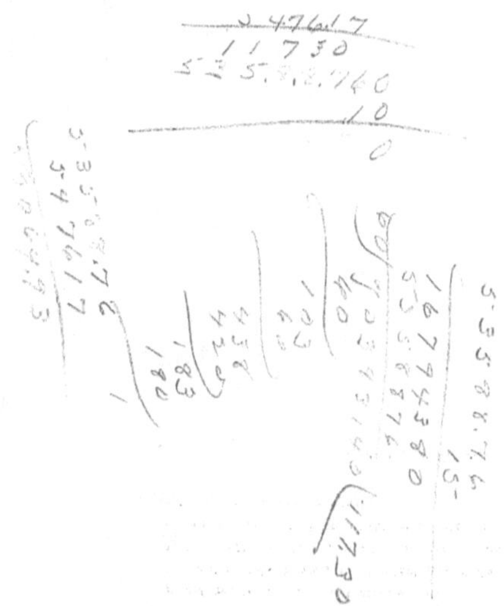

Jury award calculations written on the back of the judgment. (Buntin Case 1.)

McCuddy" because "the proof shows that he was seeing her with as much freedom and regularity as desired, without the slightest interference from his wife or anyone else." Earlier, Bettie Moore Buntin showed up at the only deposition she attended in person in the Buntin Case 1. The witness was Fergus McCuddy, called by New York Life. He testified under oath regarding his daughter's "strong personality" and "unimpeachable moral character" and asserted that she was a "very efficient business and office woman."

Rogers Caldwell's saga followed Tom. The only English-speaking newspaper in Brownsville reported on his multiple convictions, then the Tennessee Supreme Court's reversal of the state convictions for financial fraud on grounds of "manifest prejudice" against him and lack of a fair trial. Caldwell's announcement that he was returning to his financier role, after having left a trail of ruination of others, also made national news, extending to Brownsville. Caldwell was the only member on either side of the Palmer's family lines whose notoriety extended to far south Texas, however. News of their Tennessee and Kentucky families' life events never reached them by public means. Elizabeth Sinclair Buntin experienced tragedy, in the vein of her Edwards' family, when husband William Allison died in a sanitarium after murdering a younger business rival. Their son, while on home leave during World War II, excused himself from the dinner table, went into the bathroom, and killed himself with a shotgun. In a joyous affair, Tom's sister, May, married at Longview on the sixty-fourth anniversary of their Caldwell grandparents' wedding. Her brother's absence was conspicuous in the *Society* page's photos of three generations of Buntins and Caldwells.

Betty's work court reporting and as a legal secretary for multiple judges at the Cameron County Courthouse led the pair to befriend several lawyers and judges. The Palmer's neighborhood would have been considered *déclassé* by their former social peers in Kentucky and Tennessee. In Brownsville, the legal community lived on upscale Levee Street and Boca Chica Boulevard in $10,000 houses. Neighbors included Pan Am pilots, flight engineers, public works engineers, and steamship operators. Tom told friends that he was an orphan and had attended Tulane University in New Orleans. Betty claimed that she was orphaned as a child and raised by a rich uncle who sent her to an exclusive girls' school, but that he committed suicide after the Wall Street crash of 1929. People found them obviously well-educated, with Tom particularly knowledgeable about stocks and bonds. Tom was also considered deeply devoted to his wife. Once, as he and a friend walked together, the other man paid particular attention to an attractive woman who passed them on the street. When the friend ribbed his walking partner for not even giving her a "glance," Tom told him that his wife had been a "beautiful woman." The sentiment was admirable but left an impression upon his friend that Tom was a "very peculiar guy" for not at least noticing a "slick chick."

The first decennial census taken after the Palmers arrived in Brownville occurred in mid-April 1940. The census taker on their doorstep asked intrusive questions, the kind that may have made people on the lam squeamish. However, it was well known that their answers would be protected from disclosure for seventy-two years, until the far future in 2012. Thomas D. Palmer was recorded as age thirty-four (his actual age was thirty-eight) and born in Tennessee. The woman recorded as his wife, Betty, was age thirty-two and born in Alabama. The family had moved back into the W. St. Francis house, rented for $22.50 per month. Betty Ann was age seven; Jane, age six; David, age four; Margaret, age two; and Duncan, age one. Their parents' highest educational level was each listed as "H-4" (twelfth grade). Each was employed, he for forty-eight hours per week as a sales manager at Patteson Motors for $1,200 per year, and she as a steno secretary, putting in thirty-six hours per week for $720 per year. The combined total of their annual salaries was $43,000 in current dollars, meager given the size of their family, but more than the breadwinners of other resident families on their street. The fathers and mothers of the Perez, Costello, Garcia, Vera, Gray, Hart, and Guerra households made considerably less as a grocery clerk, cashier, seamstress, house painter, longshoreman, and trucker.

Reminders of the couple's precarious existence together may have surfaced in unexpected ways. *My Favorite Wife* premiered in Louisville in May 1940, fifteen years after Betty's first job there. The movie opened in Brownsville at the Capitol Theatre that following July under a promotion that posed the question regarding what happens when "a man has one wife too many." The comedic story was an adaptation of the "Enoch Arden" poem, featuring Cary Grant as Nick Arden, who remarries seven years after his wife, Ellen (played by Irene Dunne), has disappeared at sea following a shipwreck. Ellen Arden is rescued and shows up after Nick's second marriage, to hilarious and heartwarming consequences. If the Palmers saw the movie that summer, an unlikely date night given their seemingly unmanageable lives, did they think their real-life outcome would be the same or did they realize that happy endings were hit-and-miss?

Not long after the census taker appeared and the Dunne-Grant comedy was nominated for several Academy Awards, Tom registered for the first peacetime draft in U.S. history in anticipation of the country's entry into World War II. He did not have to register at that time because the pre-war conscription limited the draft to men between twenty-one and thirty-six. Tom's correct age was thirty-eight. Further, the required documentation should have been a deterrent because it was not protected from disclosure, like the census. Perhaps it was his military training combined with a sense of duty to country, but he registered as a thirty-five-year- old in October 1940. The precinct's registrar described Mr. Palmer as white, six-feet, one-inch tall, 145 lbs., with brown hair, blue eyes, and a ruddy complexion. Tom gave the information for the personal section of the card, listing his birthday as June 5, 1905, his birthplace as Carroll County, Tennessee (over a hundred miles west of Nashville, where he was born), and his wife as "Mrs. Betty McClinton Palmer." Above his signature was an all-capitalized acknowledgement on federal D.S.S. Form 1: "I AFFIRM THAT I HAVE VERIFIED THE ABOVE ANSWERS AND THAT THEY ARE TRUE." In Nashville, Tom Buntin's sons, Daniel, Thomas, and Rogers, filed their own cards in the young men's draft.

The W. St. Francis rental house became available for sale in late 1940 when the owner lost it to foreclosure. Betty and Tom were raised in houses owned by their parents so home ownership would likely have been emphasized as a family value. Tom bought the house in mid-November 1940, in his name only, with a $200 down payment. The balance of $1,800 was financed through the seller, who had acquired the property during foreclosure. Monthly payments were $15. There was some reason he bought the house in his name only. The couple must have pondered, either before or after the transaction, what would happen if Tom died. Texas was one of the few community property states in the 1930s and 1940s, which meant that each spouse in a marriage, whether recognized under civil law or common law, owned an automatic one-half interest in real estate, regardless of whether the husband or wife purchased the property.

If probate occurred, Betty would be required to produce documentation of a civil-law marriage, which she could not do, or a common-law marriage, which would raise questions within the courthouse and community. Undoubtedly to avoid this possibility, the two began to orchestrate gaining title in both their names. To that end, their first step on December 5, 1940, as "T.D. Palmer and Betty McC. Palmer," was to sell the house to car dealer Otto Manske.

In Kentucky during this period, Betty McCuddy's disappearance created uncertainty regarding the substantial inheritance that her great-uncle left her, especially given her presumptive-death date on the legal horizon. Fidelity Trust filed suit in a Logan County court in Russellville as George B. Edwards' estate executor and trustee and as statutory guardian of three-year-old Robin McCuddy, Betty's nephew and Fergus's only grandchild. The company sought a declaration of rights to establish disposition of the estate's remaining funds. Betty's total share of the McCuddy family bequest and the residuary estate was valued at about $44,000, almost $1 million in current dollars.

Twenty-one Edwards' family defendants were named, starting with Betty, who was also "sued as an unknown defendant" because Fidelity Trust did not concede that she was dead and referred to her throughout the pleading as to whether she was "in fact dead." Fergus was also sued, as well as J. Connelly Edwards and a first cousin of Betty's from Russellville, twenty-two-year-old George Edwards Duncan. Duncan was contemplating law school and would later accept his first job as an attorney in southeast Texas. The "McCuddy Case 1" spanned two years, generating over 400 pages of court filings and orders. Judge Doyle Willis issued judgment on May 21, 1941, finding that Betty McCuddy "is dead and that she departed this life intestate on the 6th day of November 1938." He appointed Fergus, her father, as her estate administrator.

The legal issue in the McCuddy Case 1 then centered on the consequence of the deaths of Mary Edwards Duncan McCuddy (who died in 1933) and her children Bill (who died in 1936) and Betty (who was declared dead in 1938). On behalf of Robin McCuddy, Fidelity Trust argued that the contingent-death clause in the will should be interpreted as follows: mother Mary died first, extinguishing her rights; her son Bill died next, but left a child, Robin; her daughter Betty was adjudged dead as of a later date and left no children, thus, the deceased, childless sibling's (Betty's) share should be awarded to Robin, the surviving child of her brother.

Fergus claimed that Betty's share went to him as her heir, next-of-kin, and the administrator of her estate and not to his only grandchild and namesake. His theory was that, following his wife's death, his daughter's fifty-percent interest in George B. Edwards' specific bequest of $30,000 became payable when she turned thirty in 1937, which was a little over a year before the date of her legally adjudged death. The judge read the will as clearly vesting Betty's interest in her nephew, without even addressing her father's argument. Fergus also lost his claim to Betty's inheritance of a share of the residuary estate, which was awarded to the child Robin.

In June 1941, the month following the Russellville judgment, the staged orchestration of title to the Palmer house in Brownsville was completed when Otto Manske sold the W. St. Francis house back to "T.D. Palmer" *and* "wife Betty McC. Palmer." At this point, the couple was clearly listed in the deed together as owners, and Betty was pregnant again. Mary Ellen, their last child, was born in late October 1941, of two legally dead parents. New York Life lost its appeal in the Buntin Case 1 and, in mid-June 1941, asked for the Tennessee Supreme Court's review, which was denied. The Chief Justice chided the insurance company for claiming that Betty McCuddy was Buntin's "paramour," stating that the reference was a "stronger characterization than the proof justifies" and was unsupported by any evidence in the record of "lewd relations" or a "disgraceful liaison" between the two. There were no dissenting opinions. Having unsuccessfully exhausted all avenues of appeal, New York Life paid Nashville Trust almost $60,000, the amount having increased since the jury verdict after interest was added.

In addition to helping with the house, for reasons that probably were not disclosed to him, Otto Manske hired Tom at Pipkin-Manske Motors. He appears to have befriended and valued his salesman. Tom Palmer was often featured in classified ads promoting Pipkin-Manske's used Fords, inexplicably photographed in a left-side profile highlighting the prominent

Tom Palmer, 1941. Far right in photo at right. (The Brownsville Herald.)

left ear. In the ads, he assured his "many friends and customers that he is ready and anxious" to sell them a car "on their own terms." In another promotion, he recommended a 1939 Ford Economy "60" Tudor Sedan, a "Thrifty Sixty," as the best value on the lot for $450 and a "good family car."

Tom and Otto attended a Ford Motor Company dealer and salesman meeting in San Antonio in 1941 and the two stood side-by-side in a large Pipkin-Manske advertising photo published around that same period. Sometime after late summer 1941, however, the relationship ended (which may or may not have been associated with Tom's drinking), and Tom took a job selling auto parts at Red Tough's Oldsmobile used car sales and service shop. World War II crushed the new car business, and Manske emphasized publicly that wartime conditions forced him to curtail operations and staff and concentrate on the used car market and service operations. Yet, Tom was a used car salesman, not a new car salesman, so the war was a questionable excuse for Otto to lay off an experienced employee.

The new job was a step down monetarily, so the Palmers needed to supplement their income. Tom opened "Palmer's Service Station," selling Sinclair products and used cars at 620 W. Elizabeth St. He urged readers to "make your ration coupon take you farther" with a used car, such as a Model A Ford coupe. The racy, red LaSalle luxury coupe he drove when secretly meeting Betty eleven years earlier was now a distant memory.

By the late 1940s, New York Life sought to return to Texas's lucrative life insurance market after leaving in protest in 1907 due to the legislature's enactment of the compulsory investment law. The company re-secured its business license effective January 2, 1948, by paying $440,000 in back taxes, penalties, and interest on Texas policies. This event was momentous for Tom and Betty. It meant that offices would be established throughout the state in major cities, one step closer to them.

Chapter 12

A Different New Life

Tom's troubles were increasingly apparent outside the Palmer-family iden-tity that Betty and he created in Brownsville. He made his living selling and servicing autos, but cars were also an undoing. A "Mr. Palmer" of 1017 W. St. Francis reported to Matamoros, Mexico, police on a weekend in early January 1944 that he parked his car on a city street and was then unable to find it. Six months later, *The Brownsville Herald* described an upcoming judicial hearing in Matamoros "in the case of Thomas David Palmer of Brownsville," following his brief stay in the Mexican border town's jail on charges associated with a traffic accident in front of police headquarters. The public exposure must have concerned the couple. And Tom hurt himself badly, breaking a hip after falling off a curb, which left his left leg about three inches shorter than his right one. He walked with a noticeable limp after.

Another front-page newspaper article in September 1947 highlighted that Thomas D. Palmer pled guilty in the Cameron County Court at Law to driving while intoxicated on Lincoln Street and was fined $116.45. The legal community knew Betty quite well as a "very fine" woman. Few, how-ever, claimed publicly to know Tom as well, except for his reputation for drinking and that his permanent handicap from the fall compounded his problems. Nevertheless, the courthouse crowd viewed the couple's plight sympathetically.

The possibility of discovery weighed on them as his name appeared in the Brownsville newspaper, publicly associated with DUI incidents. He and Betty had used some real-life fragments in their invented story—telling people she had a rich uncle from Kentucky and using family names, like "Margaret Ross" and "William Duncan," for their children's names. It was possible that someone would pick up the thread and unravel their lives. Worse, in a moment of weakness, Tom confided in Bill Mooberry, a lawyer friend, that his name was not Palmer. Though he may have trusted Mooberry, lawyers were notorious gossips, especially in bars. The couple began to consider a momentous step: moving the family.

Cameron County Judge Oscar Cromwell ("O.C.") Dancy was one of the Palmer's most consequential acquaintances through Betty's work. Dancy had served as county judge for eleven years when the Palmers landed in the Lower Rio Grande Valley, and, after taking a one-year hiatus, he served another twenty-eight years in the elective position. A county judge was the presiding authority of the county's governing body, the commissioners court. O.C. and his wife Leva's first son, Oscar Jr., was studying law with a law firm in Orange, Texas, when Betty and Tom arrived in Brownsville in 1931. Though the firm's primary office was in Houston, 100 miles west of Orange, the junior Dancy and his wife Margaret elected for small-town life in Orange. They became well-known through his work and the couple's involvement in community service, until shortly after World War II, when the Dancys returned to Brownsville following Oscar Jr.'s discharge from the U.S. Navy.

Oscar and Margaret were slightly younger than Tom and Betty. Their oldest child, Bettie Marrow Dancy, was born two months after Betty Ann Palmer, which also made her a few months older than Jane Palmer. Bettie and Betty Ann were good friends. Orange beckoned the Dancys back when Oscar was offered a position with a law firm and the Sabine Title Company. Sometime in early 1947, the two families made plans for the Palmers to follow the Dancys in the move. Tom's 1947 appearance in Betty's workplace, to plead guilty to a DUI charge, likely confirmed thoughts of relocating. New York Life's license to do business in Texas was under consideration as well (and was reinstated in early January 1948), which meant a field office could be established in Brownsville as an international border city. The life insurance company was unlikely to open an office in the sleepy town of Orange.

Orange is in southeast Texas near the Gulf of Mexico. In the nineteenth century, monumental longleaf pine forests straddled the east Texas-west Louisiana border, just north of the town. Longleaf pines, the redwoods of the South, encompassed some 90 million acres of southern landscape at the time Europeans first made contact with indigenous inhabitants. Enterprising settlers saw the acreage in another dimension: those forests contained over 400 billion board feet of lumber. There were numerous small-scale logging operations in Orange by the mid-to-late nineteenth century. However, two transplanted Pennsylvanians, Henry Jacob Lutcher and G. Bedell Moore, expanded the enterprise in 1877 by establishing the Crescent and Star Mill, the largest in Texas at the time. Over 100,000 board feet of lumber could be milled in twenty-four hours. Longleaf pine flooring was shipped around the world, including Russia and Europe.

The logging lasted only four decades, leaving about 13,000 acres of the South's original forest. The "cut out and get out" period made Orange immensely rich. Longleaf pine wealth allowed Frances Ann Robinson Lutcher to buy three, pre-Tiffany decorative arts windows from J&R Lamb Studios at the 1893 World's Columbian Exposition in Chicago for a Presby-terian church she planned to have constructed on Green Avenue. She then added forty-six more windows to the studio's portfolio and church design, as well as the church's thirty-six-foot-diameter opalescent stained-glass dome, which remains the only such dome in this country. Her affluence lured New Yorker Willis Carrier to Orange to chill her church, where he designed a "special refrigerating plant for use in the summertime." The system was reported to be the first of its kind west of the Mississippi River. Two years after the church's opening in 1912, the minister reported that the cooling system substantially increased attendance in the summer to around "fifty or sixty percent" of the congregation's membership.

At least one tourist in 1920 found the town's public buildings "wonder-ful," but lamented that the town itself was "dead," with as "many Buicks as Fords." He eagerly went on to Galveston. The Great Depression halted economic progress and any semblance of tourism for a period. However, the oil and gas industry, spawned by the prolific Spindletop oilfield in nearby Beaumont, singularly helped sustain Orange's economy until World War II.

Beginning in 1931, Martin Dies Jr. served as the area's congressional representative, holding the seat his father held for a decade previously. Dies did not hide his antipathy to federal government programs that helped people during a financial crisis. Nonetheless, he was determined to secure federal support to improve Orange's economic position in the build-up to the country's entry into World War II. With help from fellow Texas Demo-crats (Vice President John "Cactus Jack" Nance Garner and Speaker of the

U.S. House of Representatives Sam Rayburn), Dies ensured that Orange's shipyards were awarded federal contracts to construct "tugboats, oil and deck cargo barges, small tankers, minesweepers, and submarine chasers," later expanded to include surf-landing boats and destroyers.

As a result, the town's population mushroomed from 7,000 in 1940 to 60,000 by the end of the second world war. A housing development of 257 pastel-colored homes, called "Navy Park," was constructed by the U.S. Navy in east Orange as temporary housing to support the vast influx of military personnel and shipyard workers and their families. Navy Park was followed by Riverside, the largest federal public housing project in the nation, comprised of 2,000 prefabricated buildings erected quickly on the low, marshy area to the east of Navy Park, on the Sabine River. Schools were added quickly as well, including the one-story Tilley Elementary School on East Park Avenue, built in Riverside between 1942 and 1944.

The influx of residents peaked during World War II, and, while the post-war population decreased, it held at 35,000 in 1947, still a tremendous jump from pre-war conditions. The Palmers joined the remaining influx of residents, though for entirely different reasons than work opportunities. They posted the "nice well-built 5-room house with large porch" on W. St. Francis for sale in spring 1947. However, the house did not sell quickly, and the family stayed in Brownsville for another year. In late July 1948, the house finally sold for $3,750, with Betty signing the deed as "Betty McC. Palmer."

The move must have been particularly difficult for the Palmer children. Betty Ann and Jane were teenagers in high school. David, age twelve, was an honor-roll student and boxing star at St. Joseph's Catholic Academy. Margaret (age ten), Duncan (age nine), and Mary Ellen (age eight) were in elementary school. Betty Ann, Jane, and Bettie Dancy were at an age where departures meant get-togethers in which everyone professed undying friendship for all time no matter where each was located. One such event, a farewell party, was held for the three girls on July 24, 1948. A few days later, Betty Ann Palmer celebrated a final outing with friends by rising at 4 a.m. for a fishing excursion in the Brownsville channel leading to the Gulf of Mexico. On July 25, the Dancys left Brownsville. Jane Palmer left on July 28 and Betty Ann departed on August 2.

While the oldest Palmer girls were in the news because of a flurry of social events to send them off to their new lives, their parents kept a low profile. Finding an affordable home to buy was a priority. The prices were right in Riverside, but the city of Orange never incorporated the acreage into municipal limits because the houses and associated infrastructure were not built to code. The area had also flooded three years earlier and the federal government then offloaded the substandard development to a private firm from Dallas. Prices were reasonable for the "temporary" Navy Park homes in east Orange. They were still intact, having been built of steel frames and joists on concrete piers and covered with sugar-cane-derived fiberboard finished with metal lath and stucco. However, neither of the housing development locations was ideal because a car was needed to go downtown for work or shopping. The Palmers could not always count on having a vehicle that worked, notwithstanding Tom's employment as a car salesman.

A neighborhood on the north side of downtown and Green Avenue was appealing because of its location, though homes were costlier. Betty and Tom decided on that area, buying a wood-frame, one-story house at 1001 Orange Ave. on August 16, 1948, for $9,000. They paid $3,000 in cash and financed the rest through the sellers at $95 per month. The deed and lien named the buyers as "Thos. D. Palmer and wife, Betty Palmer." The house was well situated for the children and their parents. St. Mary Catholic Church's elementary school, staffed by Dominican sisters, was catty-corner. Public schools were also nearby. Anderson Elementary School, a two-story brick building with a dome on top and lots of windows, was two blocks to the north. Stark High School was about six blocks to the southwest. Riverside's Tilley Elementary School was farther, about ten blocks to the east. However, it was one story, providing suitable accessibility for Duncan, who navigated on crutches.

Oscar Jr.'s connections with

Anderson Elementary School. (Ellen Beasley, Orange, Tex. Preservation Plan.)

Lutcher Stark High School. (Orange Peel Yearbook, 1950.)

the legal community in southeast Texas made the Palmer's
decision to move economically
viable. Betty, an experienced
court reporter and legal secretary,
landed a court reporting job with
Judge F.W. Hustmyre in the 128th
District Court of Orange County
before they left Brownsville. She
settled in quickly at the Art Deco
courthouse, about nine blocks
south of their house. Hers was a
walkable commute. Tom found
work after they arrived as a parts
manager at Osborne Motors, a
Cadillac and Oldsmobile sales
and service store next to the
courthouse. He stayed with the
store until 1952 and then took a
job as a salesman at Lack's Auto
Associate Store downtown, also
walkable from home. He then
moved to Montgomery Ward in

*Orange County Courthouse. (Beasley, Pres-
ervation Plan.)*

*Downtown Orange, ca. 1950s. (Dr. Howard
Williams, Heritage House Museum.)*

Beaumont, twenty-four miles west of Orange, about eight to ten months
later. He commuted on the public bus.

The family fit into the neighborhood well. They were considered good
neighbors, friendly to all, and kind-hearted. People respected the parents
for their deep involvement in raising their children while each worked full-
time. Everyone took an interest in the Palmer children and sympathized
that their parents always "had a run for it caring for all those children."
Sandra Sample lived with her father and sister in the house at 912 W.
Cypress Ave., catty-corner from the back of the Palmer's house. She was
a year younger than Duncan and two years younger than Margaret, and
often saw their younger sister, Mary Ellen, walking to school. Sandra felt
bad for the Palmer children. They told her that they had no relatives at
all. Even as a child, the absence of any extended family whatsoever struck
Sandra oddly.

For adults, assimilating well like the Dancys meant joining clubs and social groups. Townspeople understood why Betty and Tom were unable to participate. Mrs. J. Cullen Browning, wife of the editor of *The Orange Leader*, knew that Betty's "day and night" work and home-life schedule made it unlikely that she would join the local Business and Professional Women's Club. She nominated her anyway. No one was offended when the court reporter turned down the invitation after receiving a unanimous vote of the membership in favor. Tom was also viewed as extremely hard working, a "hustler and a good salesman," though debilitated physically. When the family was enumerated for the 1950 census in mid-April, the "married" parents each reported working 50 hours the previous week. It was the only census in which the entire family was counted together. Tom, claiming Tennessee as his birthplace, gave his age as forty-four (he was forty-eight). Betty still identified Alabama as her state of birth. The children's ages ranged from eight to seventeen.

As they settled into their new town, the six Palmer children were active and popular. In her senior year of high school in 1950, "Liz," formerly Betty Ann, had matured into a tall, attractive young woman. Her face was thin, like her father's, and she inherited her mother's dark hair and likeness around the eyes. She excelled in acting, was a member of the Future Teachers of America, and, with her height, played on the girls' basketball team. Jane, a junior in the 1950-1951 school year, was about the same height as her older sister, and had a bit more worldly look than Liz because she wore make-up. Both girls were in the Horizon Club, associated with the Camp Fire Girls. David, in ninth grade, was a handsome young man. He was in the Spanish Club, not surprising since he may have been bilingual from growing up in the Valley. Margaret started junior high (seventh grade) in 1950, a pretty girl with dark, short, curly hair, and dark eyes. She uncannily resembled Betty McCuddy in her senior-year photo at Ward-Belmont. Duncan was boyishly cute and active at school, serving as vice president of the junior high Chapel Club, whose purpose was to "develop leadership, foster fellowship, and present worshipful programs." In high school, he was in the Rod and Reel Club and volunteered as a library assistant.

Betty built a local reputation for proficient court reporting, no small feat. At Belknap three decades earlier, she learned to take shorthand from one speaker, who might interrupt his own thoughts, but it was a singular interruption. In court, lawyers talked over each other and the witnesses, though never the judge. She left the Orange County court system for a higher-paying position in the courthouse in Jefferson County, an adjacent county, starting January 1, 1953. Her recommendations included the Jefferson County Bar Association, individual attorneys, and friends of Judge L.H. Hightower, her new boss. People realized that she made "good money," "probably more than he did," but her neighbors also knew she took on night work for extra money, because they heard her typing "way up into the early morning hours."

The 1953 *Orange City Directory* listed "Thos. D. Palmer" and wife "Elizabeth" at 1001 Orange Ave. His occupation was identified as "salesman." The father of six had moved from Montgomery Ward to Lack's Television and Appliance Center, also in downtown Beaumont. Their lives seemed safer in southeast Texas than in the Valley, but there were ominous signs. A photographer from *The Beaumont Journal* once photographed Betty as she walked in a hallway of the Jefferson County Courthouse following a trial in which she was court reporter. The black-and-white photo showed a smiling, handsome woman with strong features. She wore a short-sleeve shirtwaist dress with stand-up collar and light-color, open-toe sandals. It was not clear from the photo whether she even knew that an unnerving event—her image being captured for publication—had occurred.

A realization of a worst-case encounter happened in a courtroom. As Betty sat in the court reporter's chair preparing for a trial, a man walked in. She immediately recognized him as her first cousin from Russellville, George Edwards Duncan, a co-beneficiary of their Great-Uncle George B. Edwards' will. Duncan and his wife moved to Beaumont in 1945, three years before the Palmers, after he graduated from the University of Virginia School of Law. He had joined a Beaumont law firm and was one of the lawyers in the case before her. She had last seen him in 1929 when she was twenty-two and he was twelve, around the time that their great-uncle died. The lawyer was in his early-to-mid thirties during the trial and did not recognize her, reflecting how little attention

(Hearst Communications, Inc.)

litigators paid to the women who memorialized their performances before judges and juries. His litigation practice was extensive, so it is remarkable that the two cousins had not crossed paths before.

Betty clearly had not known there was such close family in southeast Texas when she and Tom moved there in 1948. Her cousin's failure to recognize her did not mean the Palmer's true identities were safe.

Chapter 13

Unraveling

Though they did not know it at the time, Betty and Tom's alternate lives began to unravel in mid-summer 1952, before the unnerving courtroom encounter with her family member. Respess Chatfield, an investigator in New York Life's Atlanta office, received a phone call from Bill Finney, a Nashville attorney with the law firm that represented the insurance company in the Buntin Case 1. Finney claimed, "I've got something on Buntin." His tip was based on a cascade of communications, starting with person one in Nashville who told a lawyer (person two), who then told Finney (person three) that Buntin was alive. One could not have blamed Chatfield for reacting skeptically. For all he knew, the chain of talk was nothing more than the game of "Gossip" played at housewives' parties where a new product, Tupperware, was sold.

Additionally, Chatfield may have hesitated in encouraging Finney, who wanted him to come to Nashville. The insurance company had spent more than $100,000 over the previous twenty years chasing tips and the elusive trail of Tom Buntin. They had even sent paid agents to South America. Zelma Brown Lipscomb, an ex-Marine from Robertson County, swore in an affidavit for New York Life that he saw Buntin, whom he knew only as a wealthy Nashvillian who spent summers in Robertson County before he disappeared in 1931, in Panama. The witness claimed Buntin drank at various locations in Colón, the gateway city to the Panama Canal on the Caribbean side, when Lipscomb was stationed in the Panama Canal Zone from 1931 to 1934.

After serving in the U.S. Navy, John McClellan, a childhood friend of Tom's, moved to Panama in the early 1930s to work in his father's foreign trade business in Central America and South America. He was in the lobby of the Bolivar Hotel in Lima, Peru, around 5 p.m. in mid-January 1935, when he spotted a man in a dark suit entering the hotel. As the man removed his hat, John recognized Nashville's Tom Buntin, even though he had not seen his friend for six years. He was surprised, waived, and approached to greet him. When McClellan was about eight feet away, the man turned around and left quickly. John followed him outside, but the street was crowded with revelers celebrating the 500th anniversary of the founding of the colonial city. He lost sight of his friend. New York Life subsequently paid McClellan $500 for his time and expenses in an unsuccessful effort to search for Tom in Peru, Ecuador, and Colombia. Nashville Trust called a Robertson County attorney and the county sheriff as witnesses in the Buntin Case 1 to assassinate Lipscomb's character. Through cross-examination of McClellan, the trust company inferred that his tip about seeing Buntin was simply a ploy for a paid vacation in South America on New York Life's dole.

New York Life also deposed three Peruvian workers with the help of a translator in mid-January 1940 during the Buntin Case 1. Each man testified under oath at the U.S. Embassy in Lima and each separately identified a photo of Tom Buntin as the American they had seen more than once at a country club and bar in Lima. Their sightings occurred during the same time period as McClellan's encounter. The evidence of Buntin's presence in South America did not convince the trial court judge or jury or the appellate courts in the first insurance lawsuit. The trust company and the Tennessee courts, including the head of the state's Supreme Court, belittled the foreign witnesses. Chief Justice Grafton Green described the Peruvians as not of a "higher type" of witness based on their stations in life (a doorman, bartender, and taxicab driver) and cast doubt on the veracity of their sworn testimony.

As it turns out, Brownsville Municipal Airport was the top international airport on the U.S.-Mexico border in the 1930s and 1940s and Tom *did* travel south by plane, documented as far as Mexico City, though for what reason is unknown. Documentation is also lacking with respect to whether he went into the southern hemisphere. He had, after all, shared "queer" ideas with a Nashville friend years earlier about traveling in remote South America. A flight from Brownsville to the Panama Canal Zone or Lima took less than a day and no passport was required at the time. Where Tom would have found the money to pay for his travels is unknown.

Notwithstanding the expensive investigative and litigation history of the case, Chatfield was professionally obligated to follow up on Finney's call that summer of 1952. The tip started with a certified public accountant and tax expert in Nashville, John Sebastian Glenn. Glenn was a devout Catholic who spent a career helping clients fight fraud. He suffered a stroke in late June 1952 and lingered for a week before dying on July 3. Possibly aided by a pang of conscience, the man disclosed to Albert Stockell, either shortly before his stroke or in his last week of life, that he had heard from Tom Buntin, who was somewhere in Texas. Stockell practiced law with J. Connelly Edwards (Betty McCuddy's cousin, who suffered James Caldwell's rebuke during his cross examination of the elder man in the Buntin Case 1). Stockell then asked another law partner of his, Bill Finney, to call Chatfield with the information.

Why Tom and John Glenn were in touch is unknown. The two men's offices were near each other in Nashville's "Wall Street of the South" business district in the 1920s. However, the accountant was not publicly associated with the same social circle as that of the Buntins and the Caldwells. Glenn often represented the state or federal government in income tax-recovery cases or he was hired by corporations to conduct forensic financial analyses when internal financial wrongdoing was suspected. There is no evidence that he was connected with the investigations or prosecutions of Rogers Caldwell, nor with any Caldwell or Buntin business matters.

Chatfield thought that there was "almost nothing to go on but hope" because the Lone Star State was vast. His company re-established offices in Texas in 1948 following a forty-year hiatus from selling insurance there because of an early twentieth-century discriminatory state law targeting out-of-state insurance businesses. In the four years since New York Life re-secured its business license in Texas, the company's network of agents and investigators faced an uphill hurdle to establish a statewide network of connections.

Wallace Murray, an investigator in the Dallas office, was tasked to start looking for Buntin in the late summer of 1952. The dead ends multiplied over the next year. Glenn was dead and Bill Finney, age forty, died of a heart attack a few months after he called Chatfield, though his partner Stockell, the middleman of the tip, was still alive. Walter Hall of Citizen State Bank in the town of Dickinson, Texas, reported to Murray that there was no one matching the profile within seventy-five miles of Houston. Hall thought a person named "Tucker," a bookkeeper turned chicken farmer, fit the description and should be checked out. The lead fizzled. Augustine Celeya of Brownsville volunteered to the investigator that the Buntin man was buried in a potter's field in the city, but New York Life drew the line at exhuming bodies randomly. Included in Murray's list of people to consult in southeast Texas, a little over seventy-five miles east of Houston, were Lutcher Stark, "money man" of Orange, and J. Cullen Browning, editor of *The Orange Leader*.

Murray was joined in his search by Richard Beyea, New York Life's inspection department manager in the Dallas office. Through insurance contacts, they found an insurance agent in north Texas, originally from the Valley, who said that their description "tallied" with a Tom Palmer he had known in Brownsville. Murray and Beyea traveled to south Texas. They carried scant documentation (Tom's 1929 pilot's license photo) to appointments with local credit bureaus and police departments. There, in the spring of 1953, they learned that the man whom they knew as Tom Buntin was Tom Palmer. Palmer had moved to southeast Texas, far up the Texas Gulf Coast from south Texas. The exact way in which Murray and Beyea learned this information is unknown, but they hastened to the largest city in the region, Beaumont.

When a disappeared policy holder was found, New York Life's standard operating procedure was to have a representative photograph the person holding a current issue of the *Saturday Evening Post* or *Life* magazine with the date clearly shown and to have him write that "I am alive on this date" and sign the statement. The two investigators were ready to purchase a magazine.

Wallace Murray spotted an aging man with the tell-tale ear on the street in downtown Beaumont around May 3, 1953. He tracked the man's movements for a month and finally went to his house in Orange where Tom Buntin and Betty McCuddy admitted their identities around June 3. Murray reported to Respess Chatfield that he believed he had found the missing man. With Chatfield's approval, Murray called New York Life's inspector in the Memphis office, Albert Alexander (who had known Tom), to ask that he travel to southeast Texas to identify Tom Buntin definitively. The two men visited the Lack's store (Tom's employer) in Beaumont on June 12, 1953. Alexander recognized the man and "verified without question" that he was Buntin.

Broadway National Bank in Nashville received the unwelcome news—that the insurance company wanted its money back—on June 22, 1953. Every man who attended the meeting that day had a relationship with Tom or Betty and blatant professional conflicts of interest that had existed since the Buntin Case 1. J. Connelly Edwards (Betty McCuddy's cousin) represented New York Life. Laurence Howard (the bank's lawyer) was Tom's friend and rescuer back in Buntin's jail days. Broadway National Bank assumed the trustee role for Tom Buntin's insurance proceeds in January 1951 when Nashville Trust Company's president, Louie Phillips, moved to the bank as its president. The news in the meeting was also unpleasant for personal reasons of Phillips'. He and Bettie Moore Buntin had quietly married on New Year's Day 1944.

Phillips said the bank would fight the case. He was given large, glossy, black-and-white photos of Tom and Betty and a photo of Tom holding a periodical dated earlier in the month. Laurence Howard tried to forestall a lawsuit or at least keep Mrs. Louie Phillips out of the fray. He subsequently wrote J. Connelly Edwards that "further examination of the details would constitute merely an unnecessary probing of old wounds" and "no good" could result. He thought it "best to leave the matter as is without further discussion." He added that Bettie Moore Buntin Phillips denied the photos were of her first husband.

New York Life had spent more than a small fortune of its policyholders' and shareholders' money and no small measure of its corporate dignity in the relentless and fruitless investigation and the Buntin Case 1 battle. On November 5, 1953, the company secured an injunction in a Davidson County chancery court against Broadway National Bank and Nashville Trust Company freezing an undisclosed amount of remaining funds from Thomas Craighead Buntin's life insurance policies and enjoining Bettie Phillips and her three adult sons from accessing the money. J. Connelly Edwards procured the injunction immediately. In a procedural move described the next day as "most extraordinary," he did not file the bill of complaint and proposed order first with the court clerk—making the documents public—but sought out one of the two court chancellors (judges) in person. He interrupted Chancellor Thomas A. Shriver in trial, handing him both documents. Shriver signed the injunction order from the bench and let Edwards keep the original complaint, an "unprecedented" action.

The "secret suit" failed to be kept in the dark despite—or possibly because of— Edwards' bold tactics. That same day, the court clerk called

Nashville's largest newspaper, *The Tennessean*. John Seigenthaler, the police and court beat reporter, took the call. Seigenthaler was later described by U.S. Attorney General Robert F. Kennedy, his boss at the U.S. Department of Justice, as a person of "integrity and honesty" and of "excellent character." When he took the clerk's call, the twenty-six-year-old had been an investigative journalist for only three years. He was still learning his trade. His physical stature and features at the time would not have made an indelible impression on witnesses, but he was scrappy, and an incipient powerhouse. Readers enjoyed his narratives, which vividly described the brazenness of bandits in everyday places familiar to Nashvillians. The writings typically appeared as front-page, above-the-fold stories, consuming more column-inches than his cohorts' articles.

John Seigenthaler, 1953. (The Tennessean — USA TODAY NETWORK.)

The physical placement of a story in a print newspaper was extremely important, not only to the writer, but to the story itself. Many readers focused on their favorite topics—sports, society, or cartoons—which were rotely assigned to dedicated sections. For other, non-routine news, location was selected by news editors who gauged potential popular appeal. Expanded appeal drove sales, which drove advertising revenue. Editors' intuition was based upon their experience and not necessarily upon the importance of the content. "Above-the-fold" on page one was literal: placement above the horizontal crease across the paper after the section was folded for distribution. The placement was a prime location since the featured photos and headlines in the print newspaper on newsstands caught people's eye. With enough human interest then generated, the Associated Press ("AP") and the United Press ("UP") might syndicate (distribute) the story nationwide and, possibly, worldwide. At the time of the phone call, none of Seigenthaler's previous stories had achieved blockbuster status or extended to readers beyond *The Tennessean*'s circulation area.

The clerk explained that a chancery court judge wanted to see Seigenthaler about a story. When the reporter showed up in person, the judge offered a few tantalizing crumbs about a man who had been missing from Nashville for decades but had been discovered. According to the judge, the man volunteered to return to Nashville to testify in a case involving an insurance company called New York Life if the identities of his wife and children were protected. Despite pointed questions, the reporter's news source refused to disclose the identity or location of the man and his family. Except for the injunction order, the lawsuit records were redacted to prevent the press or anyone else outside the case from accessing the details. Which of the chancery court's two chancellors tipped off the reporter is unclear. In a next-day quote, Shriver claimed that he could not recall "much" of what was in the bill of complaint when he signed the injunction order. The other chancellor, William Wade, ended up with the case. Wade may have been the source of the leak and then maneuvered to be assigned what was sure to be high-intrigue, high-visibility litigation.

Seigenthaler returned to the office and mentioned the visit to his editor, Coleman Harwell. The man became "unglued," instantly recognizing that the case involved Tom Buntin. The injunction had to be covered immediately. When contacted for the story, New York Life's General Counsel Ferdinand Pease confirmed that "we have talked to Mr. Buntin" and an unnamed official reported that Buntin "knows the petition has been filed." The insurance company's top lawyer refused to reveal Tom's assumed name or where he was located, citing concerns that "he might vanish again." Strangely, an ancillary lawyer on the case, who claimed he was not "very well acquainted with the suit," commented on the record to the reporter that he thought Buntin "might be in Texas."

"Buntin Alive, Suit Declares," appeared in *The Tennessean*'s morning edition of November 6, but reached only those readers in the newspaper's circulation area. Tom's photos were dated (having been taken in the 1920s) and bore little resemblance to him as a fifty-one-year-old man. In one, he was dressed as a pirate for a costume party. The other was a formal photo of Tom as a young man showing the prominent left ear. The Phillips refused to comment on the story. Son Thomas C. Buntin Jr. declared, "I'm just like the man from Missouri—I have to be shown" that the man was his father. Elsie and May Buntin Murray professed to know only what they read in the newspaper that morning. Rogers Caldwell claimed it was "very unlikely that Buntin had been found" because he was "too well known."

Seigenthaler got a huge break from the inept or purposeful on-the-record comment that Buntin might be found in Texas. Silliman Evans served as *The Tennessean*'s president and publisher and, under his leadership, the newspaper had become known as one of the South's "liveliest and most powerful papers." He was a native Texan who started his journalism career under Amon Carter, publisher of the *Fort Worth Star-Telegram*. He then served as a political reporter in Austin, followed by a stint in Washington, DC. This experience made Evans extremely well-connected in his home state. He and editor Harwell directed Seigenthaler to head to Texas to find Tom Buntin, the legally dead man, and his current family.

The second huge break was in the courthouse files, which were not redacted in one crucial way. The injunction revealed the partial name of the individual as "Palmer aka Buntin." Confidently, Silliman Evans wanted to contact New York Life himself, but even he could not pry any information out of the Home Office. He was told by various contacts that New York Life's management "on high" told staff that leaking the company's internal memo on Buntin or discussing the case was a "firing offense." The reporter was leaving for Texas and sweating it—where to start? It was a rhetorical question to himself. Seigenthaler knew that his best strategy was to "track the trackers," to find out where New York Life's agents, whose names he did not know, had been.

Evans used his Texas connections to call on Bill Kittrell, who founded the Texas Press Clipping Bureau and was a public relations businessman in Dallas. Kittrell was also a veteran operative and lobbyist for the state's Democratic Party. He was the man with the "can of oil" who ensured that the party machine ran smoothly. The publisher warned Seigenthaler that the Texan was the real thing—"Stetson, string ties, and boots." Lady Bird Johnson called Bill one of the best storytellers she ever knew. Seigenthaler immediately loaded up his suitcase with multiple spiral-bound writing pads

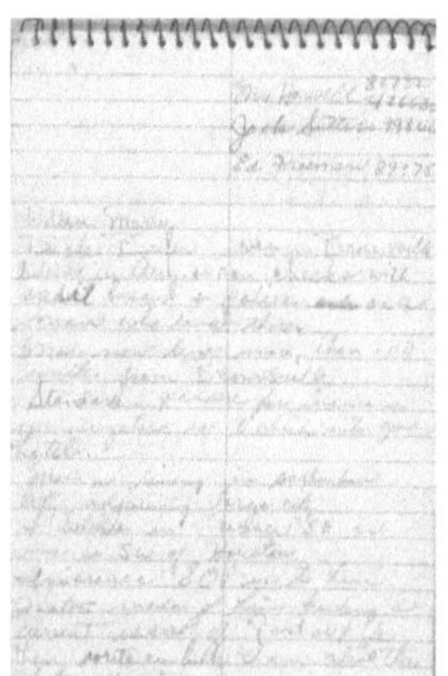

and flew out on November 9, 1953, to meet the powerbroker in Dallas. The Texan was already lining up contacts and motels around the state, without knowing where Seigenthaler wanted to start. Quickly, the reporter learned Murray's and Beyea's names. When

(J. Seigenthaler Papers, Special Collections Library, Vanderbilt Univ.)

he contacted each investigator separately, Beyea denied he had ever heard of a Buntin. Murray admitted openly he had located the man and then ineffectively backtracked, saying he could not talk about the matter.

With Kittrell's expansive network as a resource, the reporter visited in whirlwind style Fort Worth, Houston, and El Paso, and planned to end his travels in Harlingen, in the Lower Rio Grande Valley. Kittrell put him in touch with men in each city with their own contacts that gave Seigenthaler's pursuit further leverage: John Van Cronkite, Governor Allen Shivers' right-hand man; Van Kennedy, Democratic Party official in Corpus Christi; Bill Watts of *The Brownsville Herald*; and Ralph Gilliland, Chief Deputy U.S. Marshal, in San Antonio. Everywhere Seigenthaler traveled, he checked motels, airports, credit bureaus, and the Better Business Bureau office to pick up the trail of Murray and Beyea and lead him to Tom Buntin, aka Palmer.

Harwell and Evans, back at the paper, were keeping things very "hush, hush," even among their staff. Seigenthaler needed support, so they swore one reporter, John Fetterman, to secrecy and gave him a dedicated office for the assignment. Taped to the wall of the windowless, locked room was a large, 1953 Mobilgas map of the southwestern U.S., which Fetterman used to track Seigenthaler's movements.

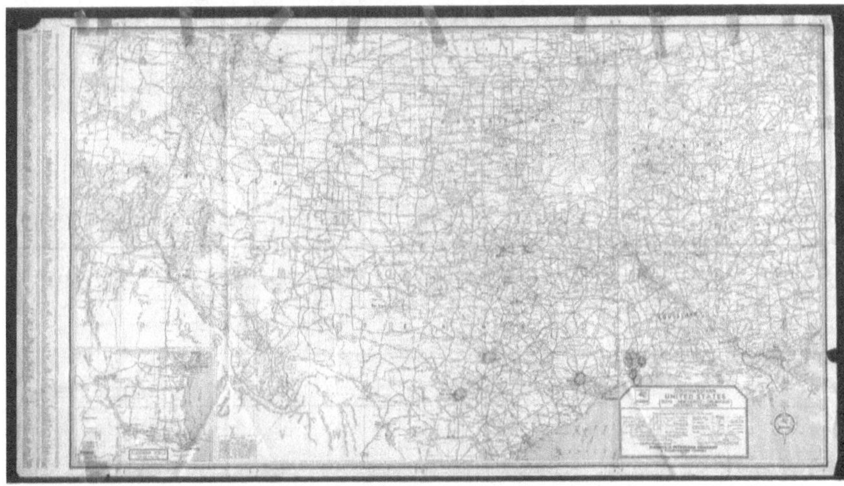

(J. Seigenthaler Papers, Special Collections Library, Vanderbilt Univ.)

Seigenthaler was soon at the end of his rope chasing dead leads. He had spent a lot of the newspaper's money, which worried editor Harwell but not publisher Evans. His final trip was to Harlingen in the Lower

Rio Grande Valley where he met with Cameron County Sheriff Boynton Fleming. The curmudgeon did not want to spend time with the out-of-state reporter. The past several months had been busy with a wave of burglaries by, in the sheriff's words, "wetbacks" coming across the Rio Grande River due to a severe drought in northeastern Mexico. Seigenthaler sensed the sheriff knew something, but his developing investigative skills failed to elicit any information. He resolved to return to Nashville, empty-handed and disappointed in his journalistic abilities.

The day of departure, Seigenthaler decided to say goodbye to Sheriff Fleming at the restaurant he frequented. For whatever reason, the lawman had experienced a change of heart and offered only one insight: "I have one hint, look for a citrus city." Seigenthaler was stunned and elated, rushing back to his motel to call Fetterman to look at the map taped to the wall. Fetterman had already circled the places the reporter had visited—Fort Worth, Dallas, Houston, El Paso—or might go—Austin and San Antonio. Seigenthaler thought the "citrus city" had to be in the Rio Grande Valley because the area was a huge producer of fruit. Texas was so large that the map cut off the Valley below a line running roughly between Corpus Christi and Laredo. Fetterman moved in closely to try to read the fine print in the map's insert for south Texas. He could not find anything promising, so he returned to the larger portion of the map and began tracing the cities and towns going up the Texas Gulf Coast. He was at the extreme upper coast, bordering Louisiana, when he exclaimed "Orange, there's an Orange, Texas!" The closest large city was Beaumont, so he circled Beaumont, nearby Port Arthur, and Orange. Dolph maps of all three cities were available, so Seigenthaler soon had detailed layouts of each place.

Seigenthaler flew back to Dallas and beelined to New York Life's office in the 900 Petroleum Building even though it was a Saturday, November 14. A custodian let him in the locked office after he introduced himself as a New York Life employee named Hugh Wellington Vester. (Hugh Wellington Vester was a real person, a friend of Seigenthaler's from high school.) "Vester" found the Buntin file in an unlocked cabinet, but it was empty except for the redacted court records. As he started rifling files throughout the cabinet, the custodian came in and became suspicious. He then ran out to take the elevator down, presumably to alert the police or security. Seigenthaler bolted and exited down the stairs to ground level, and then went to a theater several blocks away where he called Kittrell, who picked him up.

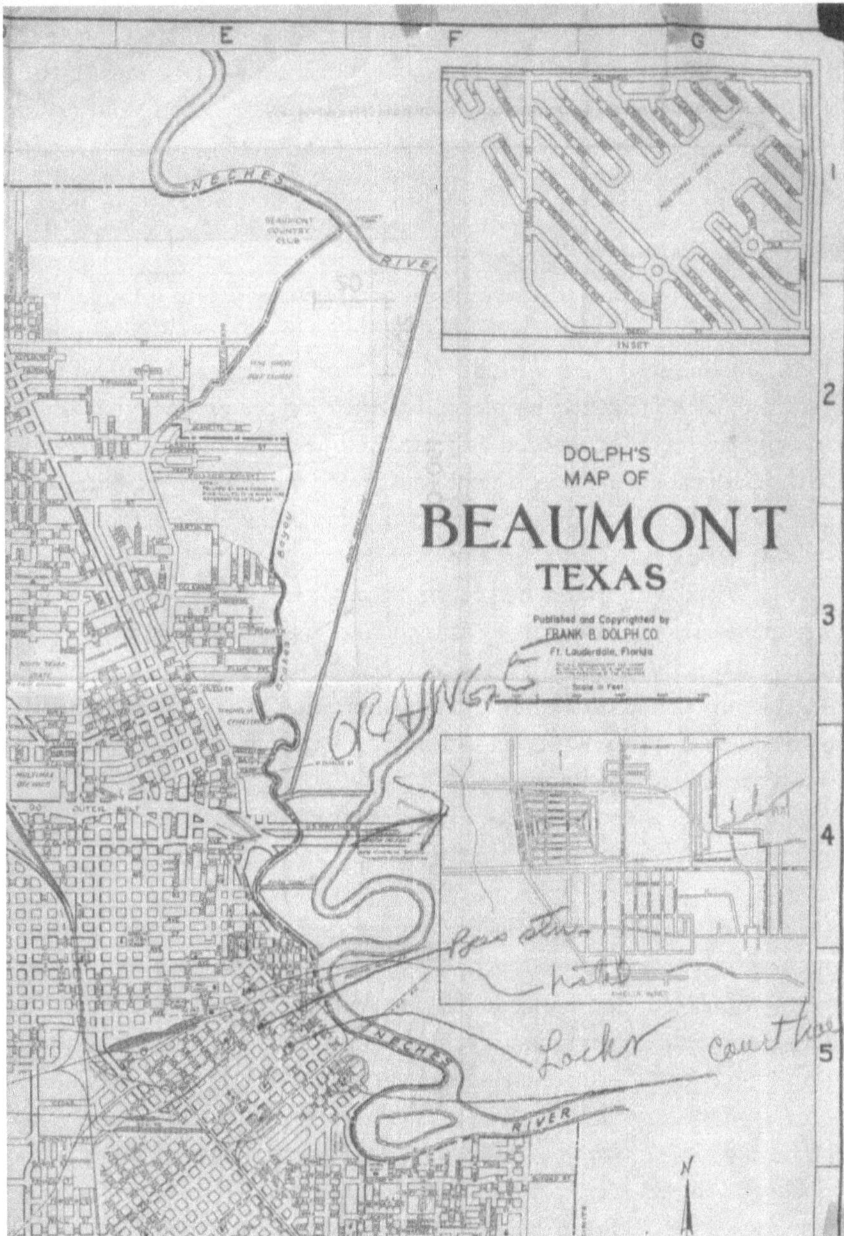

(J. Seigenthaler Papers, Special Collections Library, Vanderbilt Univ.)

The sheriff's unexpected tip and Seigenthaler's sleuthing paid off when a response to his and his newspaper's queries about Orange suggested that New York Life agents had gone to Beaumont. He arranged a flight to Houston on Braniff Airways on November 19, and then flew from Houston to the Beaumont airport. Kittrell, of course, had connections in southeast Texas and put Seigenthaler in touch with Beaumont lawyer Gaston Wilder. Gordon Browning, editor of *The Beaumont Enterprise*, was another connection through Silliman Evans. Browning, a Tennessean by birth, was related to a former Tennessee governor, his namesake, and agreed to let Seigenthaler work in the newspaper's offices.

The young reporter checked into a motel on the road to Orange where he found the agents had stayed. He had been in Texas for days and was "beat." His editor called with an ultimatum: after Beaumont, wrap up and come back. Seigenthaler pleaded for help on the ground, that he had a real lead. Harwell conceded and assigned Jimmy Holt, a photographer for the newspaper. The assignment "ticked off" Holt, however, because he had to leave home for an undetermined period a few days before his first wedding anniversary.

A "real lead" was a stretched claim. In fact, there was little to go on. The only image Seigenthaler carried was the old 1920s photo of Buntin with the bad left ear. On Saturday, November 21, 1953, the newspaper cohorts dined in downtown Beaumont. Holt continued to complain about the oppressive heat and ubiquitous swamps. He planned to leave soon, which would make his bride happy.

Paul Johns, New York Life's lead investigator in the Atlanta office, testified in the Buntin Case 1 trial that a missing person, or a suicide, was relatively easy to identify because "every man, certainly, has on him one or more or a great many marks of identification," "his face for one thing" and "his "clothing is labeled, his tie is labeled," "his shoes have numbers," and there are "laundry marks on his clothes." The time was long past where clothes could be useful in identifying Tom Buntin. He had probably long ago pawned that distinctive ring that Bettie Moore Buntin described to Johns over twenty years earlier. Distinctive physical features rarely lose their uniqueness naturally, however.

On the sidewalk after dinner, Seigenthaler gave Holt "hell" for being such a gripe. As he did so, he looked over the photographer's shoulder and saw a tall, thin man with blond hair turning sandy gray and a bent left ear, limping along the sidewalk, suggesting he had a bad left hip. He was walking away from them, going in the opposite direction. The reporter grabbed Holt. They watched the man enter a store and buy a pint of whiskey. Holt followed inside and came out saying, "It's him!"

They were close to the main drag in downtown Beaumont, near the bus station where the man went. Seigenthaler followed the man inside and, following the man's lead after he limped away from the ticket counter, bought a ticket to Orange, twenty-four miles to the east. Holt drove the rental car, following behind the bus. The man exited on Green Avenue, on the north side of downtown Orange as shown on the reporter's map. He then walked north on oak-lined Ninth Street to a modest house with a detached garage in the rear of the tiny corner lot. The house faced north, on Orange Avenue. Holt picked up Seigenthaler and they returned to the motel for the night. Holt's plan to escape for home was thwarted, but he was now "all in," notwithstanding an important anniversary. The next morning, both men, wearing "Texas blue dungarees" to try to fit in, attended Sunday services at several churches in Orange but did not see the man with the bent left ear. They did not know where he worked, so they spent the rest of the day driving around the "Golden Triangle" (Orange, Port Arthur, Beaumont) stopping at service stations and restaurants.

On Monday, November 23, the two Tennesseans staked out early. They sat low in their rental car on Ninth Street at the intersecting road to the immediate south (Cypress Avenue), next to the Sample's house at 912 W. Cypress. Their car faced north. Around 7 a.m., the man and a woman exited the rear or south side of a house that faced north on Orange Avenue. The 1950 Oldsmobile in their garage at the rear of the lot had no license plate and four flat tires, suggesting to Seigenthaler that the two were "down on their luck." The couple walked south on Ninth Street, passing the car but the two took no notice of the men inside. Two children walked out the front door of the house and headed north on Ninth Street towards what appeared to be a school at a Catholic church in the next block.

Seigenthaler and Holt focused on the adult couple who boarded a bus at Green Avenue. After following the bus to downtown Beaumont, they saw the two go their separate ways after leaving the bus station. Seigenthaler and Holt hurried to lawyer Wilder's office and looked at Orange's city directory under "1001 Orange Avenue," finding "Thomas D. and Elizabeth Palmer," phone number "TUxedo 8-3616." The lawyer recognized Elizabeth Palmer immediately as Betty Palmer and advised that she was a court reporter and had an office in the Jefferson County Courthouse nearby. The directory indicated that Tom Palmer worked at the Lack's television and appliance store in downtown Beaumont. Holt bolted to take exterior photos of the courthouse and Lack's.

Seigenthaler and Holt debated how to approach the Palmers and ended up following them that day and the next. They were "clearly in love," holding hands and window shopping the downtown Beaumont stores, decorated for the Christmas season. The debate widened through phone calls to Nashville with Evans, Harwell, and Fetterman. Everyone but Seigenthaler wanted him to approach Tom Palmer first. Seigenthaler won the argument with a plan to approach the woman—whom he now knew as Betty McCuddy of Russellville, Kentucky—first.

The reporter finally had enough information and a strategy to confront Betty, which he resolved to do on Wednesday, November 25, 1953, the day before Thanksgiving. Back in Nashville, Charles Harwell told *The Tennessean*'s staff that morning to "leave early or you'll be locked in" that night. Everyone stayed.

Chapter 14

Exposed

As Thanksgiving Day in 1953 approached, the Palmers knew they had been discovered six months earlier by New York Life. They understood that the insurance company's lawsuit was filed in secret in a Davidson County court and that Tom's first family was aware of the discovery but had agreed that he need not return to testify. Betty and Tom believed they had not been exposed in Nashville beyond a small circle of lawyers and judges and Tom's immediate family, who would not be inclined to spread the news. To the couple's understanding, the entire matter had been kept quiet in Nashville, had not reached the newspapers, and had not spread to Russellville. There was no need to tell their six children or anyone in southeast Texas. John Seigenthaler was a name unknown to them. Jimmy Holt was also an unfamiliar name although, for the past two days, the photographer had captured their images with telescopic lens as they went about their lives, walking to work from the bus station, talking with friends on the street, and buying groceries.

Early Wednesday morning, November 25, the couple boarded the bus to Beaumont. Tom was a reader, which meant he probably worked puzzles as well. Erudite gamemaster Albert Morehead's 1952 series of crossword puzzles was popular during that time and may have engaged Tom on the bumpy ride to work. Puzzle No. 44 foreshadowed the next phase of their life. The clue to Number 33 Down was "Dark period." Betty, a reader herself when she had time in her former life, could have helped with answers as needed. The clue to Number 38 Across read "Judicial opinions." If Tom hesitated

(*The Tennessean – USA TODAY NETWORK.*)

because only the second letter of the answer was filled in, "i" (from "night," the answer to Number 33 Down), Betty would have resolved the matter by whispering "dicta," as an experienced court reporter and legal secretary would know.

Betty may have used her commute time to catch up reading *The Orange Leader.* The newspaper's headline from the day before declared, "U.S. Calls for Junking of Soviet Peace Plan." Her attention was likely drawn to the photo in the top right, however. The feature attraction of the Orange Jaycee Christmas parade the upcoming Saturday, two days after Thanksgiving, was a team of real reindeer from Alaska. Mary Ellen, their youngest at age twelve, may have no longer believed in Santa Claus, but would be excited to see the exotic animals.

With no grandparents, aunts, uncles, or cousins, the Palmer family was close. It was also expanding. Daughter Jane Herring delivered her first child a month earlier in Orange, but the mother and baby had returned home to Washington State. Betty and Tom's first child, Betty Ann Burton, was due to deliver her first baby at the Orange City Hospital the past Sunday but was overdue. She was staying with her parents because husband William was stationed in Korea at a U.S. Air Force base and would hear the joyous news from afar. At Tom's age of fifty-one and Betty's age of forty-six, the couple may have thought of the day they could retire to enjoy their family. That possibility may have seemed entirely out of reach for years because money was tight and would continue to be. They would have been concerned that Duncan be able to care for himself after they died and be assured of a final resting place near them.

The couple arrived in Beaumont, parting ways as they did every working day, with Betty heading to the courthouse and Tom heading to the Lack's store. Thanksgiving week was quiet in the courthouse as the lawyers and judges fled town for football games, especially the Texas A&M University and University of Texas rivalry match ritually held on Thanksgiving. Betty often took transcription work at night to make extra money but there was probably none that week, and she may have been glad. A quiet week and long holiday weekend were welcomed, and the grandmother would have looked forward to celebrating a new grandchild's birth.

Seigenthaler went to the Jefferson County Courthouse at noon and found the small office with a marker on the door that read, "Betty Palmer, Court Reporter." It was empty, so he waited. When Betty arrived, he introduced himself and asked if she was the former Betty McCuddy and whether her husband was the former Tom Buntin. She said, "of course, you're right," and closed the door. After a moment, Betty called Tom at work saying that there was "someone here who knows someone we used to know in Nashville." The Lack's store was only a few blocks from the courthouse, so Tom arrived shortly and the three walked to a coffeehouse. Seigenthaler was beside himself because he could not find photographer Holt. Tom said that he would go to Nashville to interview with the newspaper there if his wife and children were kept out of the story. Perhaps sensing that this was an unrealistic expectation by someone who had no real leverage in the situation, he then asked Seigenthaler to take them home.

Holt was still missing in action. All three sat in the front seat, with Seigenthaler driving, Betty in the middle, and Tom on the passenger side. Tom said he did not want to ask any questions about Nashville, but Betty filled the silence by asking so many questions about her Russellville family that Seigenthaler later concluded she had been interviewing him. She wanted to know, for example, if her father and brother were alive, but did not ask about her mother. Tom interjected gently that if she asked more questions, they would have to be let out, but she continued talking. He did not become angry or try to stop her and Seigenthaler thought they were kind to each other and acted in a deeply affectionate way.

The reporter's obvious question was why the two left their lives, families, friends, and money in 1931. Seigenthaler thought to himself that Betty had been pregnant, but never asked or reported on his speculation. The timing of Betty Ann's birth does not support this notion. There was a simple response. As Betty explained, "We were in love. Money didn't mean much to us. If money had meant anything we wouldn't have done what we did." She lamented having to tell their six children "we are two people when all this time they think we have been two other people. If we had wanted to be those people, we would never have changed in the first place. It's bad to have to tell them one thing for so many years and then to change it suddenly. It was just that we were in love, and we wanted to change our lives."

The tense journey ended at 1001 Orange Avenue in the late afternoon, where the driver informed his passengers that their story would be in the paper the following morning. Tom declared, "We won't come out." Following his newspaper's policy, Seigenthaler offered them a form to sign that sold the newspaper their story's exclusive rights for $1,000 plus twenty-five

BUNTIN AND BETTY McCUDDY, 6 CHILDREN FOUND IN TEXAS

Traffic Officer Wounds Wife In Home Scuffle

Leonard Miller Faces Charges, Suspended; Milliron Probes Cause

'Love' Given As Reason Couple Left

Admit Identity, Tell Tennessean Reporter 'Money Didn't Mean Much'—Both Now Holding Jobs

By JOHN SEIGENTHALER, Staff Correspondent

ORANGE, Texas—Thomas C. Buntin and Betty McCuddy are living as man and wife in a white frame house in this small citrus center in southeast Texas.

They live under the names of Thomas D. and Betty Palmer at 1001 Orange st.

They are the parents of six children, four girls, the oldest two of whom are married, and two boys. One of their daughters presented them with a grandchild in October, and another daughter is expecting childbirth at any moment.

Buntin, a wealthy Nashville insurance executive, disappeared from Nashville 22 years ago, leaving his wife and three children. Two months after Buntin's disap-

Staff photo by Jimmy Holt.   Copyright 1953 by Tennessean Newspapers, Inc.
ORANGE, Texas—In this rambling house at 1001 Orange st., live the 'Thomas D. Palmers' and their children.

(The Tennessean – USA TODAY NETWORK.)

percent of profits if the article was syndicated by one of the wire services, such as AP. They refused. Resigned to publication of their identities, they were concerned for their children and how they would explain that evening that their parents were not the people they had believed them to be. No matter how they described their history and choices, the news would be shocking and might be physically harmful to pregnant Betty Ann. That difficult conversation with Betty Ann, Margaret, Duncan, and Mary Ellen lasted late into the night.

On Thanksgiving morning, November 26, 1953, Nashville woke to the blaring headline across the top of the front page: **"BUNTIN AND BETTY McCUDDY, 6 CHILDREN FOUND IN TEXAS,"** by John Seigenthaler, Staff Correspondent. A secondary headline read "'Love' Given as Reason Couple Left." The stories were accompanied by above-the-fold photos of Betty striding to work and Tom leaving the Beaumont bus station. Silliman Evans had called the AP to tip off the service about a "blockbuster" story that would be in the morning edition. He then called the president of New York Life to inform him of the news coverage. Paul Johns, the insurance company's investigation agent in Atlanta was "scared out of his wits," afraid that the Home Office would think he was a source for the details behind the story. In fact, he *had* called Seigenthaler at his parents' home a few days earlier and Mrs. Seigenthaler told Johns that her son was in Texas on an assignment, so he knew the reporter was on the correct trail.

Texas Highway Patrolman C.C. Bearden arrived at the Palmer house that holiday morning, bringing in *The Orange Leader*, which had been left on the sidewalk. Shrubs shielded most of the numerous windows on all sides of the house, but the shades were also drawn. A metal-barred storm door protected a wood door with a small peephole. Tom, still in his night robe, opened both doors after seeing the lawman on the small stoop. Texas Governor Allan Shivers sent Bearden for "official confirmation" of the couple's identity at the request of Tennessee Governor Frank Clement because the Buntin name was prominent in Nashville. The patrolman was unclear why further confirmation was needed, however, and felt that the contact was intrusive.

The paper that was unfurled in the living room screamed a banner headline for all of Orange to see: "'Legally Dead' Pair, Missing for 22 Years, Located in Orange." Betty murmured out loud, "What will this do to us in Orange?" Farther down the front page, it was comforting to see the related headline that the "City's Heart Goes Out to Palmer Family."

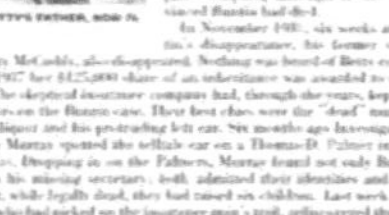

Former Playboy and Secretary Who Disappeared
22 Years Ago Are Found Living in Texas Town
Buntin Used To Work
In Valley Bean Fields
McCuddy-Buntin Tale Of Wide Interest
THEY LIVED 22 YEARS IN SECRECY
BETTY McCUDDY
... as she looked in 1931
BETTY BUNTIN
... found 22 years later
TOM BUNTIN
... man she ran away with
THOMAS BUNTIN
... as he looks now
CAME BACK FROM 'DEAD'
TO CLAIM A FORTUNE
$50,000 Life Insurance Plot Uncovered After 22 Years
PRESUMED DEAD, Thomas C. Buntin and his secretary, Betty McCuddy,
looked this way in old photographs which were kept under lock in State of Tennessee.
'DEAD' FOR 22 YEARS
Tennesseans are found deep in heart of Texas
BETTY'S FATHER, NOW 76
RESURRECTED COUPLE
MODEST HOME

The article extended "sympathetic hearts" from "Orangeites" to the family and commended Tom and Betty's commitment to their jobs and successful parenting of six children. As early as the parents could with the time differences, they called David, age eighteen, who was a Marine serving at the Fort Bliss Army post in El Paso. When the press contacted him to ask what he thought about the fact that his parents were not the people he knew them to be, he replied that learning about his father and mother's past "boosted" his admiration for them "more than ever." The newspapers in Washington State reached Jane, age twenty, who refused to comment.

Thanksgiving lunch in the Palmer house became a belated dinner, reported as "silent and miserable." *The Beaumont Enterprise*, open on the table, featured black-and-white photos of a young Tom looking headlong into the camera without smiling and a young, sweet-faced Betty with a fashionable chin-level bob haircut and a lock of hair pulled down in the middle of her forehead. The youngest Palmer, Mary Ellen, looked at the photo of her mother from over two decades earlier, and said, "I've never seen that picture of mother before," drawing smiles from the people in the room. One of the children asked if they would have to change their last name to "Buntin," to which Betty replied, "no." The Christmas parade, featuring Santa Claus and the real reindeer from Alaska, was eclipsed, and forgotten.

Through the AP, Seigenthaler's sensational story of the beleaguered Palmer's lives appeared in multiple newspapers in every state in the nation, all forty-eight at that time. In Montana, for example, readers of *The Missoulian* learned of the "socialite" Nashvillian who had been found with his secretary in a small Texas Gulf Coast town, while Bangor, Maine, residents opened their papers to read about a "couple declared dead" but found "married" in Texas. UP distributed the news worldwide. Readers of *The Age* in Melbourne, Australia, saw the news of American "runaways," a "playboy" and his "pretty secretary," while *The Sun-Herald* in Sydney headlined the curiosity of a "legally dead but living" couple. Spanish-language newspaper readers marveled at the story of *la secretaria* who had absconded with *el jefe* for so many years. "Secrecy" themed many headlines and stories. In Vancouver, British Columbia, *The Province* was amazed that the couple had "lived 22 years in secrecy," while *The Evening Review* in East Liverpool, Ohio, focused on how the Palmer's "love idyll," an "old secret," was shattered.

Sometimes the facts were inexactly reported. *The Los Angeles Times* wrote that the two had "eloped" to Texas, while readers in Tasmania, Australia, were told that the case only involved a "woman back from 'the dead'." *The*

News from New York City; Melbourne, Australia; Manchester, England; Wilmington, Del.; Nashville.

Straits Times in Singapore connected the discovery to Tom's insurance but in the wrong way, reporting that his first wife had taken out the policies on him and he would now claim the money as a "dead" man. The article also lost the storyline in translation, noting that, with Betty's inheritance money from her "grand uncle" "in the kitty," the Palmers would "be able to come back to life, reimburse the insurance company, reward [her] nephew and everyone will be happy."

Newspapers far afield from southeast Texas clamored for updated images of Betty and Tom, who refused. Some of the coverage then shifted focus to the children. High school yearbook photos of the four oldest Palmer children ran on the front page of Nashville's primary paper. Other articles led by exploiting the children's forced and painful reckoning with their parents' double lives. Tom and Betty had enough and called a stop, especially when they learned that the National Broadcasting Company was sending a Houston cameraman for a telecast planned to air on either "The Camel News Caravan," anchored by John Cameron Swayze, or the Dave Garraway show over Thanksgiving weekend, reaching all locales in southeast Texas. Tom declared that the press "had had their inning" and that he would talk about the "weather, football, duck hunting or anything else—except our life. That is the attitude my wife and I will maintain." They would not cooperate further.

Seigenthaler tried to get them to sit down together for a follow-up story, which Tom refused in a "no" said "pleasantly." The reporter was not offended and thought Tom's response "was the talk of a gentleman and salesman, one who likes people and does not want to give offense." It also gave him insights into why Thomas D. Palmer was popular in Orange and Brownsville. The couple also refused to answer his questions regarding whether they were married. New York Life's secret-suit petition claimed that they were but did not detail how or when. Legal advisors quoted in newspapers opined that they were likely to be considered as married under common law.

Notwithstanding the Palmer's understandable rejection of further interviews, the story was irresistible. The couple who plunged from fortune into poverty for love in the depths of the Great Depression brought more high-visibility coverage, for themselves and for Orange. *Life* magazine's December 7, 1953, issue featured the article, "'Dead' for 22 Years," with photos of Betty and Tom at the time they disappeared and recently, as well as their Texas house and Betty's dad, Fergus. *Time*'s coverage of the same date was salacious. Young Betty was described as a "dark, quiet girl," while young Tom was a "tall, fragile, handsome young man" who had "moods of burning exhilaration" followed by "moods of suicidal depression." By the time he disappeared at the age of twenty-eight, he "seemed to be fizzing toward self-destruction like a lighted skyrocket." In other news coverage, Tom was labeled a "playboy" and Betty an "heiress." The only accurate label was that Betty was an heiress, formerly.

Why did the runaway pair captivate a global audience? Their story had all the essentials for prurient relish: fortunes, romance, intrigue, sex (though not overtly discussed at the time), and disgrace—only lacking murder. The human-interest aspect of their saga's scales also tipped in favor of broad public appeal because they were high-society, wealthy elites who transformed their lives through sacrifice and secrets, a novel approach to self-determination. When the story broke, people had one of two reactions, either "for" or "against" what the couple had done. Many readers, regardless of culture or place of origin, empathetically appreciated that Miss McCuddy and Mr. Buntin made a conscious decision to join in life. Their plight led to struggles involving money, kids, and work—all experienced by regular people, but hardships the two would have never known in their former world. Supporters found inspiration in the pair's "true love" and Tom's jettisoning of a "life of pampering, security, and position to face the world on his own two feet" and show the world that he was "capable and upright." The "against" side saw the decline of civilization in their willful actions, succinctly reflected by "Mrs. J.," a Nashville resident. Cloaked in anonymity, she excoriated Tom and Betty and their supporters for "washing all principles of a great nation right down the drain."

But what about Orange itself? Did Orange turn its back on the couple and their children or did its people continue to befriend them? Neighbors and friends rallied around the family, at least initially. Their home land-line phone number was public information and supportive calls quickly overwhelmed them, so the telephone's handset was taken off the hook. Daughter Margaret's Sunday school class sent her flowers. When she called her teacher to thank the group, the sixteen-year-old teenager cried, "What will people think?" Her teacher advised her to "put on powder and lipstick and be in church as usual." J. Cullen Browning, editor of *The Orange Leader*, said that he knew Betty and Tom well and that they were "highly respected citizens" who had reared six "outstanding" children. He claimed to have called "many" of the town's residents and found no one who criticized the family.

Orange Mayor Sid Caillavet vouched for Betty, whom he said he knew better than Tom. Betty's boss, Judge Hightower, praised her as a "woman of fine integrity" and a "very efficient reporter" and welcomed her to return to work the following Monday. George E. Duncan, Beaumont lawyer and Betty's cousin, was astonished to learn of the court reporter's real identity and that he had encountered her without recognition. Patrick Doom, owner of the Lack's store in Beaumont, thought Tom was a "wonderful person of high character" and impressive "ability and honesty."

One resident shrugged off the situation, giving a historical perspective that "Texas is made up of people who ran away to Texas and changed their names. There is an old saying, 'What was your name before you came to Texas?'" The Lone Star State, after all, was an early attraction for Tennesseans of "broken-down fortunes." Still, the small city of Orange was church-filled and the topic was sensitive enough that the Dancy's names were kept out of the media coverage. Today, there are people who call them both bigamists and recoil that Orange made its name in *Life* and *Time* because of their double lives.

And then there were the families that Betty and Tom left over two decades earlier. *The Tennessean* tried to reach Bettie Moore Buntin Phillips on Thanksgiving Eve, to no avail. Silliman Evans called his friend Rogers Caldwell to ask him to discuss with the Buntin family what they wanted to do. The publisher sensed from the conversation that some of the family supported Tom. Rogers, in poor health, could not travel to Texas, so the family sent Rachel Adelia Craighead Buntin Wilmot. Rachel was Tom's first cousin and the daughter of his Uncle Charley (his early real-estate boss) and Aunt Jane Buntin. Tall and attractive like her relative Rachel Adelia Carter Craighead, Rachel was invited in 1937 to perform a screen test for the role of Scarlett O'Hara in *Gone with the Wind*. The antebellum Rachel would have coveted playing this starring lead character. While in Orange, Mrs. Wilmot wore black and kept her face shielded by a veil on her hat. She stayed briefly and, when she left, Betty and Tom took her to the airport in Beaumont. The three chatted before she boarded but there were no embraces, just an affectionate pat between Rachel and Tom.

In Russellville, Fergus fretted over whether to call his daughter or wait for her to try to reach him. His second wife, Nan, assured him that his daughter would get in touch. He wondered if her voice would sound strange to him. He and Nan both worried about not causing Betty, Tom, and their Texas family any harm or problem if they connected. Betty put an end to the wondering when she contacted her seventy-six-year-old father, "Mr. Mac" as he was now known. She spent several days with him December 11th weekend after the news story broke. In a flurry of visits, they went to the bank where he still worked, followed by a drive to Flint Ridge to

(News-Democrat and Leader, Russellville, Ky.)

see her Uncle Ross McCuddy, and then made a call on her mother's close friend Mrs. Hal Meyers. Mrs. Meyers declared Betty "as sweet and pretty as ever."

Awkwardly, the local paper identified her as "Mrs. Betty McCuddy Buntin-Palmer," but otherwise was upbeat about Betty's reappearance and her joy in seeing Russellville "still beautiful." Stepmother Nan spoke to the press on her husband's behalf, denying reports that Betty would travel to Nashville, but Betty did visit there with her cousin, lawyer J. Connelly Edwards. She then spoke with reporters briefly, declaring that her father was "wonderful, really wonderful." She also "expressed a hope" that her children would visit Russellville to see her hometown and "get acquainted" with their grandfather. She did not see her nephew, Robin, during the trip because he was in his first semester of college at Duke University.

As soon as she read the Thanksgiving-day story, Elsie Buntin had an operator place a long-distance call to "TUxedo 8-3616" in Texas, the phone number given to her to reach Thomas David Palmer. She asked him first if he was her son who disappeared from Nashville in September 1931, to which he replied, "yes." The rest of the call was described as "happy," but "somewhat formal." Elsie told her son that she planned to visit him in Texas. Whether it was Elsie's age (seventy-seven) or the awkwardness of a visit with Betty McCuddy Palmer and Elsie's newly found grandchildren, she did not travel to the citrus city. Tom went to her four months later, in early April 1954. After reserving a room at the Noel Hotel under the name "Tom Buntin," he ended up staying at Elsie's house at 1607 Eighteenth Ave., South, near Vanderbilt University. She had sold the Kensington Place "castle" home and downsized to the Eighteenth Avenue property about the time the Palmers decided to move from the Lower Rio Grande Valley to southeast Texas.

Mother and son visited inside for hours upon his arrival and then left together in her chauffeur-driven car, returning well after dark. Reporters were still waiting outside the house, but neither would comment on reuniting or where they had been. The media captured only photographs: Tom escorting his mother up the front stairs of the house and a side profile in which each had turned toward the cameras—possibly startled by the flash—Elsie wearing dark-tinted glasses even though it was night and a prematurely aged Tom looking surprised.

(The Tennessean –
USA TODAY NETWORK.)

Introducing himself as "Tom Buntin," Tom Palmer visited old friends in town. One of the first on his list was Charles ("Chick") Davitt Jr., who now ran the upscale Davitt's men's clothing store. The shopkeeper was surprised when a man opened the door and asked, "Do you recognize this man?" He instantly knew it was Tom Buntin, who had "just grown older—that's all." They talked of "old times," but Davitt would not reveal further information to reporters about the conversation. Failing to pry information out of Tom, his mother, or any other visited person, the newspapers speculated as to whether the legally dead man discussed his legacy in the trust that Rachel Carter Craighead had established for the Buntins, of which Elsie and May were the current beneficiaries. Unnamed attorneys advised in one news article that Tom might have to sue the Craighead estate's trustee, Nashville Trust Company, formerly headed by Bettie Buntin Phillips' husband, if he sought a share in the valuable commercial properties held in the trust.

The Tennessean received many letters from all over the country regarding its exposure of the Palmers, many directed to the reporter. Some writers complimented Seigenthaler on his investigative journalism. One was Bill Gilliland. The high-profile bookshop owner in Dallas was certain that his uncle, Ralph Gilliland (the U.S. Marshal in San Antonio who was on the reporter's initial contact list), and Bill Kittrell were pleased with the story. His letter closed by advising Seigenthaler that he could now "settle down and get married after the honeymoon or before." Many of the people who wrote were livid. Mrs. Mae Scott Ingalls of Pasadena, California, eighty years of age, asked Seigenthaler if he was proud to have brought "misery into the lives of 10 or more persons" especially with Christmas approaching. Mrs. M.H.

Alberts of Los Angeles outright called him a "rat," "the lowest stinker," a "snooper," and a "slanderer" and was sure that there was a "special Hell" reserved for him. An anonymous male writer from Spartanburg, South Carolina, wished a "curse" upon Seigenthaler, whom he called a "thoroughly cheap and contemptible thing."

Part Four

AFTER

Chapter 15

FORTUNES, REVISITED

When the Buntin/McCuddy/Palmer story was published, *The Orange Leader*'s newsman Ralph Ramos predicted that the couple would quickly "resume their normal way of life" and "headline readers" would forget them. The couple hoped so as well, vowing that they would change nothing about their lives. Howard Van Arsdell, Tom's former co-worker at the Nashville insurance company, now lived in Fort Worth. He begged for people to "let sleeping dogs lie" and leave the couple in peace. Ramos's prediction, the Palmer's wishes, and Van Arsdell's unfortunate proverbial plea turned out not to be the case, at least in the short term. Tragedy immediately followed the exposure, causing the "flood of interest" in the Palmers to become a "tidal wave of sympathy overnight," reaching coast to coast.

Betty Ann went into labor the evening after *The Tennessean*'s blockbuster story appeared. She delivered a stillborn daughter, who was named Barbara Ann. People speculated that the shock of learning her parents' real identities caused her to lose the baby, which also cast blame on reporter Seigenthaler. The city hospital's attending physician was disinclined to support this theory, however. The young woman hemorrhaged before the birth. This "very rare" event, according to the doctor, separated the baby from the placenta. Baby Barbara Ann was buried the next afternoon in Orange's Evergreen Cemetery following a service at the Cove Baptist Church. The Red Cross cabled the news to her father overseas and he returned, though not in time to attend his firstborn's burial.

The notoriety also lasted beyond Ramos's forecast because there was the matter of money: Tom Buntin's life insurance proceeds and the inheritance that Betty McCuddy had foregone. On November 5, 1953, New York Life had filed the not-so-secret lawsuit (the "Buntin Case 2") to recover its money and immediately secured an injunction against the bank and Tom's first family. The insurance company asserted a legal point that had not been first raised in the Buntin Case 1 until New York Life's final (and losing) appeal to the state supreme court. The company now claimed that the Buntin Case 1 judgment was "fraudulently obtained" through Tom's manufactured evidence—his 1931 will—to mislead New York Life, the judge, and the jury.

This type of fraud was called "extrinsic fraud." The crime is one of the few ways that a previous judgment could be overturned because judges do not like to revisit old cases. Chancellor Wade rejected the argument in the Buntin Case 2, however. Following the sensational newspaper exposé of the Palmer's identities, New York Life appealed Wade's decision to the Tennessee Supreme Court. The pleading is ironic in tone, a bit sarcastic, and laden with explanations of the unfairness of its legal situation. The company noted that the legally dead Thomas Craighead Buntin could sit in the courtroom audience of the Buntin Case 2 to listen to the parties' arguments about the fate of his life insurance proceeds decided in the Buntin Case 1, which judgment concluded that he had likely committed suicide. The plaintiff also asserted that because Buntin was an insurance man, he was knowledgeable about insurance matters and should not be entitled to benefit his first family by fooling the insurance company or the Tennessee courts. Broadway National Bank countered that, even if fraudulent action had taken place, it was merely "intrinsic fraud," a minor procedural defect that did not justify the extraordinary step of setting aside a previous case's outcome.

On April 27, 1956, the Tennessee Supreme Court issued its decision on the appeal. Chancellor Wade's judgment in favor of Broadway National Bank was reversed, but the five-member court was splintered in its conclusion, three to two. Judicial decisions tend to be mind-numbingly bland and devoid of emotion. Italics, used to emphasize tone, are sparingly used. The published opinion in the Buntin Case 2 must rate near the top of the state's highest court's use of italics, most certainly reflecting the majority's outrage and indignity. In numerous italicized references to Buntin's extrinsic fraud, the court emphasized that he committed a *gross fraud upon the Court*" and New York Life and this "*after-discovered fraud*" caused "*Our*

Courts, this very Court" to be *"imposed upon and fooled and defrauded."* Chief Justice Burnett also smacked down Wade for ruling that the insurance company's policy (a contract) should have been written to prohibit a policy holder from committing fraud. According to the justice, it was not New York Life's responsibility to protect itself from fraud in its contract. It was the courts' duty to decide the question of fraud and to *"protect the rights of those that are defrauded."*

Chief Justice A.B. Neil joined in the majority opinion, agreeing that Buntin had perpetrated a deceit that would not be judicially forgiven. Neil had a unique vantagepoint since he was the very same judge who presided over the Buntin Case 1 over fifteen years earlier, at which time he expressed incredulity that Buntin could still be alive. Now on the state's supreme court, he described the case as involving "the great forum of conscience" and seemed to relish returning the insurance company's money, observing that "equity delights in doing justice."

In the spring of 1957, George B. Edwards' estate and 1941 judgment in the McCuddy Case 1 were once again under judicial scrutiny. The "McCuddy Case 2" ensued after Betty Palmer was found with six living children. When she visited her dad and stepmother shortly after the newspaper stories of her and Tom's discovery, speculation began regarding what would happen to her share of the "sizeable estate" that was awarded to nephew Robin years earlier. Louisville's Citizens Fidelity Bank and Trust ("Citizens Fidelity") had succeeded Fidelity Trust and now oversaw the Edwards' estate. A vice president of the bank and trust was contacted by a Louisville reporter at home during his Thanksgiving dinner and grilled over turkey and cranberry sauce. The reporter demanded to know how Betty Palmer's discovery impacted Betty McCuddy's inheritance. A representative of the bank and trust company contacted Betty shortly after to discuss "any interest she might have under the Edwards' will trust." She responded by claiming her remaining inheritance in the various trusts left in her great-uncle's will.

Instead of going to court immediately, Betty spent about three-and-a-half years negotiating an arrangement to resolve the now-disputed inheritance. Betty, nephew Robin (now an adult at age twenty-one), and Citizens Fidelity met in Louisville several times to try to work out some of the "doubts and uncertainties which have arisen due to the circumstance that the said Betty Edwards McCuddy (now Betty Palmer) is living." After meeting in early May 1957, they reached consensus and signed a Compromise Agreement dated August 22, 1957. The document noted that the "most pleasant family relationships exist" between aunt and nephew and that they wanted to avoid harm to the relationship, as well as the "trouble, annoyance, and expense" if she sued to recover her inheritance. Robin agreed to pay Betty $35,000 in cash from his inheritance funds, which is almost $400,000 in current dollars. She agreed to relinquish all claims against him and Citizens Fidelity and the two relatives agreed for Robin to pay two-thirds of the legal fees and Betty to pay one-third.

On August 23, 1957, the Palmer children (including unrepresented minors Duncan and Mary Ellen) each endorsed the seven-page Compromise Agreement. The agreement included a clause that the document would not be binding unless it was made part of a judgment. A week later, Citizens Fidelity formally filed the McCuddy Case 2 in Logan County Circuit Court in Russellville seeking Judge Thomas Noe's "advice" about the Compromise Agreement. A few days after the petition was filed, Betty, her six children, and Fergus submitted an Entry of Appearance. Each signatory acknowledged they had read the petition and exhibits, agreed to join with the bank and trust company to resolve the case, and waived notice of all further proceedings in the case. Citizens Fidelity received the judge's approval of the document in a final judgment issued in late November 1957, which protected the company as trustee during the remaining years of its responsibility. George B. Edwards' estate was finally resolved twenty-eight years after his death and four years after his great-niece's real identity was revealed.

Chapter 16

Evergreen Cemetery

Evergreen Cemetery was established around 1840 to bury settler families of Green's Bluff in southeast Texas. It eventually became a highly visible location, after the Orange County Courthouse was built across the street and the city of Orange expanded on adjacent, filled swampland. Today, the graveyard's location is unremarkable. The population has dwindled, downtown historic Orange has been intentionally demolished, and successive hurricanes have swept over the land, resulting in further disinvestment. After a rain, shallow groundwater squishes through visitors' shoes as they walk along the headstones. Starting from the front, on Border Street, and heading toward the back, visitors pass ornate granite mausoleums embodying the past wealth of Orange. The monumental crypts include those of the longleaf pine baron families—the Lutchers, Starks, and Browns. If Tom Buntin had followed the path of his birth entitlement, he would have been interred in a similarly elaborate manner with the Daniel Franklin Carter family in Nashville's historic Mount Olivet Cemetery. The Carter's burial setting includes an Italian-marble structure and plot so large that the mausoleum site has its own section in the tony cemetery.

As visitors amble toward the rear of Orange's graveyard, they head toward the municipal wastewater treatment plant. A scent of sewage often wafts through this burial section. Near the last few rows, five flat markers lay next to each other. There is no indication that others visit these burial sites and there are no mementos. To fully read the inscriptions, visitors might have to kick off a crawfish mound or find a long stick and, more cautiously, scrape away a mound of stinging fire ants. The markers read, left to right: "Thomas David Palmer, 1902–1966" (his exact date of birth is not noted, just the year, and, in symmetry, only the year of death is inscribed); "Betty McCuddy Palmer, June 27, 1907–Nov. 26, 1972"; "Jane Palmer Lindsey, Jan. 23, 1934–Feb. 12, 1999"; and "William Duncan Palmer, Sept. 3, 1938–Jan. 15, 1998." The most recent marker is from 2013 when Bill Lindsey, Jane Palmer's second husband, was buried next to her. Barbara Ann Burton, the baby that Betty Ann lost in childbirth in 1953, is also buried in the cemetery, most likely in the children's section though a visible marker is not apparent.

(Photos by author.)

No one who knew Betty McCuddy as a young adult in Kentucky or Tennessee questioned whether she could make it on her own in the world—she could. Texans who knew her, but not her background, considered her intelligent, a hard worker, and a mother who "carried the burden" of the family. Tom Buntin was viewed as a fragile man in his young adulthood in his birthplace. His Nashville friends thought him incapable of self-sufficiency or able to support a family on his own. Nashville Trust said he had "neither the physical, mental nor moral stamina to meet the vicissitudes of life." New York Life was harsher, calling him a "dissatisfied, maladjusted, and depraved character," a "libertine and a degenerate." The characterizations could not have been more wrong about Tom. To get his start in Brownsville, he picked beans in the searing sun of the Lower Rio Grande Valley fields all day for seventy-five cents. Texas friends and employers considered him smart, a "hustler" of sales, and a dedicated family man. He endured difficult circumstances, maintained a loving relationship with Betty, and helped raise six children successfully.

The couple stayed in Orange for seven years after their secret was splashed across the globe. The only other news they made during the remainder of their short lives were their obituaries. During their last years in the "citrus city," Tom switched jobs, leaving television and appliance sales for the Lee and Company real estate firm in Beaumont. Betty continued her work in Beaumont as a court reporter. Margaret, Duncan, and Mary Ellen lived with them in Orange while finishing school. After Duncan graduated from Stark High School, Betty and Tom moved to a ranch house in suburban Beaumont in 1959. The Palmer children connected with their mother's family in Kentucky, but not with their father's family in Tennessee and there seems to have been no reciprocal interest expressed by the Buntins in Nashville at that time.

Tom's last workplace move was to another real estate firm in Beaumont. Following a cancer diagnosis, he retired. Betty's first cousin, Beaumont lawyer George Edwards Duncan, prepared his will in February 1964. The document is titled the "Last Will and Testament of Thomas Craighead Buntin" and he signed the same name in shaky handwriting. His birthdate in the first paragraph was left blank. Bettie Moore Buntin is identified as his first wife and Betty Edwards McCuddy Palmer as the woman to whom he is "presently married to and residing with." All nine of his children were also identified. Betty was named as his independent executrix and he left his property to her, providing that, if she died before or contemporaneously with him, the six Palmer children would inherit in equal shares. He "made no provision" for his three Buntin sons stating that "each of them has been amply provided for by their mother and grandmother, and I am confident that each is well launched on his own career and enjoys an earning capacity in keeping with his station in life."

At age sixty-four, Tom died at the Hotel Dieu Hospital in Beaumont during the afternoon of Monday, October 3, 1966. Private services were held at the Westminster Presbyterian Church in Beaumont the following day. His death certificate lists coronary heart disease as the immediate cause of his death, with pulmonary insufficiency due to emphysema as an underlying condition. A simple obituary was published in the local newspapers, requesting that contributions be made to the American Cancer Society in lieu of flowers. Survivors identified in the announcement were Betty, Elsie (who died in 1971 at age ninety-three), the Palmer children, his sister May Winston Buntin Murray, and nineteen unnamed grandchildren. Unmentioned were other survivors: Bettie Buntin Phillips (who died in 1978 at age seventy-five), son Daniel (who died in 2001 at age seventy-eight), son

Thomas (who died in 2000 at age seventy-five), and son Rogers (who died in 2012 at age eighty-five). Tom's death also dredged up the scandal, resulting in news articles across the country, often titled colorfully. Coverage focused upon the funeral held for a man already "declared legally dead," who had also been a one-time "socialite" and "playboy." *The New York Times* ran his obituary as the "missing man" who had two identities.

After suffering a heart attack on Thanksgiving Eve 1972—the nineteenth anniversary of discovery—Betty died three days later, on November 26th, at her daughter Betty Ann's home in Orange. She was sixty-five and identified in her death certificate as "Betty Edwards Palmer." Her death passed quietly in the newspapers, with no coverage beyond southeast Texas. All six of her children survived her at that time. Fergus, her dad, had died in 1963 at age eighty-five. Today, there are no surviving Palmer children, though there are generations of Palmer descendants.

John Seigenthaler's career was launched by the Palmer story, described as "one of the most unusual 'beats' in newspaper history." He won a National Headliner Award for his coverage of the couple, a prestigious recognition of "journalistic merit." In 1962, he was named editor of *The Tennessean*. Tom Palmer sent him a congratulatory telegram, noting that he took "personal pride" in Seigenthaler's promotion. The telegraphed signature was "Tom Buntin." Seigenthaler enjoyed a career at the newspaper, then served as an aide to U.S. Attorney General Robert F. Kennedy. He later became editorial director of *USA Today* upon its founding and was a creator and director of the First Amendment Center at Vanderbilt University. John Seigenthaler died in Nashville in July 2014.

In the post-World War II period, the 2500 block of Kensington Place rapidly turned over to house Greek fraternities associated with Vanderbilt University. After thirty-two years as a Buntin residence, Elsie sold the Kensington Place castle mansion around 1947 to Sigma Alpha Epsilon ("SAE"), Louie Phillips' fraternity. Vanderbilt University bought the property in 1977 but allowed its continued use by SAE, whose members have been known to vandalize the historic house during football season. Today, the property is valued at $4.4 million.

The Palmer's house at 1001 Orange Avenue in the "citrus city" was in decline by the 2000s. "Miss Ruby," a wizened and locally popular Cajun woman, rented it for years. A real estate firm bought the vacant house in 2017 but made no repairs or improvements. In 2019, the company secured approval from the Orange Historical Commission to demolish it. The lot is vacant today.

(Photo by author.)

(Photo by John Backer.)

NOTES

Abbreviations used in the notes:

Names

ACCA	Aeronautical Chamber of Commerce of America, Inc.	GED	George E. Duncan
		GG	George Gale
		GMT	G.M. Trammell
AEE	Arthur E. Edwards	HF	Harold Fuqua
BEM	Betty Edwards McCuddy	HSK	Hester Sinclair Kirkman
BF	Bill Finney	HVA	Howard Van Arsdell
BGM	Bettie Gould Moore	ID	Isaiah DeShazer
BK	William "Bill" Kittrell	JB	John Burch
BMB	Bettie Moore Buntin	JCB	Jennie Craighead Buntin
BMBP	Bettie Moore Buntin Phillips	JCE	James (J.) Connelly Edwards
BMP	Betty McClinton Palmer	JD	John Dougherty
BNB	Broadway National Bank	JEC	James E. Caldwell
BP	Betty Poage	JECr	Jennie Erwin Craighead
CEA	Charles E. Anstett	JH	Jimmy Holt
CFBT	Citizens Fidelity Bank and Trust	JHE	Joseph H. Erwin
		JHM	J. Harb Milliken
CN	Charles Nelson	JJM	John J. McClellan
CptWAB	Captain William Allison Buntin	JOB	Jake O'Brian
		JP	Jane Palmer
CTT	Cumberland Telegraph and Telephone	JPH	Jane Palmer Herring
		JRB	J. Robert Bogan
DCB	Daniel Carter Buntin	JS	John Seigenthaler
DFC	Daniel Franklin Carter	JTS	John Thomas Shugart
DPP	David Preston Palmer	JWM	Rev. John Wright Moore
EAP	Elizabeth Ann Palmer	LBH	Laurence B. Howard
ECB	Elsie Caldwell Buntin	LLD	L.L. Daugherty
ELS	Elizabeth Louise Sinclair	LMP	Louis ("Louie") M. Phillips
ERT	E.R. Tallmadge		
ESB	Elizabeth Sinclair Buntin	MBM	May Winston Buntin Murray
FCTC	Fidelity and Columbia Trust Company		
		MCM	Margaret Connelly McCuddy
GBE	George B. Edwards		

MDM	Mary Duncan McCuddy
MED	Mary Edwards Duncan
MEP	Mary Ellen Palmer
MRP	Margaret Ross Palmer
MWB	May Winston Buntin
NTC	Nashville Trust Company
NYL	New York Life Insurance Company
OCD	Oscar C. Dancy
PAJ	Paul A. Johns
RAC	Rachel Adelia Carter Craighead
RCC	Rogers Clark Caldwell
RCCB	Rogers Clark Caldwell Buntin
RFM	Robert Ferguson McCuddy
RWB	Robert W. Benson
RWW	Robert W. Washington
SE	Silliman Evans
SS	Sidney Souers
TBLC	Tallmadge-Buntin Land Company
TBT	T. Bush Taylor
TCB	Thomas Craighead Buntin
TDC	Thomas David Craighead
TDP	Thomas David Palmer
TH	Tinsley Harrison
UW	University of Wyoming
VU	Vanderbilt University
WAB	William Allison Buntin
WDP	William Duncan Palmer
WGB	Walter G. Bowerman
WRM	William Ross McCuddy
ZBL	Zelma Brown Lipscomb

Newspapers

AE	*The Adairville Enterprise*, Adairville, Ky.
Age	*The Age*, Melbourne, Australia
AN	*The Auburn News*, Auburndale, Ky.
BA	*The Breckinridge American*, Breckinridge, Tex.
BDN	*The Bangor Daily News*, Bangor, Maine
BE	*The Beaumont Enterprise*, Beaumont, Tex.
BH	*The Brownsville Herald*, Brownsville, Tex.
BJ	*The Beaumont Journal*, Beaumont, Tex.
BVE	*Bridger Valley Enterprise*, Lyman, Wyo.
CDC	*The Charleston Daily Courier*, Charleston, S. Car.
CDL	*The Cheyenne Daily Leader*, Cheyenne, Wyo.
CE	*Chicago Examiner*, Chicago, Ill.
CJ	*The Courier-Journal*, Louisville, Ky.
CLC	*Clarksville Leaf-Chronicle*, Clarksville, Tenn.
CN	*The Chattanooga News*, Chattanooga, Tenn.
CP	*The Centennial Post*, Centennial, Wyo.
CST	*The Casper Star-Tribune*, Casper, Wyo.
CT	*Chicago Tribune*, Chicago, Ill. (also *Chicago Daily Tribune*)
Dem.	*The Democrat*, Russellville, Ky.
DM	*The Daily Mail*, Hagerstown, Md.
DW	*Daily World*, Opelousas, La.
ER	*The Evening Review*, East Liverpool, Oh.
FR	*The Frankfort Roundabout*, Frankfort, Ky.
FWST	*Fort Worth Star-Telegram*, Fort Worth, Tex.
HL	*The Herald-Ledger*, Russellville, Ky.
HP	*The Houston Post*, Houston, Tex.
HSB	*Honolulu Star-Bulletin*, Honolulu, Hi.
HTH	*Hawaii Tribune-Herald*, Hilo, Hi.

KN	*Kingsport News*, Kingsport, Tenn.
KR	*The Kemmerer Republican*, Kemmerer, Wyo.
KT	*The Kingsport Times*, Kingsport, Tenn.
LAT	*Los Angeles Times*, LA, Ca.
LB	*The Laramie Boomerang*, Laramie, Wyo. (and *The Laramie Daily Boomerang*)
LMA	*Lubbock Morning Avalanche*, Lubbock, Tex.
LR	*The Laramie Republican*, Laramie, Wyo.
Mercury	*The Mercury*, Hobart, Tasmania
Miss.	*The Missoulian*, Missoula, Mont.
MM	*The Mississippi Messenger*, Natchez, Ms.
NB	*Nashville Banner*, Nashville, Tenn.
NDL	*News-Democrat & Leader*, Russellville, Ky. (also *The News-Democrat*)
NUA	*Nashville Union and American*, Nashville, Tenn.
NYDN	*New York Daily News*, New York, New York
NYT	*The New York Times*, New York, New York
NYTrib.	*New York Tribune*, New York, New York
OL	*The Orange Leader*, Orange, Tex.
PAN	*The Port Arthur News*, Port Arthur, Tex.
PBP	*The Palm Beach Post*, West Palm Beach, Fl.
PCDN	*The Park City Daily News*, Bowling Green, Ky.
Province	*The Province*, Vancouver, British Columbia
RB	*The Republican Banner*, Nashville, Tenn.
RDR	*The Roswell Daily Record*, Roswell, N. Mex.
Rec.	*The Record*, Orange, Tex.
RM	*The Russellville Messenger*, Russellville, Ky.
RN	*Riverton News*, Riverton, Wyo.
SE	*Suburbanite Economist*, Chicago, Il.
SFE	*San Francisco Examiner*, San Francisco, Ca.
SH	*The Sun-Herald*, Sydney, Aus.
SLPD	*St. Louis Post-Dispatch*, St. Louis, Mo.
Sol	*El Sol*, Phoenix, Az.
SR	*The Spokesman-Review*, Spokane, Wa.
ST	*The Straits Times*, Singapore
Tenn.	*The Tennessean*, Nashville, Tenn. (also *The Nashville American* and *The Nashville Tennessean*)
Tenn. Mag.	*The Tennessean Magazine*, Nashville, Tenn.
TH	*The Tulia Herald*, Tulia, Tex.
TN	*The True Northerner*, Paw Paw, Mi.
VG	*The Vermont Gazette*, Bennington, Vt.
VMS	*Valley Morning Star*, Harlingen, Tex.
WSTCSL	*Wyoming State Tribune – Cheyenne State Leader*, Cheyenne, Wyo. (also *The Wyoming Tribune*)
WT	*The Wheatland Times*, Wheatland, Wyo.
WW	*The Wheatland World*, Wheatland, Wyo.

Manuscript Collections and Repositories

BCAH-UTA	Briscoe Center for American History, University of Texas at Austin, Austin, Tex.

BR-UL Belknap, Inc. Records, Boxes 8 and 9, University of Louisville Archives and Special Collections, Louisville, Ky.

JS-VU John Seigenthaler Papers, Box 146, Folder 8 (Buntin Case 1), Folders 9 and 10 (Reporter's Notebook), Folder 11 (Research Materials), Special Collections Library, Vanderbilt University, Nashville, Tenn.

KHS-FF Kentucky Historical Society, Frankfort Ky.

LBJL-UTA Lyndon Baines Johnson Library, University of Texas at Austin, Austin Tex.

LCA-RK Logan County Archives, Russellville, Ky.

LCPL-RK Logan County Public Library, Russellville, Ky.

SC-LSU Special Collections, Louisiana State University, Baton Rouge, La.

THL-BT Tyrrell Historical Library, Beaumont, Tex.

TSLA-NT Tennessee State Library and Archives, Nashville, Tenn.

WSA-CW Wyoming State Archives, Cheyenne, Wyo.

Lawsuits

Buntin Case 1 *NTC v. NYL* files, including the Circuit Court (pleadings, discovery, and testimony), Court of Appeals, and Tenn. Supreme Court records, are found at TSLA-NT under Davidson Co. Equity Case No. 40097.

Buntin Case 2 *NYL v. NTC* files, including the Circuit Court (pleadings, discovery, and testimony), Court of Appeals, and Tenn. Supreme Court records, are found at TSLA-NT under Davidson Co. Equity Case No. 73888.

McCuddy Case 1 *FCTC v. BEM et al.* files (pleadings, discovery, and testimony) are found at LCA-RK under Logan Co. Circuit Court Case No. 8665.

McCuddy Case 2 *CFBT v. BEM et al.* files (pleadings, discovery, and testimony) are found at LCA-RK under Logan Co. Circuit Court Case No. 8665.

The Families
xi-xii   Compiled by the author.

Prologue: Summer 1931 at Rock Rest
xiii   *TCB had the flu*: Buntin Case 1, BMB test. (Jun. 10, 1940), 1:119.

xiii   *spooky caves in Robertson Co.*: see, e.g., Hugh Walker, "Cheek a Mur-
                derer—Or Maligned?," *Tenn.*, Dec. 26, 1978, 4-A; Claudette Stager,
                "Bell Witch Cave [Tenn.]," National Register of Historic Places Nom-
                ination Form (Washington, D.C.: U.S. Dept. of the Interior, National
                Park Service, 2008), Section 8:7.

xiii   *"sultry or oppressive," weather data*: J.H. Agee, Lewis A. Hurst, and H.
                Jennings, U.S. Dept. of Agriculture, and R.F. Rogers, Tenn. Geological
                Survey, *Soil Survey of Robertson Co., Tenn.* (Washington, D.C.: Govern-
                ment Printing Office, 1914), 7, 8.

xiii   *limestone quarrying, oxen hauling to build stone houses*: Linda O'Neal,
                "Rock Jolly [Tenn.]," National Register of Historic Places Nomination
                Form (Washington, D.C.: U.S. Dept. of the Interior, National Park
                Service, 1973), Section 7.

xiii   *DFC buys Rock Rest in 1847*: "Turnip Patch with a Past," *Tenn. Mag.*,
                Nov. 20, 1949, 7.

xiii   *sour-mash methods superior to bourbon production*: Charles E. Röbert,
                *Nashville and her trade for 1870: a work containing information valuable
                alike to merchants, manufacturers, mechanics, emigrants and capital-
                ists* (Nashville: Roberts & Purvis, 1870), 103, 107 (113, 117 of 496, pdf
                version).

xiv   *exclusive store*: "Grace's Shop Will Move to Newer Quarters," *NB*, Dec.
                31, 1932, 2.

xiv   *alpaca shawls, Paris 1931 couture shows*: Honore Booth, "World of Fash-
                ion," *Tenn.*, Jun. 21, 1931, 25.

xiv   *county road conditions*: Agee *et al.*, *Soil Survey of Robertson Co.*, 7.

xiv   *supper party*: "Announcements," *Tenn.*, Jun. 21, 1931, 12.

xiv   *Tom's break-in*: Buntin Case 1, LBH test. (Jun. 10, 1940), 1:135-136.

xv   *State Fair September 21-26*: "The Bigger Tenn. State Fair is the Grand
                Event of the Year," *Tenn.*, Aug. 30, 1931, 8.

xv   *"fe-e-e-ro-shus" animals, "high-wire performers"*: "Tented City of Circus
                to Rise Early Today; Two Performances Scheduled," *Tenn.*, Sept. 10,
                1931, 1.

xv   *the adults made plans for the horse show*: Buntin Case 1, GG test. (Jun. 10,
                1940), 1:162.

xv   *gave her $1.50, "all the money ... in the world"*: Buntin Case 1, BMB test.,
                1:129, 1:107.

xv   *denied photos were of her husband*: Buntin Case 2, Circuit Court on
                remand, NYL Response, (filed Aug. 27, 1957), Ex. A, LBH letter to JCE
                (Jul. 10, 1953), Transcript, 33.

Part One - Tom

1.   Elsie, Dan, and Their Son, Tom

3   *boarding houses and cottages*: see, e.g., "For Sale," *NB*, Jun. 23, 1900, 7;
           ibid., Jun. 8, 1901, 10; "For Rent," *NB*, Aug. 23, 1902, 7.

3   *Elsie and Dan together on Thanksgiving Eve*: "Society," *Tenn.*, Nov. 29,
           1900, 8.

3   *1901 dance*: "Dance of the Cotillion Club," *Tenn.*, Jan. 12, 1901, 8.

3   *coquetry and flirtation, "worthless dudes"*: Sue Lynn McGuire, "Fannie's
           Flirtations: Etiquette, Reality, and the Age of Choice," *Register of the Ky.
           Historical Society* 93, no. 1 (Winter 1995): 47.

4   *"get you a monkey," "cheaper and a great deal nicer," "left about as bad …
           Appomattox*: "See Here Girls," *Ladies Home Journal and Practical House-
           keeper* 4, no. 9 (Aug. 1887): 11, cited in McGuire, "Fannie's Flirtations,"
           53.

4   *"few female graces," "captivating powers," "rudeness"*: "Modesty," *MM*,
           Feb. 3, 1806, 4.

4   *"ripple … initiated few"*: "Nashville Society," *CJ*, Apr. 28, 1901, Section
           2, 8.

5   *"No marriage … interest," "statuesque loveliness," "superb … rose pointe"*:
           "Nashville Society," *CJ*, Jun. 16, 1901, Section 2, 8.

5   *"lady of fine social standing and abundant means"*: *Williams v. Buntin*, 4
           Tenn. App. 340, 342 (Tenn. Ct. App. 1927).

5   *"myriads … lamps," "glowing frame"*: "Nashville Society," *CJ*, Jun. 16,
           1901, section 2, 8; *honeymooned in Asheville*: ibid.; *then Old Point Com-
           fort*: "Nashville Society," *CJ*, Jun. 30, 1901, Section 2, 8.

5   *DCB's $110,000 sale, largest real estate transaction in Nashville*: "The Cast-
           ner-Knott Building," photo and caption, *Tenn.*, Dec. 22, 1901, 44.

5   *"Athens of the South"*: Christopher K. Coleman, "From Monument to
           Museum: The Role of the Parthenon in the Culture of the New South,"
           Tenn. Historical Quarterly 49, no. 3 (Fall 1990), 140.

5   *"Kentucky Trinity," "maiden, equine, and julep"*: Robert W. Brown, ed.,
           Book of Louisville and Ky. (Louisville: Louisville Convention and Public-
           ity League, 1915), 41 (45 of 126, pdf version).

5   *DCB's arcade trips, Rockefeller's structure, "one of … places"*: "Arcades
           Elsewhere – Daniel C. Buntin Returns from a Tour of Inspection,"
           Tenn., Feb. 1, 1902, 4.

5   *pregnant ECB's last social events before TCB's birth*: Ada Scott Rice, ed.,
           "Society, Mrs. Macquire's Card Party," *Tenn.*, Feb. 11, 1902, 8.

5   *TCB born in RAC's home*: TCB, Delayed Certificate of Birth, File No.
           D-557771, May 28, 1964, Ancestry.com, Tenn., U.S., Delayed Birth
           Records, 1869-1909, database online.

6   *birth certificates for six other babies*: Certificates of Birth, File Nos.
           327-332, Mar. 16, 1902, Ancestry.com, Tenn., U.S., City Birth Records,
           1881-1915, database online.

6   *TCB's date of birth, delayed birth certificate*: TCB, Delayed Certificate of
           Birth, File No. D-557771, May 28, 1964.

6   *"Master" Tom*: "Society," *Tenn.*, Jan. 15, 1909, 7; "Society," *Tenn.*, Feb. 2,1909, 7.

6   *"servants ... originally owned by the Carter family"*: "Passing of Old Home That Served as Headquarters for Gen. Grant," *Tenn.*, Jan. 12, 1913, C-5.

6   *Jack Horner pies, ices, and bonbons*: Ada Scott Rice, ed., "Society," *Tenn.*, Dec. 12, 1903, 6.

7   *traveled to Florida, ranches in Tex. and Wyo.*: *"Society, Brief Mention,"* NB, Apr. 6, 1908, 5; "Social Happenings," *Tenn.*, Aug 30, 1910, 7; "Personals," *Tenn.*, Oct. 1, 1915, B-14.

7   *Tom stayed with the Caldwells*: "Society," *Tenn.*, Jan. 15, 1909, 7; "Society," *Tenn.*, Feb. 2,1909, 7.

7   *RAC married TDC in 1859*: *Williams v. Buntin*, 4 Tenn. App. at 342.

7   *"ready wit and sparkling humor," "versed ... literature," "ornament ... social affairs"*: "Thomas D. Craighead," *Tenn.*, May 27, 1898, 4.

7   *JECr married CptWAB in 1869*: "Married," *NUA*, Mar. 10, 1869, 4.

7   *RAC adopted DCB*: "Mrs. Thomas D. Craighead Adopts D.F.C. Buntin," *Tenn.*, Feb. 14, 1901, 6.

7   *"lucky ... spot," "one of ... community," DBC managed DFC's estate*: "Tenn. State News," *BB*, Feb. 22, 1901, 1.

7   *RAC's $400,000 inheritance from her father*: "Estate of Daniel F. Carter," *RB*, Mar. 27, 1874, 4.

7   *"all the ... child"*: *Meriwether v. Fourth & First Bank & Trust Co.*, 285 S.W. 34 (Tenn. 1925).

7   *foster mother*: "Craighead Estate Goes to Heirs of Daniel Buntin, Supreme Court Holds," *Tenn.*, Jun. 20, 1926, 14.

9   *JCB's activities as a club woman*: "Funeral Today for Mrs. Buntin," *Tenn.*, Jun. 17, 1930, 3.

9   *guardian sued TDC as CptWAB's estate executor*: "Guardian Sues the Executor," *Tenn.*, Feb. 25, 1897, 5.

9   *DCB in Venezuela*: John Trotwood Moore and Austin Powers Foster, "Daniel Carter Buntin," *Tenn. the Volunteer State, 1769-1923* (Chicago: S.J. Clarke Pub., 1923), 4-6; *permission to travel the Orinoco River*: "News and Gossip," *Tenn.*, Oct. 27, 1903, 2.

9   *Canadian timber dispute*: *Ayres v. The Graham Steamship C. and L. Co.*, 150 Ill. App. 137 (1909).

9   *lawsuit with tenants*: "Arcade May Be Abandoned," *Tenn.*, Jul. 6, 1902, 11; "Summer Street Tenants Accept," *Tenn.*, Aug. 9, 1902, 7.

9   *$200,000 cost*: Mrs. Donald Drummond, Junior League of Nashville, "The Nashville Arcade [Tenn.]," National Register of Historic Places Nomination Form (Washington, D.C.: U.S. Dept. of the Interior, National Park Service, 1973), Section 8.

9   *full of tenants, DCB as general manager*: "Big Loan to Arcade," *Tenn.*, Jul. 21, 1903, 5; "Wanted," *Tenn.*, Oct. 22, 1903, 9.

9   *"hamburger to a $5,000 diamond"*: Drummond, "The Nashville Arcade," Section 8.

9   *DCB as general manager of JEC's bank and trust*: "Amalgamation of
           Local Banks," *Tenn.*, Mar. 14, 1906, 9.

9-10   *family moved to Franklin Turnpike rental house*: *Vaulx v. Buntin*, 153 S.W.
           481 (Tenn. 1912); *breach of contract, $4,000 in damages*: ibid.

10   *Buntins moved to Chicago in 1908*: "Society," *Tenn.*, Oct. 2, 1908, 7; *Nash-
           ville City Directory 1909* (hereafter "*Nashville City Dir. year*") (Nashville:
           Marshall-Bruce-Polk Co., 1909), 244.

10   *DCB incorporated TBLC in 1907*: "As Ass't Manager," *Tenn.*, Jul. 19, 1908,
           17; "C.L. and E.R. Tallmadge No Longer Partners," *RDR*, Jan. 25, 1908, 1.

10   *"high-rise," "high-class" apartment homes and rental rates*: A.J. Pardridge
           and Harold Bradley, *Directory to Apartments of the Better Class along the
           North Side of Chicago* (Chicago: Pardridge and Bradley, 1917), 2, 4; *exam-
           ple "flat" amenities and interior decoration*: ibid., 3, 9; *"modulating vapor
           heating," "abundance of base plugs," "device … beverages"*: ibid., 3, 27.

10   *1512 Dearborn Pkway rental flat location*: Sanborn Map Co., Sanborn
           Fire Insurance Map (Chicago, 1910), 2: Sheet 79, loc.gov/collections/
           sanborn-maps; *cook and butler*: U.S. Bureau of the Census, Thirteenth
           Census of the U.S.: 1910—Population Schedule, Chicago, Enum. Dist.
           No. 1, 21st Ward, Sheet No. 15A (enumerated Apr. 16-30, 1910), lines
           42-47.

11   *Palmer House Hotel brownie creation*: palmerhousehiltonhotel.com/
           about-our-hotel/thebrownie/.

11   *Rasmussen Riding Academy*: Sanborn Fire Insurance Map (Chicago,
           1910), 2: Sheet 79.

11   *Palmer mansion*: "Potter Palmer's New House," *CT*, Nov. 6, 1882, 5; *no
           doorknobs, servant always on duty*: John Handley, "Museum Quality,"
           CT, Jul. 19, 2000, Section 9, 16-17.

11   *Ward mansion (4700 Kimbark Ave.)*: "Movements of Society People," *CT*,
           Oct. 29, 1899, 42; "News of the Society World," *CT*, Apr. 10, 1909, 11.

11   *ECB and society events in Chicago*: Joan Candour, "In the World of
           Society," *CE*, May 16, 1912, 5; *"very old and influential family," "thought
           … woman"*: ibid.

11   *raised funds for "destitute crippled children"*: "Society News and Notes,"
           CE, Apr. 1, 1911, 7.

11   *"The Yards"*: Lester Armour, "The Meat-Packing Industry in Chicago,"
           Chicago (Chicago: American Pub. Corp., 1929), 113.

11   *"ghettoes," "slums," "Little Hell"*: Harvey W. Zorbaugh, *The Gold Coast
           and The Slum: A Sociological Study of Chicago's Near North Side* (Chi-
           cago: Univ. of Chicago Press, 1976, 1983), 5; *"Smoky Hollow"*: ibid., 33.

12   *child killed at least once a year*: "Children Killed and Maimed by Speed-
           ing Street Car," *CE*, May 16, 1912, 1.

12   *fell out of a Pullman car*: Buntin Case 1, Dr. JB test. (Jun. 7, 1940), 1:68.

12   *"protruded … angle," "very large"*: ibid., NTC Declaration (filed May 19,
           1939), 1:8.

12   *Buntins left Chicago in 1912*: "News of the Society World, Personal
           Items," *CT*, Sept. 29, 1912, 61.

12   *lived briefly at Melrose outside Nashville*: Margaret Lindsley Warden, "More Change for Melrose," *Tenn. Mag.*, Nov. 12, 1950, 8.

12   *moved to west-end house in town*: *Nashville City Dir. 1912*, 194.

12   *moved to 2500 Kensington Place*: ibid. *1913*, 164; ibid. *1914*, 157; ibid. *1915*, 155.

12   *Kensington Place primary living space square footage*: Metropolitan Nashville and Davidson Co., Assessor of Property, 2500 Kensington Place, General Property Information, padctn.org; *description of house*: "Large Warehouse; Fine Residences," *NB*, Sept. 24, 1909, 6.

12   *Longview party before TCB left for the academy*: "Social News, Dance at 'Longview'," *Tenn.*, Jun. 19, 1917, 8.

12   *TCB's appearance*: Culver Military Academy, *The Roll Call 1918 Yearbook* (Culver, Ind.: First Class, 1917-18), 254 (144 of 212, pdf version).

12   *Culver, largest private military instruction school in U.S.*: Daniel McDonald, *A Twentieth Century History of Marshall Co., Ind.* (Chicago: Lewis Pub. Co., 1908), 2:353.

12   *TCB joined Black Horse Troop*: Culver Military Academy, *Culver Military Academy Catalog* (Culver, Ind., 1918), 14.

13   *on sports teams*: Culver Military Academy, *The Roll Call 1918 Yearbook*, 254 (144 of 212, pdf version); Culver Military Academy, "Enter Indoor Baseball as Topic of Conversation," *The Vedette* 21, no. 19, Mar. 9, 1918, 1 (23 of 153, pdf version).

13   *placed in swimming competitions*: "C Company Wins," *The Vedette* 23, no. 13, Jan. 25, 1919, 1 (9 of 170, pdf version); "Natatorial," *The Vedette* 23, no. 18, Mar. 1, 1919, 2 (30 of 170, pdf version); "Natatorial," *The Vedette* 23, no. 20, Mar. 15, 1919, 2 (38 of 170, pdf version).

13   *ECB or ECB and DCB visited Culver*: "Social News, Personals," *Tenn.*, Mar. 24, 1918, Society Section, 4; "Social and Personal," *The Vedette* 21, no. 22, Mar. 30, 1918, 2 (37 of 153, pdf version); "Easter Visitors," *The Vedette* 21, no. 23, Apr. 6, 1918, 1 (40 of 153, pdf version); "Social and Personal," *The Vedette* 21, no. 29, May 18, 1918, 2 (69 of 153, pdf version).

13   *Buntins enumerated in Wyo., 1920 census*: U.S. Bureau of the Census, Fourteenth Census of the U.S.: 1920—Population, Laramie, Albany Co., Wy., Enum. Dist. No. 2, Sheet No. 7B (enumerated Jan. 1-17, 1920), lines 98-100.

13   *TCB attended Cascadilla School to prep for Cornell's entrance exams*: "The Culver Legion, from Acheson at Cornell," *The Vedette* 24, no. 16, Feb. 14, 1920, 3 (15 of 170, pdf version).

2.   A Father's Legacy

14   *six feet tall, blue-gray eyes, red hair, "florid"*: DCB, Passport Application, No. 189951, Davidson Co., Tenn., Feb. 9, 1921, Ancestry.com, U.S. Passport Applications, 1795-1925, database online.

14   *"happy faculty … at ease," "in all things," "actuated … fail"*: I.S. Bartlett, ed., "Daniel C. Buntin," *History of Wyo.* (Chicago: S.J. Clarke Pub., 1918), 2:303-304.

14   *encounter with an armed train robber during train trip from Cheyenne to*

Laramie: "Overland Limited Robbed at Cheyenne," *KR*, Apr. 7, 1916, 5; "Gets in His Work on the Overland Train," *LR*, Apr. 5, 1916, 5.

14, 16   *"ill fame," disorderly houses"*: Robert T. Shannon, compiler, ed., annotator, *A Compilation of Tenn. Statutes*, V (Nashville: Tenn. Law Book Pub. Co., 1918), Ch. 7, n.3, n. 4, 5263.

16   *"splendid," "quick," "remarkable executive ability"*: Bartlett, "Daniel C. Buntin," *History of Wyo.*, 2:303-304.

16   *ERT and brothers brought midwestern "home seekers" to the Pecos River Valley*: "More Homeseekers," *RDR*, Jan. 23, 1904, 1; "Another Train Load," *RDR*, Sept. 10, 1904, 5.

16   *ERT and brother's legal problems*: "Sues the Tallmadges," *RDR*, Jun. 29, 1905, 4; "Chicagoans Held for Fraud," *CT*, Apr. 30, 1906, 2.

16   *syndicate to build a railroad from the Tex. Panhandle to the Mexican border and connect with Mexico City*: "For a New Railroad," *RDR*, Aug. 16, 1905, 1.

16   *DCB promoted the railroad in Tex. Panhandle, bought land*: Ada Scott Rice, ed., "Society, Social Notes," *Tenn.*, Aug. 11, 1905, 6; Bartlett, "Daniel C. Buntin," *History of Wyo.*, 2:304; Moore and Foster, "Daniel Carter Buntin," *Tenn. the Volunteer State*, 3:5-6.

16   *Wyo., U.S. population growth 1900-1910*: U.S. Bureau of the Census, Thirteenth Census of the U.S. Taken in the Year 1910, Statistics for Wyo. (Washington, D.C.: Government Printing Office, 1910), Supplement for Wyo., 568.

17   *Buffalo Bill and the Shoshone Irrigation Co.*: Phil Roberts, "Watering a Dry Land: Wyo. and Federal Legislation," *Encyclopedia*, Wyo. State Historical Society, entry posted Oct. 28, 2019, https://wyohistory.org/encyclopedia/watering-dry-land-wyoming-and-federal-irrigation.

17   *TBLC bought 60,000-acre cattle ranch in the Big Laramie River Valley*: "As Ass't Manager," *Tenn.*, Jul. 19, 1908, 17; *Haley Ranch and others*: "Half Million Spent by Tallmadge-Buntin Company Since May 1," *LB*, Nov. 30, 1908, 4.

17   *increased holdings to over 200,000 acres by 1908*: "Carload of Easterners," *LR*, May 28, 1908, 2.

17   *$115,000 hotel investment*: U.S. Senate, Committee on Irrigation and Reclamation of Arid Lands, *Private Irrigation Projects, Carey Act*, 62nd Congr., 1st sess.,1912, 6.

17   *free excursions*: e.g., "Tuesday, Aug. 18th is the Day for Our Second Free Homeseekers' Excursion," advertisement, *TN*, Aug. 14, 1908, 6; "Free Trip from Allentown to Laramie, Wyo.," *MC*, Jun. 2, 1908, 3.

17   *railcars used for overnight accommodations*: "Free Homeseekers' Excursion," advertisement, *TN*, Aug. 14, 1908, 6.

17   *small groups*: "Carload of Easterners," *LR*, May 28, 1908, 2.

17   *seventy-five people per trip*: "Large Tallmadge-Buntin Party Coming the 23rd," *LB*, Jul. 17, 1908, 1.

17   *party of 175 "land seekers" in 1908*: "Tallmadge-Buntin Company Has Large Party Coming," *LB*, Jul. 1, 1908, 1.

17   *fifty-six bought land, "at least … ends"*: "Many Land Buyers in Eastern Party," *LB*, Jun. 8, 1908, 1.

17   *"invested heavily," J.F. Ward bought 5,000 acres*: "Easterners Invest Heavily in Tallmadge-Buntin Land," *LB*, Jul. 24, 1908, 1.

17   *Carey Act land for 50 cents/ac. and ranges of water rights costs*: Craig O. Cooper, *A History of Water Law, Water Rights & Water Development in Wyo., 1868-2002* (Riverton, Wyo.: Cooper Consulting, 2004), 29; "Government Land Opening Under Carey Act," *SE*, Feb. 26, 1909, 7: Clarence T. Johnson, *Tenth Biennial Report of the State Engineer to the Governor of Wyo., 1909-1910* (Cheyenne: S.A. Bristol, 1910), "Agreement," State Engineer and TBLC (Aug. 2, 1910), second para., 92.

17, 19   *$500,000 per month*: "As Ass't Manager," *Tenn.*, Jul. 19, 1908, 17; *sales of 500 farms*: advertisement, *LR*, Sept. 5, 1908, 2.

19   *Jan. 1909 sales*: "Real Estate Sales Recorded Yesterday," *LR*, Jan. 15, 1909, 5.

19   *largest sale to J.H. Falkingham, 240 acres*: "Real Estate Transfers," *LR*, Mar. 17, 1909, 8.

19   *"apparently unlimited capital"*: "Carload of Easterners," *LR*, May 28, 1908, 2.

19   *$15,000 for first payment on James Lake construction project*: "Half Million Spent by Tallmadge-Buntin Company Since May 1," *LB*, Nov. 30, 1908, 4; "Developing the Arid Farm Lands," *LB*, Jun. 17, 1909, 1; "To Begin Work on Great Irrigation Ditch Soon," *LB*, Jul. 31, 1908, 1.

19   *contractors missed deadline*: "Pushing Irrigation Work," *CDL*, Jan. 31, 1909, 3.

19   *acquired Whitehouse and Palmer ranches*: "Red Buttes Ranch Sold to Easterners," *LR*, May 19, 1909, 1; *Hart ranch and Pioneer canal, total cost at least $245,000*: "Purchase Price Paid for Big Land Deal," *LR*, May 19, 1909, 1.

19   *opened Laramie office for Lake Hattie project, scope*: "Permanent Office Established Here," *LB*, Jun. 17, 1909, 1.

19   *200,000 acres v. 100,000 acres*: compare "Carload of Easterners," *LR*, May 28, 1908, 2, and "Developing the Arid Farm Lands," *LB*, Jun. 17, 1909, 1.

19   *TBLC approved in 1910 to finish the Riverton/Wind River project*: Cooper, *A History of Water Law*, 49.

19-20   *Rosecrans telegram, financing secured, "strange," $25 "for any charitable purpose," "based on facts," "means business," "criminal," "keep settlers … false dope," "four-year apprenticeship," "postponement business"*: "Are the Telegrams Bona Fide," *RN*, Sept. 24, 1910, 1.

20   *TBLC sold remaining land to Wyo. Land and Credit Co. in Apr. 1910*: "Has Sold its Lands," *LR*, Apr. 25, 1910, 1.

20   *Riverton/Wind River project sold to Wyo. Land Board*: "Closing Deal with Tallmadge-Buntin," *RN*, Aug. 6, 1910, 1.

20   *TBLC sold James Lake stock to committees*: "Have Sold their Interests," *LR*, May 21, 1912, 1.

20   *ERT turned to selling Great Plains' lands*: see, e.g., "Kansas," *CT*, Jun. 22, 1917, 24.

20   *Buntins moved from Chicago to Nashville*: "Where They Are," *CE*, Sept. 29, 1912, 15.

20   *Buntins spent summers of 1912 and 1913 in Laramie*: "Here to Spend the Hot Summer Months," *LR*, Jul. 9, 1913, 4; Joan Candour, "In the World of Society," *CE*, May 16, 1912, 5.

20   *DCB reneged on land sale due to nearby oil production*: *Riedesel v. Towne*, 206 P.2d 747, 748 (Wyo. 1949); *spurned buyer acquired land when DCB failed to pay taxes*: ibid. at 747.

20   *MWB born*: Feb. 8, 1914, Ancestry.com, U.S., Social Security Applications and Claims Index, 1936-2007, database online.

20   *DCB tried again in Laramie; willing to rent land at lower prices:* "Buntin Booms Laramie Plains," *CP*, Mar. 14, 1914, 1.

20   *Palmer said DCB unsuccessful*: "Taking Supplies to Red Buttes Ranch," *LR*, Mar. 1, 1916, 8.

20   *DCB bought water co.*: "Laramie Water Company is Sold to Daniel Buntin and Prominent Nashville Banker," *LB*, Aug. 1, 1917, 1; *Big and Little Laramie River dams*: "Will Take Views of Irrigation Plant," *LR*, Dec. 14, 1910, 8; "Preparing for Dam for Water Company," *LR*, Dec. 16, 1910, 1.

20   *"seven figures*: "Laramie Water Company is Sold," *LB*, Aug. 1, 1917, 1.

20-21   *"heap" of debt and money*: *Caldwell v. Roach*, 12 P.2d 376, 378 (Wyo. 1932); *"keep it afloat"*: ibid. at 378.

21   *"no doubt be widely advertised," "probable … there"*: "Laramie Water Company is Sold," *LB*, Aug. 1, 1917, 1.

21   *water co. sold*: "Brief News Notes from all Parts of Wyo.," *BVE*, Apr. 23, 1918, 7; "Laramie Water Co., Acquired Today by Illinois Capital," *LB*, Apr. 4, 1918, 1.

21   *DCB declared Wyo. as permanent address*: DCB, WWI Registration Card, Serial Number 113, Order Number 134, Local Board for the Co. of Albany, State of Wy., Sept. 11, 1918, Ancestry.com, WWI Draft Registration Cards, 1917-1918, database online.

21   *left Nashville for "exceptionally urgent business" in Laramie*: "D.C. Buntin to Arrive from Tenn. Sunday," *LB*, Apr. 4, 1919, 3.

21   *DCB, ECB returned to Nashville in fall 1920*: "Forced to Go South for Health this Winter," *LB*, Oct. 8, 1920, 2; *"pay no attention to business," "complete rest"*: ibid.

21   *$20,000 income from RAC's trust*: *Williams v. Buntin*, 4 Tenn. App. at 342.

21   *DCB, ECB's Hawaiian cruise*: DCB, Passport Application, Feb. 9, 1921; *"floating palace"*: "Hilo Greets Hawkeye State," *HTH*, Mar. 17, 1921, 1, 6; "Two Palatial Liners Sail for this Port," *SFE*, Feb. 16, 1921, 13; *passed through the Panama Canal*: "Hilo Greets Hawkeye State," *HTH*, 1; *brief stop in Laramie*: "D.C. Buntin and Wife Arrive after Winter Trip to Hawaiian Islands," *LB*, Apr. 1, 1921, 8.

21   *DCB's health, "seemingly … indisposition"*: Maude Ingham, "Society and Women's Page," *LB*, Apr. 2, 1921, 3.

21   *"many new people"*: "D.C. Buntin and Wife Arrive," *LB*, Apr. 1, 1921, 8.

21   *DCB suicide*: "Bad Health Causes Tragic Death Here of Daniel Buntin,"
          Tenn., Jan. 19, 1922, 1.

22   *dead when doctor arrived*: DCB, Certificate of Death, File No. 101, Jan.
          20, 1922, Ancestry.com, Tenn., U.S., Death Records, 1908-1965, database
          online.

22   *services and burial*: "Funeral Saturday for Dan C. Buntin," *Tenn.*, Jan.
          20, 1922, 16.

22   *JHE's "embarrassing condition" of finances*: Alice Pemble White, "The
          Plantation Experience of Joseph and Lavinia Erwin," *La. Historical
          Quarterly* 27, no. 2 (Apr. 1944), 58, SC-LSU.

22   *JHE's suicide*: ibid., 16; *head stuck in a drainage barrel*: "Donaldson, April
          25," *CDC*, May 16, 1829, 2; *"wet death, dry feet"*: Francois Mignon, "Plan-
          tation Memo, 1966," *DW*, Mar. 27, 1966, 5.

22   *"worked right," "'dead one'"*: "Barrett Eastman, Writer, Ends Life," *CE*,
          Jan. 16, 1910, 1.

22   *"accidentally," "through the body," "supposed"*: "A Dangerous Wound,"
          Tenn., Jul. 25, 1903, 8.

22   *WC suicide by gunshot, "unbalanced" mind*: "Boy Suicide," *CN*, Jan. 27,
          1908, 1.

22   *"incurable malady"*: "Bad Health Causes Tragic Death Here of Daniel
          Buntin," *Tenn.*, Jan. 19, 1922,1.

22   *"he had … nuisance to his family"*: NYL v. NTC, 159 S.W. 2d 81, 83
          (Tenn. 1942).

23   *"paresis," "softening of the brain," "feared … syphilis"*: Buntin Case 1, Dr.
          TH test. (Jun. 7, 1940), 1:83.

23   *DCB's probate filings, assets, will instructions*: DCB Will (filed Aug. 17,
          1922), District Court, Second Judicial District, Albany Co., Wyo.; ibid.,
          (filed Jul. 25, 1924), County Court, Davidson Co., Tenn.

23   *Chicagoan's claim*: "Chicago Man Sues Estate of Dan C. Buntin," *NB*,
          Jun. 9, 1924, 3.

23   *Tex. lawsuit to recover property in Happy*: "Citation by Publication," *TH*,
          Aug. 24, 1923, 9.

23   *JEC's bank filed for sale of DCB lots*: "Chancery Sale," *NB*, Jan. 24, 1925, 12.

23   *RAC's disposition of her property*: Buntin v. Plummer, 46 S.W.2d at 61;
          Williams v. Buntin, 4 Tenn. App. at 343, 345.

23   *RAC conveyed Rock Rest to DCB and ECB*: Williams v. Buntin, 4 Tenn.
          App. at 346.

23   *TCB's and MWB's right to RAC's estate through DCB upheld*: Meriwether
          v. Fourth & First Bank & Trust Co., 285 S.W. 34 (Tenn. 1925).

23   *protégé of "Miss Puss" won suit challenging TCB's and MWB's inheritance
          from DCB's estate*: Williams v. Buntin, 4 Tenn. App. at 361.

23-24   *TCB and MWB sued aunt over RAC property entrusted to DCB*: Buntin v.
          Plummer, 46 S.W.2d at 60.

24   *DCB's suicide "preyed" on TCB's mind "a great deal"*: Buntin Case 1,
          BMB test., 1:130.

24   *"financial reverses" did not justify suicide*: ibid., JD test. (Jun. 11, 1940),
          1:184.

24   *mental illness did justify suicide*: ibid., Court of Appeals, NTC Def.-in-
          Error Reply Brief and Argument (May 5, 1941, filed May 13, 1941),119;
          "curse of one of the social diseases," TCB feared for himself: ibid., 118, 119.

3.   **Mr. and Mrs. Thomas Craighead Buntin**

25   *"pretentious," "landscape gardening"*: UW, *The Wyo. Student* 20, no. 16
          (Laramie: Associated Students of the Univ. of Wyo., Feb. 1, 1918), 2, 3.

25   *TCB president of the freshman class and yearbook editor*: "Tom Buntin,
          Betty Moore are Married Here This Morning," *LB*, Sept. 28, 1922, 5.

25   *TCB joined Alpha Tau Omega fraternity*: "Betty Moore Weds at Laramie
          Thursday," *WSTCSL*, Sept. 29, 1922, 6.

25   *debate team alternate*: "Teams to Represent Wyo. U. in Debates
          Announced at Laramie," *CST*, Dec. 17, 1920, 2.

25   *"lamentable failure in forensics," "interesting and instructive," "exception-
          ally well attended"*: *1922 Wyo Yearbook* (Laramie: Junior Class of the
          Univ. of Wyo., 1922), 175 (179 of 282, pdf version).

25   *TCB second lieutenant in campus ROTC*: *1922 Wyo Yearbook*, 91 (95 of
          282, pdf version); *"beauty sleep"*: ibid., 191 (195 of 282, pdf version).

26   *BGM, TCB started UW in the fall of 1920, freshman class of 180*: *1921 Wyo
          Yearbook*, 84-85 (88 of 282, pdf version).

26   *Rev. JWM fell between two railcars*: "Rev. Moore is Mangled," *CDL*,
          May 8, 1907, 4; *dies after amputations*: "Injury Fatal," *WT*, May 8, 1907, 4.

26   *insurance claim was denied:* "Items of Interest from Our Exchanges,"
          WW, Jun. 28, 1907, 2.

26   *BGM's mother was head librarian at Cheyenne's Carnegie Library*: Wil-
          liam Rideout, M.D., and Elizabeth Cuckow Thorson, ed., *The Carnegie
          Library* (Cheyenne: Laramie Co. Public Library, 2017), 60, 62.

26   *"handsome, affable young man," raccoon coat, touring car*: "Casperites
          Recall Buntin at State U.," *CST*, Nov. 27, 1953, 1.

26   *TCB as dice instructor, "importance ... points"*: *1921 Wyo Yearbook*, 235
          (238 of 282, pdf version); *slow to put on "goloshes," "in great gobs of fre-
          quency"*: ibid., 224 (228 of 282, pdf version).

26   *he drank*: Buntin Case 1, BMB test., 1:98.

26   *BGM an actress*: *1921 Wyo Yearbook*, 112-113 (116 of 282, pdf version).

27   *dramatic role in "The Lesser Evil"*: Clara Dodds, "Society," *WSTCSL*.
          Apr. 24, 1921, 6; "Cheyenne Girls in College Plays," *WSTCSL*, Jan. 29,
          1922, 7.

28   *DCB, ECB met BGM, they liked her*: Buntin Case 1, ECB test. (Jun. 11,
          1940), 1:169.

28   *TCB attended ROTC camp in summer 1921, does well*: *1922 Wyo Yearbook*,
          193 (197 of 282, pdf version); *TCB and others traveled after camp*: ibid.

28   *motored to Cheyenne for Frontier Days*: "Tom Buntin Goes to Cheyenne
          Today," *LB*, Jul. 25, 1921, 5.

28   *cowgirl Lorena Tricky's trick-riding and bronc-riding win*: G.B. Dobson,

"Frontier Days," *Wyo. Tales and Trails,* wyomingtalesandtrails.com/frontierdays4c.html.

28   *"to the surprise … friends" BGM and TCB married:* "Betty Moore Weds," *WSTCSL,* Sept. 29, 1922, 6; "Tom Buntin, Betty Moore are Married," *LB,* Sept. 28, 1922, 5; Statement of Application for a Marriage License, Albany Co. Book F, p. 564 (Sept. 28, 1922), WSA-CW.

28   *ECB, MWB had returned to Nashville:* "Women's Activities, The Personal Side," *Tenn.,* Sept. 14, 1922, 8.

28   *"if she was … for her":* Buntin Case 1, ECB test., 1:170.

28   *"exceptionally well known and very popular" couple:* "Tom Buntin, Betty Moore Are Married," *LB,* Sept. 28, 1922, 5.

28   *BMB elected secretary of the Associated Students of UW:* "Additional Society," *WSTCSL,* Oct. 1, 1922, 7.

28   *TCB on student committee to welcome new UW president and his wife:* "Cowboy Welcome is Planned, U. President is Due Monday," *CST,* Sept. 28, 1922, 5.

29   *feted at Longview:* "Mr. and Mrs. Caldwell Entertain with Tea Dance at Longview," *Tenn.,* Dec. 9, 1922, 7.

29   *Cheyenne's Carnegie Library interior details, Mexican onyx, marble drinking fountains, bronze statuary:* Rideout and Thorson, ed., *The Carnegie Library,* 25.

29   *Leafy Lot, Hood's Waste history:* John E. Norvell, "Leafy Lot Plantation and the War Between the States," *An American Family,* entry posted Feb. 17, 2014, jenorv66.wordpress.com/2014/02/17/leafy-lot-plantation-and-the-war-between-the-states/.

29   *Longview interior features:* Shain Dennison and Judy De Palma, "Longview (Norvell-Caldwell House) [Tenn.]," National Register of Historic Places Nomination Form (Washington, D.C.: U.S. Dept. of the Interior, National Park Service, 1982), Section 7:1.

29   *BMB's attire complimented:* "Mr. and Mrs. Caldwell Entertain," *Tenn.,* Dec. 9, 1922, 7; *family hostesses, flowers:* ibid.

29-30   *two-tiered Italian chandelier, "extravagant glass solarium":* Dennison and De Palma, "Longview," Section 7:2.

30   *Mrs. TCB's photograph in Christmas edition:* "Society and its Interests," *Tenn.,* Dec. 24, 1922, Women's Section, 1.

30   *BMB, TCB returned to Wyo., live at the Palmer ranch:* "Women's Activities, The Personal Side," *Tenn.,* Feb. 14, 1923, 6.

30   *ECB, MWB visited the couple:* "Women's Activities, The Personal Side," *Tenn.,* Sept. 9, 1923, Women's Section, 5.

30   *DFCB born, Aug. 1923:* "Daniel Franklin Carter Buntin," *Tenn.,* Feb. 8, 2001, 7B.

30   *$200 per month:* Buntin Case 1, ECB test., 1:171.

30   *TCB visited ECB in Chicago:* "Personal Mention," *Tenn.,* Dec. 9, 1923, Women's Section, 6.

30   *"very good friends":* Buntin Case 1, BMB test., 1:110; *never a misunderstanding:* ibid., ECB test., 1:170.

30   *TCB secured realtor's license in Nashville, worked at the Buntin real estate firm*: "List of Licensed Realty Dealers in City Given," *Tenn.*, Apr. 13, 1924, Real Estate Section, 5.

30   *stayed in the room where DCB committed suicide, bullet hole still in the wall*: Buntin Case 1, BMB test., 1:103-104.

30   *DCB's dead letters*: see, e.g., "Advertised Letters," *FR*, Mar. 9, 1907, 3.

31   *in the "smart set"*: "Love of Fine Horses Has in No Way Abated in this Section," *Tenn.*, May 20, 1925, 8; *BMB's fashion choices*: see, e.g., ibid. ("ensemble costume in shades of blue," a "charming creation" of a hat in "flesh chiffon").

31   *Junior League work for crippled children*: Photograph, *Tenn.*, Oct. 20, 1929, Rotogravure Section, 50; *sold newspapers at Broadway and 16th Ave.*: "88 Newsgirls Will Sell Junior League Edition on Sunday," *Tenn.*, Apr. 9, 1927, 1.

31   *TCB Jr. born Aug. 1925*: TCB, Ancestry.com, U.S., Social Security Death Index, 1935-2014, database online; *RCCB born Jul. 1927*: RCCB, Ancestry.com, U.S., WWII Draft Cards Young Men, 1940-1947, database online.

31   *BMB and RCCB photograph in the newspaper*: "Society and Its Interest," *Tenn.*, Jan. 15, 1928, Women's Section, 1.

31   *TCB "very disturbed," "went to pieces," "no stomach for hardships"*: Buntin Case 1, Dr. JB test., 1:65.

31   *drinking worsened after marriage*: ibid., BMB test., 1:98; *"habit"*: ibid., 1:99.

32   *divorce in the South*: Paul R. Amato and Shelley Irving, "Historical Trends in Divorce in the U.S.," *Handbook of Divorce and Relationship Dissolution*, Mark A. Fine and John H. Harvey, ed. (Routledge Handbooks Online, 2005), 44.

32   *"responsible family member"*: McGuire, "Fannie's Flirtations," 63, n. 78.

32   *"drunk and staggering"*: Buntin Case 1, JD test., 1:182.

32   *"I might as well kill myself," pulls gun from a safe in the stamp drawer, "his daddy," "if there is such a place"*: ibid., 1:182, 1:184.

32   *TCB's $300 per month salary at his grandfather's insurance firm*: ibid., BMB test., 1:129.

32   *"allowance"*: ibid., ECB test., 1:172.

32   *"didn't have a home … summers there"*: ibid., BMB test., 1:97.

33   *LBH comments on TCB, "man … pressure," could never earn a living on his own*: McCuddy Case 1, Stipulation, LBH depo. (Aug. 26, 1940), 20-21.

33   *"doctrine of duty," "immortal"*: James M. Hudnut, *History of the New-York Life Insurance Company 1895-1905* (New York City: New York Life Ins., 1906), foreword, 8.

33   *"earn an independent income," "have a right"*: "The Rights of the Individual and the Safeguards of Individual Rights," advertisement, *Life Insurance Courant* 25, no. 6 (Jan. 1, 1920): 280.

33   *first policy for $3,000*: Buntin Case 1, SD depo., Division Superintendent,

NYL Comptroller's Dept. (Apr. 24, 1940), submitted into evidence (Jun. 11, 1940), 2:420.

33   *1929 policies for $50,000, annual premium of $1,128*: ibid., CN test., NTC President (Jun. 7, 1940), Exs. D and E.

33   *"delicate," "not prying" inquiries*: Hudnut, *History of NYL*, 99.

34   *risk factors*: ibid., 94; *reduced life's monetary value*: ibid., 95.

34   *"aerial flights," no morphine or cocaine, medical history, "occasional" drinker*: Buntin Case 1, NYL Bill of Exceptions, (dated Jun. 7, 1940, filed Jul. 20, 1940), Ex. D, Application for Insurance, Pt. 2 (Apr. 3, 1929).

34   *"sprees," "nerves," formaldehyde, "sober enough to operate," "running mates," Merten's Turkish Baths*: ibid., Dr. JB test., 1:53, 1:54, 1:56, 1:76.

34   *TCB set up trust*: Buntin Case 1, CN test., 2.

34   *raised his sons' distribution age to thirty-five*: ibid., Ex. C, Supplemental Trust Agreement (Mar. 11, 1930), submitted into evidence (Jun. 7, 1940), 1:17.

35   *better off with him dead and with the insurance money*: ibid., BMB test., 1:103.

4.   Tom's Denouement and Disappearance

37   *BMB was awakened, TCB had a gun, it went off*: Buntin Case 1, BMB test., 1:101; *he cried when she took the gun away*: ibid., 1:125; *she hid it "somewhere back of the house"*: ibid., 1:102; *at Rock Rest*: ibid., 1:101.

37   *"extremely sensitive," had a lot of pride*: ibid., JEC test. (Jun. 11, 1940), 1:214

37   *JCB died*: "Services Held for Mrs. Jennie Buntin," *NB*, Jun. 17, 1930, 17; "Funeral Today," *Tenn.*, Jun. 17, 1930, 3.

37-38   *"I have no idea … or brain"*: JCB, Certificate of Death, File No. 13076, Jun. 16, 1930, Ancestry.com, Tenn., U.S., Death Records, 1908-1965, database online.

38   *JCB bequests, "solid silver coffee service," "handsome bracelet," "token of affection"*: JCB Will (Jul. 12, 1929), probated Sept. 23, 1930, Davidson Co., Tenn., Wills, Vol. 47-48, 1930-1932, 139-140, Ancestry.com, Tenn., U.S., Wills and Probate Records, 1779-2008, database online.

38   *"being of a good … and fretter"*: Buntin Case 1, Dr. JB test., 1:57.

38   *"addicted," "suicide theories"*: ibid., RWW test. (Jun. 11, 1940), 2:506-507.

38   *showed friends the bullet hole*: ibid., HVA test. (Jun. 11, 1940), 1:193; ibid., Court of Appeals, NTC Def.-in-Error Reply Brief and Argument, 119.

38   *"boogers," "notions," "queer ideas"*: ibid., Dr. JB test.: 1:67, 1:68.

38   *"encircling gloom"*: ibid., Court of Appeals, NTC Def.-in-Error Reply Brief and Argument, 122.

38   *traveling up the Orinoco River*: ibid., RWW test., 1:505.

38   *LBH as friend and professional peer*: McCuddy Case 1, LBH depo., 20; *"bad habit"*: ibid., 21; *represented TCB, sometimes left him in jail*: ibid., 22-23.

38   *"prominent business institutions," "employ men addicted to drink"*: "W.C.T.U. Urges Dry Planks for Major Parties," *Tenn.*, Mar. 7, 1928, 1.

38-39   *RCC gave up whiskey*: "The Rogers Caldwell Story," *Tenn. Mag.*, Oct. 20, 1963, 7.

39   *"four-plus" drinker, Dr. JB wanted to see him more frequently*: Buntin Case 1, Dr. JB test.: 1:57, 1:62.

39   *broke into the house*: ibid., LBH test., 1:135-136.

39   *sisters fled, one went upstairs, the other went outside*: "Mrs. Buntin Tells Jury Husband Showed Suicidal Tendencies," *Tenn.*, Jun. 11, 1940, 11.

39   *not charged with breaking-in and larceny*: Buntin Case 1, BMB test., 1:132.

39   *paid fine for public drunkenness*: ibid., LBH test., 1:138; *Clare Britton, release of all civil liability for $75*: ibid., 1:136-137.

39   *TCB ran his car into a gully at RCC's brother-in-law's property*: ibid., Dr. JB test., 1:63; *"pretty blue"*: ibid.

39   *"rough," "rather nasty letter"*: ibid., LBH test., 1:137-139.

39   *TCB visited ECB, she gave him his $200 allowance*: ibid., ECB test., 1:172.

40   *BMB did not believe he had been drinking*: ibid., BMB test., 1:105-106.

40   *"nothing in the world" to the letter, settled on a Coca Cola*: ibid., LBH test., 1:137.

40   *nothing had upset their family relationship*: ibid., BMB test., 1:105-106; *looked through his belongings, Hermitage Club*: ibid., 1:130.

40   *"look around"*: ibid., ECB test., 1:172-173.

40   *Rock Jolly, GG summer retreat*: O'Neal, "Rock Jolly," Sections 7, 8.

40   *invited to the horse show, GG called another friend when BMB said TCB had not come home*: Buntin Case 1, GG test., 1:162.

41   *TCB's will*: ibid., 1:153-154, and Ex. 1, 1:155.

41   *"showed plainly ... had happened"*: ibid., ECB test., 1:173.

41   *identical will, in TCB's own handwriting*: ibid., JEC test., 1:210-211; ibid., ECB test., 1:175-176.

41   *"Yankee" soldiers burned down Rock Rest on Christmas day 1863*: RAC Diaries, 1855-1911, Accession No. 89-042 (Dec. 29, 1863), 5, TSLA-NT.

41   *Victorian, wood-construction*: "Turnip Patch with a Past," *Tenn. Mag.*, Nov. 20, 1949, 8.

41   *no safe, asked WAB to entrust GG with will*: Buntin Case 1, BMB test., 1:123.

41   *"look here"*: ibid., GG test., 1:145.

41-42   *GG's impression of the will, his safeguarding of it*: ibid., 1:146-157.

42   *JEC brought the will to NTC*: ibid., JEC test., 1:210.

42   *bank account*: ibid., BMB test., 1:129.

42   *SS's relationship to the Caldwells, "gentleman," "fellow who ... the gutters," "tooted somewhere," "lower grade ones ... York," "fairly well ... drunks"*: ibid., SS depo. (Jun. 8, 1940), submitted into evidence (Jun. 11, 1940), 1:197, 1:199, 1:200, 1:202, 1:203.

42   *first outreach to ECB*: ibid., BMB test., 1:119; *PAJ role*: ibid., CEA depo. (May 9, 1940), submitted into evidence (Jun. 11, 1940), 1:251.

43   *disappearance investigations, Atlanta office*: McCuddy Case 1, Stipulation, PAJ depo., filed in open court (Feb. 5, 1941), 7.

43   *Bertillon technique*: Chloe Govan, "In the Criminal-Catching Footsteps
          of Alphonse Bertillon," entry posted Mar. 10, 2020, francetoday.com/
          learn/history/in-the-criminal-catching-footsteps-of-alphonse-bertillon/;
          Ted Yeshion, Ph.D., "Anthropometry, The First System of Identifi-
          cation," *The Forensic Teacher Magazine*, no. 23 (Spring 2014): 46-51,
          fliphtml5.com/lvgc/suwt/basic/51-70.

43   *insufficient info for Bertillonage evaluation*: McCuddy Case 1, CEA depo.
          in Buntin Case 1 (May 9, 1940), submitted into evidence (Feb. 5, 1941),
          42; *FBI needed fingerprints*: ibid., 41; *NYL failed to check several places for
          info*: ibid., 19-21.

43   *McNeilly letter to NYL*: Buntin Case 1, CN test., Ex. F, 1:21.

43   *TCB's pilot license application photo*: ibid., CEA depo., 1:259.

43   *portrait parlé*: Yeshion, "Anthropometry," 46.

43   *TCB's "mug shot"*: Buntin Case 1, BMB test., Ex. A.

43-44   *average policy of $3,000*: ibid., WGB depo., NYL Assistant Actuary (May
          9, 1940), submitted into evidence (Jun. 11, 1940), 2:429.

44   *PAJ interviewed BMB*: ibid., PAJ test. (Jun. 11, 1940), 2:303-305.

44   *TCB's ring*: ibid., BMB test., 1:108; ibid., PAJ test., 2:304-305.

44   *did not believe TCB dead, fruit business in South America*: ibid., BMB
          test., 1:305.

44   *coverage of suicides*: Hudnut, *History of NYL*, 167; Spectator Co., "NYL,
          Twenty Payment Life Policy," *Handy Guide to Premium Rates, Applica-
          tions and Policies of 181 American Life Insurance Co.'s*, 34th edition (New
          York: Spectator, 1925), 842.

44   *"self-destruction" payout, conditions*: Spectator, "NYL, Twenty Payment
          Life Policy," 842.

44   *3.4 percent suicide rate, 1895-1905, 5-10 years into policies, committed by
          merchants, merchant-workers*: Hudnut, *History of NYL*, 92-93.

44   *investigated Tom for insurability, Committee approval*: Buntin Case 1,
          CEA depo., 1:275.

44   *"survey basis," "casual inquiries," "one eye on the money"*: ibid., 1:255, 1:258;
          no rewards: ibid., 1:249.

5.   *Nashville Trust Company v. New York Life*

45   *BMB lived with ECB until 1943*: *Nashville City Dir. 1943*, 119.

45   *dealer took back the LaSalle; sold his second car for $100*: Buntin Case 1,
          BMB test., 1:109,1:117.

45   *1935 saleswoman job*: *Nashville City Dir. 1935*, 222.

45   *1937 saleswoman job, Town & Country Shop*: ibid. *1937*, 143; "Shop's Demise
          Revives Old Memories," *Tenn.*, Dec. 30, 1973, Living Section, E-4.

45-46   *"Enoch Arden" marriage laws, "to meet intelligently"*: Judson T. Landis
          and Mary G. Landis, *Building a Successful Marriage*, 2nd edition (New
          York: Prentice-Hall, 1953), 245.

46   *one Enoch Arden legal option in Tenn., "well-founded" rumor*: Tenn.
          Code Ann. § 36-4-128(a) (2020); *reappearance of Enoch Arden spouse
          under option one*: ibid. and § 36-4-128(b); *second Enoch Arden legal option,
          "contracted," "shall be regarded as dissolved"*: ibid., § 36-3-102.

46   *"due proof" of death*: Spectator, "NYL, Twenty Payment Life Policy,"
      838.

47   *LBH as TCB's intimate friend*: McCuddy Case 1, LBH depo., 16-17;
      inquiry letters to twenty-five cities: ibid., 19.

47   *"decided blond ... red coloring"*: Buntin Case 1, BP test. (Jun. 11, 1940),
      Exs. 1-12, 1:224-237; *Sing-Sing*: ibid., CEA depo., 1:249.

47   *fall 1938 letters to-fro NTC and NYL*: ibid., CN test., Ex. H, 1:24-25; Ex.
      I, 1:26-27; Ex. J, 1:27-28; Ex. K, 1:28-30; *Dec. 16, 1938, affidavit and proof-
      of-death*: ibid., Ex. L, 1:31-32; *Dec. 27, 1938, NYL's response, "the evidence
      ... not to death"*: ibid., Ex. O, 1:41.

47   *$2,000 to $2,500 spent by late 1938*: ibid., CEA depo., 1:274; CEA test.
      (Jun. 11, 1940), 1:296.

47   *NTC filed lawsuit in Feb. 1939*: ibid., Transcript, Introduction, 1.

47   *"highly nervous and excitable condition," "aggravated ...difficulties"*: ibid.,
      NTC Declaration, 1:6; *"very unusual appearance"*: ibid., 1:8.

48   *NYL's response*: ibid., NYL Demurrer (filed May 22, 1939), 1:11.

48   *twelve male jurors*: ibid., Transcript, 1:27.

48   *TCB's will disappeared*: ibid., GG test., 1:145-149; *"stiff cardboard," "Mrs.
      Thomas Buntin"*: ibid., 1:149, 1:150; *"many other" Buntin files found*: ibid.,
      1:148.

49   *NTC president cannot explain will loss*: ibid., CN test., 1:44-45.

49   *"no doubt"*: ibid., GG test., 1:154.

49   *relationship was "all right"*: ibid., Dr. JB test., 1:64.

49   *"deep affection," "interrupt the pleasantness and sweetness"*: ibid., BMB
      test., 1:99, 1:100.

49   *"up on ... in the bottom," "vicious circle"*: ibid., 1:100, 1:101.

50   *BMB dismissed South America rumors*: ibid., 1:124; *TCB had given up fly-
      ing*: ibid., 1:131; *unintelligent man*: ibid.; *"No sir ... Yes ... he wasn't smart
      about that"*: ibid.

50   *"blue and melancholy," "very peculiar," "want ... his business"*: ibid., JD
      test., 1:185.

50   *"casual conversations"*: McCuddy Case 1, LBH depo., 18.

50   *TCB and a woman might be together somewhere*: Buntin Case 1, CEA
      depo., 1:276-277.

50   *"felonious seduction"*: James M. Roberson, *Roberson's New Ky. Criminal
      Law and Procedure, Both Statute and Common Law*, 2nd edition (Cincin-
      nati: W.H. Anderson, 1927), §§ 1012-1032, pp. 1244-1269; *felony offense of
      bigamy*: ibid., §§ 1035-1040, pp. 1270-1277.

50   *"There is ... Miss Betty McCuddy, did you know her?"*: Buntin Case 1, JD
      test., 1:188; *"Yes, sir... Tom left"*: ibid.; *"not very neat," "heavy set," "by a
      long shot"*: ibid., 1:190.

51   *JD identified the woman in the photo, "mighty good," "good justice"*: ibid.
      and Ex. A; *"good salary" of $150 per month*: ibid., 1:188-189.

51   *"very untidy," "terrible condition," "nice," "always looked like her neck was
      dirty"*: ibid., HVA test., 1:194.

51   *HVA and wife friends of TCB and BMB*: "Insurance Man Knew Couple," *FWST*, Nov. 28, 1953, 2.

51   *"accounting for the tastes," "delightful," "matter of argument"*: Buntin Case I, courtroom exchange during HVA testimony, 1:195.

51   *"very attractive girl"*: "Insurance Man Knew Couple," *FWST*, Nov. 28, 1953, 2.

51   *JEC's probable appearance*: Image no. 642, W.B. Newman photograph, ca. 1937, Photographic Archives, TSLA-NT.

52   *turned the tables on the treasurer accusing him of fraud*: James E. Caldwell, *Recollections of a Life Time* (Nashville: Baird-Ward Press, 1923), 132-135 (162-165 of 322, pdf version).

52   *CTT's pole-cutting clashes*: "Another Bill Filed," *Tenn.*, Jul. 8, 1906, 11; "President Caldwell on that Pole-Cutting," *Tenn.*, Aug. 18, 1907, 7.

52   *JEC survived AT&T Vail's financial threats*: Caldwell, *Recollections*, 204-205, 206 (234-235, 236 of 322, pdf version).

52   *"never let … forget," "dignified aristocrat"*: "A Cornerstone in Banking History was Placed in 1883," *Tenn.*, Sept. 4, 1983, Business Section, 3-G.

52   *"seems to know … didn't it?"*: Buntin Case I, JEC test., 1:220; *"Yes," "they put in … looked at"*: ibid.

52   *newspaper story*: "Jury Hears Buntin May be Alive; Woman's Name Enters into Case," *Tenn.*, Jun. 12, 1940, 4.

Part Two – Betty

6.   Betty Edwards McCuddy

55   *"Dead," "died … night"*: "Dead," *HL*, Nov. 20, 1903, 1.

55   *"bright-eyed, cherry faced," "fell asleep in Jesus"*: "A Bright Child Passes Away," *Dem.*, Nov. 23, 1906, 1.

55   *"one of … Russellville," "very fashionable wedding"*: "Ky. Social Events," *Tenn.*, Jul. 18, 1902, 8.

55   *settled in Logan Co., Ky., married first cousin*: Rev. G.W. Beale, D.D., "Col. Nathaniel Pope and His Descendants," *William and Mary College Quarterly Historical Magazine* 12, no. 4 (Apr. 1904): 250.

55   *Hester of "superior cultivation," "uncommon conversational powers"*: J.M. Armstrong, "George T. Edwards," *The Biographical Encyclopaedia of Ky. of the Dead and Living Men* (Cincinnati: Western Methodist Book Concern, 1878), 315-316 (320-321 of 806, pdf version).

55-56   *William and Penelope Edwards Pope; he surveyed Louisville*: Kathleen Jennings, "The Pope Family," *Louisville's First Families* (Louisville: Standard Printing, 1920), 69-71 (14-16 of 184, pdf version).

56   *befriended Lincoln*: "A Responsible Place," *SLPD*, Feb. 22, 1887, 2.

56   *A.G. Edwards investment firm started in 1887*: "A.G. Edwards, Inc. History," fundinguniverse.com/company-histories/a-g-edwards-inc-history/.

56   *McCuddy settled in Logan Co., thirty acres of "excelent corn," $4.50 per acre, "fatning hoggs"*: Letter, Isaac B. McCuddy to Mary and Sally McCuddy (Oct. 30, 1829), Accession No. SC 1561_F1_09, McCuddy Family Papers, 1810-1858, 1, KHS-FF.

56   *Flint Ridge*: David Bosse, "Flint Ridge," Lo-64, Ky. Historic Resources Inventory (Mar. 1979); K. Gibbs, "Baylor House, Baylor-McCuddy House," Lo-64, Ky. Historic Resources Inventory (Summer 1980), "Logan Co.-Houses-Flint Ridge" folder, KHS-FF.

56   *haunted by Frances Guinn Baylor*: "Old Baylor Home, 'Flint Ridge'," *AE*, May 7, 1970, 23.

56   *"thorough institution," "moral and religious," no saloons, "attractions of vice"*: Bethel College, *Yearbook*, 1894-95, v, "Bethel College" folder, LCPL-RK.

56   *RFM activities at Bethel*: Literary Societies and Greek Fraternities, "Vignettes of Bethel, 1895," 16, 33, 59, "Bethel College" folder, LCPL-RK.

56   *RFM appearance*: Bethel College, *Yearbook*, "Editors," "Bethel College" folder, LCPL-RK

56   *GBE hired RFM at Deposit Bank*: "Mr. Hodgen Resigns," *HL*, Aug. 28, 1897, 1.

56   *MED graduated from Logan Female College in 1897, bachelor's degree*: Edward Coffman and Edward Coffman Jr., *Through My Father's Eyes, The Story of Logan Co., Ky.* (Nashville: Parthenon Press, 2004), 183.

56   *"spoken of … know him"*: "Mr. Hodgen Resigns," *HL*, Aug. 28, 1897, 1.

56   *"greatest … of the summer"*: "Russellville, Ky., Society," *Tenn.*, Aug. 23, 1901, 8.

56   *RFM promoted to cashier*: Coffman and Coffman, *Through My Father's Eyes*, 138.

56   *BEM's date of birth*: BEP, Certificate of Death, File No. 85378, Nov. 29, 1972, Ancestry.com, Tex., U.S., Death Certificates, 1903-1982, database online.

57   *Mockingbird Hill, The Oaks, Oakhill*: Mary Cronan, "Russellville Historic District [Ky.]," National Register of Historic Places Nomination Form (Washington, D.C.: U.S. Dept. of the Interior, National Park Service, 1976), Section 8:19 (the Roberts-Edwards House); *architecture and history*: ibid.

57   *"one of the … healthiest villages"*: George W. Locke and R.C. Hunt, "Synopsis of the Early History of Logan Co.," *Atlas of Logan Co., Ky. from Surveys and Recorded Plans 1877* (Owensboro, Ky.: Cook & McDowell Pub., reprinted 1980), 1.

58   *buildings likely viewed from Mockingbird Hill*: Cronan, "Russellville Historic District," Section 8:14, 20, 23, 25.

58   *county courthouse, exterior*: ibid., Section 8:10; Logan Co. Genealogical Society, Facebook postings, Jan. 1, 2021, and Apr. 7, 2021.

58   *African American settlement*: Meredith Martin, Michael Morrow, and L. Martin Perry, "Black Bottom Historic District [Ky.]," National Register of Historic Places Nomination Form (Washington, D.C.: U.S. Dept. of the Interior, National Park Service, 2010).

59   *"book of hope" white leather cover*: "Colored Leather for Bibles, Some

Gossip about the Leather Market," *Boot and Shoe Recorder* 53, Leather Section, no. 15 (Jul. 8, 1908): 97.

59   *white mob lynchings*: Coffman and Coffman, *Through My Father's Eyes*, 226.

59   *Jan. 1908 night-rider destruction*: ibid., 229; Anna Youngman, "The Tobacco Pools of Ky. and Tenn.," *Journal of Political Economy* 18, no. 1 (Jan. 1910): 36, 41; Terry Bisson, "Tobacco Terror," entry posting undated, originally published in *American History* (Sept./Oct. 2016), historynet.com/tobacco-terror.htm; "Night Riders Out Again," *NYT*, Jul. 30, 1909, 4.

59   *lynching of four Black Bottom men accused as "troublemakers," hanging tree*: Coffman and Coffman, *Through My Father's Eyes*, 230.

59   *RFM named as Deposit Bank vice-president*: ibid., 138.

59   *RFM elected to Russellville city council*: "New City Council," *Dem.*, Dec. 6, 1907, 1.

59   *WRM born Jun. 25, 1909*: WRM, Ancestry.com, U.S., Veterans Administration Master Index, 1917-1940, database online.

59   *MCM death, causes*: MCM, Certificate of Death, File No. 16730, May 10, 1919, Ancestry.com, Ky., U.S., Death Records, 1852-1965, database online.

59   *BEM childhood activities*: "Russellville," *CJ*, Mar. 14, 1914, 8; "Prize Winners," *CJ*, Aug. 12, 1917, Junior Section, 2.

59   *sent to Nazareth Academy in 1919*: untitled, *RM*, Jan. 8, 1920, 4; *leaves in May 1923*: "Russellville," *CJ*, Sept. 10, 1922, 27.

59   *"disposition … innovations"*: "Nazareth Academy," *CJ*, Oct. 27, 1922, Special Section (International Federation Catholic Alumnae), 26.

60   *BEM started senior year of high school at Ward-Belmont, fall 1923*: "Local Briefs," *RM*, Aug. 3, 1923, 3; Ward-Belmont, *Milestones Yearbook* (1924), 80.

60   *Del Vers club*: Ward-Belmont, *Milestones Yearbook* (1924), 171; *twenty-three state clubs*: ibid., 156-159.

60   *thirty-acre campus, Belmont mansion owned by Adelicia Hayes Franklin Acklen Cheatham*: "Belmont Mansion," entry posting undated, www.americanheritage.com/content/belmont-mansion.

60   *Angola, sale of plantation and enslaved persons*: Louisiana Prison Museum & Cultural Center, "History of the State Penitentiary," www.angolamuseum.org/history.

60   *"business affairs," "fill … responsibility," manage their own estates*: Ward-Belmont, *Catalogue and Announcement of the Ward-Belmont School for Young Women, 1922-1923* (Nashville: pub. not given, 1923), 22.

60   *"open to women," "every girl … stenography," diversity of careers*: advertisement, Catherine Filene, ed., *Careers for Women*, Intercollegiate Vocational Guidance Association (1920), loc.gov/resource/rbpe.07905000.

60   *"beyond the capabilities of the gentler sex," specific examples*: "Unusual Jobs for Unusual Women," *The Office Economist* 6, no. 3 (Mar. 1924): 8-9.

62   *Gregg shorthand methodology*: John Robert Gregg, S.C.D, *Gregg*

Shorthand, A Light-Line Phonography for the Millions (New York: Gregg Pub., 1929), vii.

62   *read incessantly, quoted Kipling, "good joke," "jocular side"*: "McCuddy-Buntin Tale of Wide Interest," *NDL*, Dec. 4, 1953, 2.

62   *"intelligent," "strongly independent," "steady"*: JS reporter's notes, Mrs. Warren Walton, Allensville, Ky., Box 146, Folder 9, JS-VU.

62   *"beaus," not interested in boyfriends*: McCuddy Case 1, RFM depo. (Jul. 26, 1940), 20.

7.   Betty's Great-Uncle – George B. Edwards

63   *"cup of sorrow and grief," "overflowing"*: "George E. Duncan," *HL*, Oct. 16, 1903, 1.

63   *Geo. E. Duncan (a different man than the son of Wm. M. Duncan and Eva Booker) killed in hunting accident*: ibid.; *Hester Pope Duncan's suicide*: "Miss Hester Duncan," *Tenn.*, Oct. 14, 1904, 8.

63   *GBE at Yale, William Howard Taft his roommate; receives law degree from the U. of Virginia*: "Russellville Man Dies Here," *CJ*, Dec. 16, 1929, 1.

63   *seventeen "good" lawyers*: "Logan Co.," *CJ*, Aug. 7, 1881, 6.

64   *candidate for Hawaiian position*: "Will Helm," *CJ*, Jan. 26, 1897, morning edition, 1.

63   *turned to banking*: "New Board," *HL*, Aug. 5, 1891, 4.

63   *Russellville's first millionaire*: "McCuddy-Buntin Tale," *NDL*, Dec. 4, 1953, 2.

64   *"sound as a dollar"*: "The Deposit Bank," *HL*, Jan. 12, 1906, 1; *"conservatism, safety, and soundness," "no dummies"*: ibid.; *burglar-proof safe*: ibid.

64   *"reckless firing"*: Frank Triplett, *The Life, Times and Treacherous Death of Jesse James*, as dictated by Mrs. Jesse James and Mrs. Zerelda Samuel (Chicago: J.H. Chambers & Co., 1882), 64-65 (82-83 of 479, pdf version); David Morton, *The Nortons of Russellville, Ky.* (Philadelphia: J.B. Lippincott Co., 1891), 27 (26 of 83, pdf version).

64   *$9,000-$19,000 heist*: Coffman and Coffman, *Through My Father's Eyes*, 213; "Jesse James Bank Robbery is a Famous Historical Event," *NDL*, Aug. 31, 1992, Logan Co. Bicentennial Section, 27; "Some Reminiscences," *HL*, Sept. 21, 1889, 6.

64   *James' brothers masterminded, hid out nearby*: Triplett, *Jesse James*, 65, 379 (82, 434 of 479, pdf version).

64   *GBE's thumb ring, advice to child*: John Fetterman, "Kentuckians Still Ponder Missing Betty McCuddy," *Tenn.*, Nov. 15, 1953, 16.

64   *"old fat carcass," "best of fellows," "ablest man … Kentucky," "Bourbon Democracy," "Bill"*: Walter P. Armstrong, "Letters of Roommates: William H. Taft and George B. Edwards," *American Bar Association Journal* 34, no. 5 (May 1948): 383.

64   *value of GBE assets in 1924*: Fetterman, "Kentuckians Still Ponder," *Tenn.*, Nov. 15, 1953, 16.

64   *serious illness*: "Russellville," *CJ*, Jul. 18, 1886, 7; *went south for his health*: "Russellville," *CJ*, Feb. 13, 1887, 6.

65   *GBE began will in Oct. 1924*: Office of Clerk, Logan Co., Ky., Will Bk.

Q, 280-298 (will dated Oct. 22, 1924), LCA-RK; *FCTC named as executor and trustee*: ibid., 290 (Item 18, Oct. 22, 1924); *bequests to MDM and family*: ibid., 281 (Item 4, Oct. 22, 1924); *JCE bequest*: ibid., 280 (Item 2., Oct. 22, 1924); *restrictions on the bequest to MDM*: ibid., 285 (Item 10, Oct. 22, 1924); *distribution of residuary estate*: ibid., 288-290 (Item 17, Oct. 22, 1924); *housekeeper typed the will and codicils*: ibid., 285 (Item 10, Oct. 22, 1924); *codicil 15 executed May 20, 1929*: ibid., 298.

65   *"dramatic collapse"*: "Exchange in Another Big Price Break," *PCDN*, Oct. 28, 1929, 1.

65   *"slight operation"*: "Russellville Man Dies Here," *CJ*, Dec. 16, 1929, 1.

66   *GBE's death, causes*: GBE, Certificate of Death, File No. 31910, filing date illegible, Ancestry.com, Ky. Death Records, 1852-1953, database online.

8. Belknap Hardware, Louisville

67   *BEM hair-do mid-1920s*: Buntin Case 1, JD test., Ex. A.

67   *number of kiss curls equaled number of men kissed*: Debbie L. Sessions, "1920s Hairstyles History – Long Hair to Bobbed Hair," entry posting undated, https://vintagedancer.com/1920s/1920s-long-hair-to-bobbed-hair/.

67   *1924 populations of Louisville and Nashville*: Caron's Directory of the City of Louisville for 1924 (Louisville: Caron Dir. Co., 1924) (hereafter "*Louisville City Dir. year*"), 21; *Nashville City Dir. 1924*, 7 (citing the 1920 Census population).

68   *BEM rented apt. 34 in the first Weissinger-Gaulbert building*: *Louisville City Dir. 1926*, 1314; *prestigious*: "Apartment Living, Many Louisvillians Whose Homes are Now in Flats," *CJ*, Mar. 6, 1904, 14.

68-69   *history and architectural style*: Mary Jean Kinsman, "Weissinger-Gaulbert Apartments – Third Street Annex [Ky.]," National Register of Historic Places Nomination Form (Washington, D.C.: U.S. Dept. of the Interior, National Park Service, 1977), Section 8:1; *The Inland Architect and News Record*, 40, no. 6 (1903): 6, 39.

69   *$85 per month rent for a two-room flat*: advertisement, *CJ*, Nov. 14, 1924, 21.

69   *likely furnishings, interior style of the period*: Edward Stratton Holloway, *The Practical Book of Furnishing the Small House and Apartment* (Philadelphia: J.B. Lippincott Co., 1922), 101-102, 133, 137.

69   *grocery store on ground-level floor:* advertisement, Julius Strauss's Grocery Store, *CJ*, Sept. 6, 1925, 76.

70   *Wilderness Road store, "Book Lovers' Book Shop"*: "Old Bookshop in Brown Hotel Closing Doors," *CJ*, Jul. 13, 1958, 35.

70   *BEM's first job in stenography, Belknap Hardware*: *Louisville City Dir. 1926*, 1314.

70   *Morris Belknap, classmate of GBE at Yale*: John Kleber, ed. in chief, "Morris Burke Belknap," *The Encyclopedia of Louisville* (Lexington: Univ. Press of Ky., 2001), 81.

70   *new office building in 1923 where the Galt House was located*: "New Concerns Bring $2,846,000 Capital Here in Single Year," *CJ*, Jan. 1, 1923, 22.

70   *"largest … in the world"*: advertisement, *CJ*, Jan. 1, 1926, 18.

70   *scientific principles for improved workspace, increased productivity*: Frederick Winslow Taylor, *The Principles of Scientific Management* (New York: Harper & Bros. Pub., 1911).

70   *"automatic telephone system"*: "Belknap Offices Nearly Finished," *CJ*, Aug. 10, 1923, 14.

70   *centralized coat rooms abolished*: "Physical Factors in Office Planning," *The Office Economist* 5, no. 7 (Jul. 1923): 11-12.

70   *benefits of steel office furniture over wood*: "A Co-operative Desk," advertisement, Art Metal, *The Office Economist* 6, no. 2 (Feb. 1924); "What Will Your Equipment be Worth Five Years from Today?," advertisement, Art Metal, *The Office Economist* 6, no. 5 (May 1924); "A Reasonable Expectation," advertisement, Art Metal, *The Office Economist* 5, no. 2 (Feb. 1923).

71   *"scientifically placed" lighting globes, cafeteria, dance floor*: "Belknap Offices Nearly Finished," *CJ*, Aug. 10, 1923, 14.

71   *appropriate stenographer business attire*: "Shopping with Peggy True, The Tweed Suit," *CJ*, Mar. 1, 1926, 7; *Margaret Rorke hat*: "Perfect Hat Arrives for Business Women," *CJ*, Sept. 13, 1926, 4.

71   *South Fourth Street shops, businesses on the east side, mid-1920s, walking north from Broadway*: *Louisville City Dir. 1926*, 2572 (600 block, Fourth South).

71   *"Arctic New Air"*: "Kentucky's New Cooling System," *CJ*, Jul. 4, 1926, 20.

71   *"The Untamed Lady"*: "Ky., Gloria Swanson," *CJ*, Jun. 6, 1926, 33.

71   *"super thriller"*: "Phantom of the Opera," *CJ*, Apr. 11, 1926, 33.

71   *500 block of the east side of South Fourth Street, then walking north on North Fourth Street toward the Ohio River*: *Louisville City Dir. 1924*, 2046 (500 block, Fourth South).

71-72   *Starks Building and north, Busath's, S.S. Kresge*: ibid., 2043-2044 (400 and 500 block, Fourth South).

72   *daily transportation line up at Belknap*: Image No. ULPA CS 101780, Caulfield & Shook photograph, 1929, Caulfield & Shook Collection, Photographic Archives, University of Louisville, Louisville, Ky.

72   *American Eagle display of hardware products in lobby*: "Turning Back the Clock," *Blue Grass News* 3, no. 2 (Feb. 1964), 8, Box 9, BR-UL.

72   *"a mole … baseball game … in my life"*: Roy F. Soule, "Belknap's Business, The Store that Started With a Postage Stamp and How it Stuck on the Job," *Hardware Dealers Magazine* (Aug. 1925), Box 9, BR-UL.

72   *"most complicated … instrument"*: "The Trouble of Being Right," *The Office Economist* 5, no. 1 (Jan. 1923): 10; see also, Walter Kay Smart and Louis William McKelvey, *Business Letters* (New York: Harper & Bros. Pub., 1933).

73   *color-coding system (lemon, pink, green) for stenos, internal distribution, and filing*: "Is Your Filing System a Waste Paper Bailer?," *The Office Economist* 5, no. 5 (May 1923): 7.

73   *"House Rules … Employees," "General Conduct" prohibited activities,*

sanctions for errors: "Turning back the clock. Remember when?," *Blue Grass News* 4, no. 2 (Feb. 1965), Box 8, BR-UL.

73   "*live and vital*": Rupert P. Sorelle and John Robert Gregg, *Secretarial Studies* (New York: Gregg Pub. Co., 1922), 71-72.

73   "*sloppy*" letters: memorandum of Charles W. Allen Jr., Aug. 17, 1967, Box 9, "Company notes" folder, BR-UL; "*mistreated*" words: "The Trouble of Being Right," *The Office Economist*, 5, no. 1 (Jan. 1923): 10.

74   *Fourth Street shops, businesses on the west side heading south from West Main Street*: *Louisville City Dir. 1924*, 2043 (300 block, Fourth South), 2044-2045 (500 block, Fourth South).

74   *Bon Ton's "Black-Bottom" shoe, "blackest of black velvet … touches of rattlesnake … and bow," "spike heels only"*: advertisement, *CJ*, Nov. 28, 1926, 19.

74   *Seelbach Hotel, F. Scott Fitzgerald, The Great Gatsby wedding scene*: "The Seelbach Hilton Hotel, History," historichotels.org/us/hotels-resorts/the-seelbach-hilton-louisville/history.php; *Al Capone at the Seelbach*: ibid.

74   *bridal outfit, Besten and Langan storefront*: Image No. ULPA CS 071996, Caulfield & Shook photograph, 1926, Caulfield & Shook Collection, Photographic Archives, University of Louisville, Louisville, Ky.

74   *South Fourth Street shops on the west side, heading south from the Seelbach Hotel to Broadway*: *Louisville City Dir. 1926*, 2571-2572 (500 block, Fourth South), 2572 (600 block, Fourth South).

9.   Nashville Beckons

75   "*the girl … Love Pirate*," "*pretty, young Scotch girl*": "Love Pirates," *CE*, Jan. 10, 1909, 34; "*disturbing … home*," "*gray respectability*": ibid., 35; "*girl*," "*polygamous by nature*," "*trained … penitentiary*": ibid.; *workplace rules*: ibid.

75-76   "*despairingly*," "*dashes …billows*," "*Nothing impedes her*": "Western Women," *VG*, Apr. 16, 1833, 3.

76   *BEM in Louisville three years*: McCuddy Case 1, RFM depo., 22.

76   *moved to Nashville at friend's urging in 1928, opening at James E. Caldwell and Sons Insurance Co.*: ibid., JCE depo. (Aug. 26, 1940), 12.

76   *hired as stenographer, promoted to executive secretary answering to TCB, office manager*: ibid.

76   "*mannish*," *did not care about clothes or personal appearance*: JS reporter's notes, Mrs. Byrne Evans, Box 146, Folder 9, JS-VU.

76   *1928 work and residence*: *Nashville City Dir. 1928*, 856; *1929 residence*: ibid. *1929*, 804, 827, 1345; *1930 residence*: ibid. *1930*, 775.

76   "*Miss Betty*," *spent about $300 to $450 per year*: Buntin Case 1, GMT test. (Jun. 12, 1940), 2:510.

76-77   "*very intelligent, very intellectual*": McCuddy Case 1, JCE depo., 12; "*at all*": ibid., 13-14.

77   "*very pleasant casual acquaintance*": ibid., LBH depo., 23.

77   *ELS married to WAB*: "Society," *Tenn.*, Oct. 22, 1914, 5.

77   *best manager he ever had*: Buntin Case 1, JEC test., 1:218; "*crazy*" *about his boys*: ibid., 1:209.

77   *witness refused to answer whether JEC edged out BEM*: ibid., JD test., 1:182.

77   *staff let go by TCB*: McCuddy Case 1, JCE depo., 12; ibid., LBH depo., 23.

Part Three - Betty and Tom

10.   Rendezvous and Betty's Disappearance

81   *BEM returned home*: "Russellville Notes," *CJ*, Jul. 20, 1930, 10.

81   *residuary estate funds paid to BEM and WRM*: McCuddy Case 1, RFM depo., 18.

81   *maid of honor for close friend, who moved after marriage*: "Russellville Notes," *CJ*, May 12, 1929, 6.

81   *HF a friend*: McCuddy Case 1, Stipulation, HF statement, filed in open court (Feb. 5, 1941), 1; *she tended to stay in at night*: ibid., RFM depo., 22; *HF a riding companion*: ibid., Stipulation, HF statement, 1.

81   *restless, wanted to work*: Buntin Case 1, RFM depo. (May 30, 1939), submitted into evidence (Jun. 11, 1940), 2:328.

81   *hobbies*: JS reporter's notes, Mrs. Warren Walton, Allensville, Ky., Box 146, Folder 9, JS-VU.

82   *WRM's graduation*: "U.S. Naval Academy, Annapolis, Md.," *CJ*, Jun. 11, 1931, morning edition, 18; *visit to Russellville*: "Society, Personal Mention," *CLC*, Jun. 19, 1931, 3.

82   *WRM an ensign on USS Arkansas in 1931*: U.S. Dept. of the Navy, Bureau of Navigation, *Navy Directory, Offices of the U.S. Navy and Marine Corps* (Washington, D.C.: Government Printing Office,1931), 58 (58 of 279, pdf version).

82   *"Mac" characteristics, "feminine company and conversation"*: U.S. Naval Academy, *Lucky Bag 1931* (Chicago: Rogers Printing Co., 1931), 224 (224 of 593, pdf version).

82   *distilled spirits' production in Ky. and tax revenues*: Thomas H. Appleton Jr., "Prohibition and Politics in Ky.: The Gubernatorial Campaign and Election of 1915," *Register of the Ky. Historical Society* 75, no. 1 (Jan. 1977): 33.

82   *city parking ordinance*: "City Dads Active," *NDL*, Mar. 18, 1921, 1.

82-83   *officer saw the young woman and man, "fine young lady," "virtue … reproach"*: Buntin Case 1, ID depo. (Sept. 19, 1939), submitted into evidence (Jun. 11, 1940), 2:340.

83   *"Buntin," from Nashville*: ibid., 2:335, 2:336.

83   *HF knew of the meetings*: JS reporter's notes, HF, Box 146, Folder 9, JS-VU.

83   *daily business at Shugart's*: "Country store tradition maintained by Shugarts," *NDL*, Aug. 26, 1974, 2.

83-84   *woman driving back-forth between Russellville and Franklin*: Buntin Case 1, JTS depo. (Aug. 30, 1939), submitted into evidence (Jun. 11, 1940), 2:356-357.

84   *bootlegging car, told JHM*: ibid., 2:357, 2:359.

84   *AEE spotted woman driving back-forth in front of his store*: ibid., AEE

depo. (Sept. 11, 1939), submitted into evidence (Jun. 11, 1940), 2:382; *customer asked for a beer, got a Coca-Cola*: ibid., 2:368; *"seemed to get … himself"*: ibid.

84-85   *locust-tree thicket, tore his clothes rabbit hunting*: ibid., 2:367-368.

85   *"Where the hell is she going?," "wicked sort of fellow," "Search me, I don't know," fear of slandering "someone"*: ibid., 2:369, 2:380.

85   *"nice-looking people," "sport model, sportily painted"*: ibid., TBT depo. (Sept. 11, 1939), submitted into evidence (Jun. 11, 1940), 2:392, 2:393.

86   *legacy of stills "every 100 yards" along streams*: "The History of Robertson Co.," *Goodspeed's History of Tenn.* (Nashville: Goodspeed Pub. Co., 1886), reprint by David L. Sanford, TNGenWeb Project, Tenn. Records Repository, entry posting undated, 6 (pdf version).

86   *did not pay further attention*: Buntin Case 1, TBT depo., 2:395.

86   *JTS's tip-off, followed the woman*: ibid., JRB depo. (Aug. 30, 1939), submitted into evidence (Jun. 11, 1940), 2:343-344.

86   *hooked the bumpers, sheriff jumped out with a gun, "Mr. Ed, don't do that," "Why Tom, is that you?," "all right," "Tom's girl"*: ibid., 2:345, 2:346; *"good people … good reputation"*: ibid., 2:351, 2:352.

86-87   *JHM also knew her*: ibid., JHM depo. (Aug. 30, 1939), submitted into evidence (Jun. 11, 1940), 2:362-363.

87   *sheriff informed TBT of TCB's disappearance two months later*: ibid., TBT depo., 2:396.

87   *RFM heard of the meetings from Coleman Taylor*: McCuddy Case 1, RFM depo., 13; *never confirmed the information at the time*: ibid.

87   *Russellville, Ky., intermediate airfield in 1931*: U.S. Army, Air Corps, "Air Navigation Map No. 48, Louisville, Ky. to Nashville, Tenn.," *Aeronautical Strip Maps of the U.S.* (Washington, D.C.: Air Corps, 1927, rev. Sept. 1934).

87   *J.H. Woods' story of the airplane landing in Logan Co., Ky.*: JS reporter's notes, Box 146, Folder 9, JS-VU.

87   *"visiting pilots" required to give information that Woods requested*: U.S. Dept. of Commerce, Aeronautics Branch, *Intermediate Landing Field Rules: May 20, 1930* (Washington, D.C.: Government Printing Office, 1938), #22, 2.

87   *would notify "Washington"*: JS reporter's notes, Box 146, Folder 9, JS-VU.

88   *"very distinctly," "left"*: McCuddy Case 1, RFM depo., 3.

88   *last purchase May 26, 1931, balance of $148.50*: McCuddy Case 1, GMT test. in Buntin Case 1, filed in open court (Feb. 5, 1941), 1, 3.

88   *BEM wrote a $50 check in the lobby, left around $8 in account*: McCuddy Case 1, RFM depo., 3; *"good-bye," "so-long," "something like that"*: ibid.; *11 a.m. bus, round-trip ticket*: ibid.

88   *sat near HF*: "McCuddy-Buntin Tale," *NDL*, Dec. 4, 1953, 2.

88   *planned to go to Nashville*: McCuddy Case 1, Stipulation, HF statement, 1.

88   *"only a small bag"*: "McCuddy-Buntin Tale," *NDL*, Dec. 4, 1953, 2.

88   *walked her to the Nashville bus*: McCuddy Case 1, Stipulation, HF state-
        ment, 2.
88   *trips to Nashville, often stayed at the boarding house*: ibid., RFM depo., 4.
88   *MDM played bridge, Dunbar Cave*: "Clarksvillians Are Enjoying Dun-
        bar Cave During the Hot Weather," *CLC*, Jun. 30, 1931, 3.
88   *BEM's stated return*: McCuddy Case 1, RFM depo., 19; *never went to the
        boarding house*: ibid., 5; *"cordial, pleasant," "affectionate"*: ibid.
89   *"very independent," "would not ... restraint," "thought her ... business"*:
        ibid., 11, 15; *did not lie, parents not her confidants*: ibid., 11, 14; *Grace's
        check paid, returned to the bank*: ibid., 5.
89   *balance owed of $98.50*: Buntin Case 1, GMT test., 2:511. (Fergus never
        paid the balance: McCuddy Case 1, RFM depo., 6.)
89   *discrete investigation, did not contact the police or media*: McCuddy Case
        1, RFM depo., 6, 23; *"unusually intelligent," "did not ... her trail"*: ibid.,
        7; *checked schools and a convent*: ibid.; *RFM and a former sheriff go to
        Nashville to investigate matters*: ibid., 6; *told FCTC*: ibid., 24; *BEM's
        Nashville bank account*: ibid., 12.
89   *called JCE at home Sat. evening*: ibid., JCE depo., 2; *Mrs. Frazier and her
        sister*: ibid., 3.
89   *felt his daughter was dead*: ibid., 4; *JCE returned to the Fraziers*: ibid.
90   *"some things," BEM and TCB "running around," "common talk"*: ibid.;
        JCE found facts in Nashville: ibid., 5-6; *BEM asked the cab driver when
        the Pan Am left, timing supported going south to New Orleans*: ibid., 5.
90   *JCE did not confirm BEM's New Orleans' destination but was convinced she
        went south*: ibid., RFM depo., 18; *learned of TCB's disappearance*: ibid., 16;
        *"on two or three occasions," "man of ... intelligence," "busted," "owed more
        ... pay"*: ibid., 17, 25; *"highly extravagant, rich people"*: ibid., 25.
90   *$2,900 suites*: "Hilo Greets Hawkeye State," *HTH*, Mar. 17, 1921, 1, 6;
        "Two Palatial Liners Sail for this Port," *SFE*, Feb. 16, 1921, 13.
90   *ESB and BEM*: "Locals," *NDL*, Sept. 3, 1931, 4.
90   *ESB, HSK, and/or husbands visited MDM, RFM in Russellville*: "Local
        Briefs," *RM*, May 18, 1923, 3; untitled, *RM*, Jan. 17, 1924, 4.
90   *not aware of family trying to find TCB*: McCuddy Case 1, RFM depo., 16;
        no publicity or police, possibility BEM was with TCB: ibid., 17.
91   *radio stations*: ibid., JCE depo., 11; *"agreed that if she had ... no effect ...
        all things together"*: ibid., 12.
91   *"disappeared of her own will and accord," stopped looking*: ibid., RFM
        depo., 24.

11.   Brownsville, Texas

92   *"Thomas D. Palmer ... in the city"*: "City Briefs," *BH*, Sept. 28, 1931, 6.
93   *NYL enterprise in the early 1900s*: Hudnut, *History of NYL*, 11.
93   *Tex. Robertson Act requirements for out-of-state insurance cos.*: H.P.N.
        Gammel, "Insurance—Requiring Investment in Tex. of Portion of
        Reserve Funds, H.B. No. 112," *The Laws of Tex.: Supplement Volume
        to the Original Ten Volumes 1822-1897* (Austin: Gammel's Book Store,
        1907), 316-319.

93   *motives for the Robertson Act, "good money"*: Winton C. Beard, "An Epitaph for the Robertson Law," *Journal of Risk and Insurance* 32, no. 4 (Dec. 1965): 598; *NYL withdrew from business in Tex.*: ibid.

93   *"Texas ... standpoint"*: Charles Hall, "In Our Valley," *BH*, Feb. 21, 1930, 1.

93   *"exceedingly difficult ... located," easy to change names*: McCuddy Case 1, CEA depo. in Buntin Case 1 (May 9, 1940), filed in open court (Feb. 5, 1941), 41.

94   *African American Elizabeth McClinton in Louisville, from Miss.*: Louisville City Dir. *1925*, 1317.

94   *Brownsville's 1850 population*: Antonio N. Zavaleta, "'The Twin Cities': A Historical Synthesis of the Socio-Economic Interdependence of the Brownsville-Matamoros Border Community," *Studies in Brownsville History*, Milo Kearney, ed., Univ. of Tex. Rio Grande Valley & Tex. Southmost College Regional History Series, UTRGV Digital Library, The Univ. of Tex. – Rio Grande Valley ("UTRGV") (1986), 140.

94   *Ruby Red grapefruit*: The Tex. Citrus Industry, "Our History," entry posted Oct. 7, 2015, texascitrusindustry.com/2015/10/07/texas-citrus-mutual/.

94   *Dust Bowl in Tex.*: Donald Worster, Tex. State Historical Association, "Dust Bowl," *Handbook of Tex.*, entry updated Jul. 27, 2023, tshaonline.org/handbook/entries/dust-bowl/.

94   *Valley vegetable crops*: A.H. Belo Corp., *1943-1944 Tex. Almanac and State Industrial Guide, The Encyclopedia of Tex.* (Dallas: *Dallas Morning News*, 1943), 132,146-147.

94   *"finest ... the world"*: "Forty of the Many Special Things for Which We are Thankful on this New Era Thanksgiving Day for the Lower Rio Grande Valley Activity," (no. 8), advertisement, Rio Grande Valley Corporation, *BH*, Nov. 25, 1931, 2.

94   *county problems*: H.M. Skelton, Co. Auditor, *Annual Report of the Co. Auditor, Cameron Co., Tex. (Aug. 1, 1930-July 31, 1931)*, BCAH-UTA.

94   *"Magic Valley," population*: "Importance of Rio in Development of Valley Pointed Out," *BH*, Jun. 26, 1932, 10.

94   *1931 aerial view*: Skelton, *Annual Report of the Co. Auditor*, 11; "Modern Brownsville as Seen from the Air," photo caption, *BH*, Jun. 29, 1930, 48.

94-95   *"barren ... buildings," homes, grassy lawns, flowers, palm trees*: Cipriano A. Cárdenas, "Brownsville and *The Herald* in the 1940s," *Studies in Rio Grande Valley History*, Milo Kearney, Anthony Knopp, and Antonio Zavaleta, ed., UTRGV (2005), 217.

95   *TDP's first work in the fields, seventy-five cents per day*: "Buntin Used to Work in Valley Bean Fields," *BH*, Nov. 27, 1953, 1.

95   *"excessively fatigued," "play out in ten minutes"*: Buntin Case 1, Dr. JB test., 1:66.

95   *Palmers lived at the Nel-Roy*: "Friend Recalls Palmer Couple," *VMS*, Nov. 27, 1953, 1.

96   *"new, exclusive, ultra-modern," "overstuffed," "tasteful selection"*: advertisement, *BH*, Oct. 20, 1929, 25; advertisement, *BH*, Nov. 25, 1930, 23.

96   *Nel-Roy monthly rentals, $25-$65*: U.S. Bureau of the Census, Fifteenth
      Census of the U.S.: 1930—Population Schedule, Brownsville, Cameron
      Co., Tex., Enum. Dist. No. 31-6, Sheet No. 4B (enumerated Apr. 4,
      1930), lines 58-90; *neighbors from all over, well-paying jobs*: ibid.; *TDP's
      wages*: ibid.

96   *sold their expensive clothes to have money to eat*: "Friend Recalls Palmer
      Couple," *VMS*, Nov. 27, 1953, 1.

96   *"nervous troubles"*: Buntin Case 1, Dr. TH test., 1:79, 1:88.

96   *"natural," i.e., illegitimate children in Tex. in the 1930s and 1940s*: Landis
      and Landis, *Building a Successful Marriage*, 250.

96   *premarital blood tests, reason*: Louis G. Iasilli, "The Pre-Marital Blood
      Test Law," *St. John's Law Review* 13, no. 1 (Nov. 1938): 199.

97   *congenital syphilis "fairly common"*: U.S. Dept. of Labor, Children's
      Bureau, *Infant Care*, Pub. No. 8 (Washington, D.C.: Government Print-
      ing Office, 1933), 125.

97   *blood test from the man only in Tex.*: Iasilli, "The Pre-Marital Blood Test
      Law," 199, n. 5.

97   *federal Comstock Act of 1873*: Landis and Landis, *Building a Successful
      Marriage*, 383.

97   *"chaste wedlock"*: Pope Pius XI, "Casti Connubii," *Encyclical of Pope Pius
      XI on Christian Marriage* (Dec. 31, 1930), paras. 29, 72.

97   *"deliberately frustrate," "natural power to generate life," "offense against the
      law of God"*: ibid., para. 56; *"intrinsically evil"*: ibid., para. 61.

97   *"natural," "normal relations," "continence … menstrual cycle"*: Thurston S.
      Welton, M.D., *The Modern Method of Birth Control* (New York: Walter
      J. Black, 1935, 1938), 6-7.

97   *birth of EAP*: EAP, Standard Certificate of Birth, No. 67557, Sept. 3,
      1932, 1357, Ancestry.com, Tex., U.S., Birth Index, 1903-1997 (hereafter
      "Tex. Birth Index"), database online.

98   *MDM's death*: MDM, Certificate of Death, File No. 2141, Jan. 24, 1933,
      Ancestry.com, Ky. Death Records, 1852-1953, database online.

98   *radio broadcasts, "come home"*: "McCuddy-Buntin Tale," *NDL*, Dec. 4,
      1953, 2.

98   *"a daughter, Miss … McCuddy" as survivor*: "Mrs. M'Cuddy Dies at
      Russellville," *CLC*, Jan. 21, 1933, 1.

98   *"ardent" pilot, rumor of TDP flying BMP over MDM's funeral*: "McCud-
      dy-Buntin Tale," *NDL*, Dec. 4, 1953, 2.

98   *birth of JP*: JP, Jan. 23, 1934, 1448, Ancestry.com, Tex. Birth Index, data-
      base online.

98   *August 1933 hurricane*: "Valley Gets Worst Blow Since Hurricane of
      1886," *BH*, Aug. 6, 1933, early edition, 1; *spoiled fruit was buried*: 'Valley's
      $6,000,000 Citrus Crop Movement to Get Under Way Sept. 1," *BH*,
      Aug. 27, 1933, final edition, 5.

98   *September 1933 hurricane*: "Valley Will Get Millions to Rebuild in Storm
      Area," *BH*, Sept 8, 1933, 1.

98   *anti-typhoid fever vaccines, mosquito control*: "Nearly 25,000 Given
      Serum," *BH*, Sept.13, 1933, 16.

98   *birth of DPP*: DPP, Feb. 9, 1936, 1390, Ancestry.com, Tex. Birth Index,
      database online.

99   *WRM's death*: U.S. Dept. of the Navy, Naval Historic Center, "U.S.
      Navy Airplane type SBU-1," #9792, *Casualties: U.S. Navy and Marine
      Corps Personnel Killed and Injured in Selected Accidents and Other
      Incidents Not Directly the Result of Enemy Action*, Fold3.com, database
      online.

99   *WRM's and pilot's bodies never found, only WRM's notebook*: "Navy
      Resumes Search for Air Crash Victims," *HSB*, May 2, 1936, main edi-
      tion, 1.

99   *son a little over three weeks old*: Robert F. McCuddy, Ancestry.com,
      Social Security Death Index, database online.

99   *RFM gave up hope after WRM died*: "McCuddy-Buntin Tale," *NDL*,
      Dec. 4, 1953, 2.

99   *births of the last three children*: MRP, Jun. 23, 1937, 1441, Ancestry.com,
      Tex. Birth Index, database online; WDP, Sept. 3, 1938, 1509, ibid.; MEP,
      Oct. 25, 1941, 1700, ibid.

99   *recommended quantity and material of diapers and clothes protectors*:
      Maternity Center Association, *Maternity Handbook* (New York: G.P.
      Putnam's Sons, 1932), 73; *daily disinfection and washing of diapers*: ibid.,
      93-94.

99   *"artificial feeding"*: U.S. Dept. of Labor, *Infant Care*, 90.

99   *poliovirus, risk to children under five, vaccine*: Mayo
      Clinic, "1955 Polio," mayoclinic.org/diseases-conditions/
      history-disease-outbreaks-vaccine-timeline/polio.

99   *mechanic, salesman for used car lots*: "Friend Recalls Palmer Couple,"
      VMS, Nov. 27, 1953, 1.

100   *moved to 1017 W. St. Francis rental after JP was born*: U.S. Bureau of
      the Census, Sixteenth Census of the U.S.: 1940—Population Schedule,
      Brownsville, Cameron Co., Tex., Enum. Dist. No. 31-11, Sheet No. 8B
      (enumerated Apr. 15, 1940), lines 73-79 and column 17 (location on Apr.
      1, 1935).

100   *newly built*: Cameron Co. Appraisal District, cameroncad.org, 1017 W.
      St Francis St., Property Details, Improvement/Building (main area,
      porch, carport, fence, built 1935); *square footage*: ibid., Property Details,
      Improvement/Building (main area).

100   *"very courteous … excellent education," "seedy condition"*: "'Legally Dead'
      Palmer Resided Here in 1930s," *BH*, Oct. 5, 1966, 1.

100   *"always very poor"*: "Buntin Used to Work," *BH*, Nov. 27, 1953, 2.

100   *Lincoln Street apartment*: *Wilmot's Brownsville, Tex., City Directory
      1938-39* (hereafter *"Brownsville City Dir. year"*) (Brownsville: Benj. A.
      Wilmot, Pub., 1938), 259.

100   *WDP contracted polio*: "Palmers Hope to Rebury Their Past Lives," *OL*,

Nov. 27, 1953, 3; "Youth Will Go to Lions Camp at Kerrville," *OL*, Jun. 19, 1955, 20.

100   *WDP's treatment*: JS reporter's notes, Mrs. Lula George, Brownsville, Box 146, Folder 10, JS-VU.

100   *physical therapy at home*: John Seigenthaler and Gene Graham, "Buntin's Family Rejected 1st News," *Tenn.*, Nov. 29, 1953, morning edition, 4.

100   *presumption of death in Sept. 1938*: Buntin Case 1, NTC Declaration, 1:8.

100   *TCB adjudged dead, insurance amount*: ibid., Jury Verdict (Jun. 13, 1940), 2:606.

100   *"I am of the opinion … made in this case"*: ibid., Ruling on Motion for New Trial (Jul. 8, 1940), 2:656.

101   *fraudulent concealment*: ibid., NYL Pl.-in-Error Assignments of Error, Brief and Argument (filed Oct. 18, 1940), 48.

101   *"weak moral fiber"*: ibid., NTC Def.-in-Error Reply Brief and Argument, 122; *"unnecessary," "leave the comfort … McCuddy," "the proof shows … or anyone else"*: ibid., 124.

101   *the only deposition BMB sat in on*: Buntin Case 1, RFM depo., 2:318; *"strong personality," "unimpeachable moral character," "very efficient … woman"*: ibid., 2:327, 2:329, 2:326.

101   *RCC's Tenn. convictions overturned; lack of fair trial*: "Banker Gets Re-Trial," *BH*, Apr. 20, 1932, 12; *"manifest prejudice"*: *Caldwell v. State*, 48 S.W. 2d 1087, 1097 (Tenn. 1932).

101   *started anew as financier*: "Finance Head Prepares to Regain Funds," *BH*, Aug. 31, 1932, 15.

101   *WAB's death*: "W.A. Buntin, 56, Realty Man Here, Dies at Madison," *Tenn.*, Oct. 23, 1933, 1.

101   *shot younger business competitor*: "Slayer Gives Up After Hunt Fails," *KT*, Jan. 27, 1933, 1; "Proof as to Sanity of Buntin Will Be Heard," *Tenn.*, Jul. 15, 1933, 2; *WAB's and ESB's son committed suicide*: "Soldier's Death Said by Own Hand," *Tenn.*, May 4, 1943, 7.

102   *MWB and Shade Murray Jr. married at Longview*: "Murray-Buntin Bridal Party and Wedding Guests," *Tenn.*, Oct. 17, 1939, 7.

102   *BMP's Cameron Co. court reporting, legal secretary work*: "Buntin Used to Work," *BH*, Nov. 27, 1953, 2; "Friend Recalls Palmer Couple," *VMS*, Nov. 27, 1953, 1.

102   *Palmer's background stories told to friends*: "Buntin Used to Work," *BH*, Nov. 27, 1953, 1, 2.

102   *well-educated, TDP knew stocks and bonds*: ibid., 1; *"glance," "beautiful woman," "very peculiar guy," "slick chick"*: ibid., 2.

102   *1940 census entries for the Palmer family in Brownsville*: U.S. Bureau of the Census, Sixteenth Census of the U.S.: 1940, Sheet No. 8B, lines 73-79; *1017 W. St. Francis address*: *Brownsville City Dir. 1940*, 211.

103   *"My Favorite Wife" released in May 1940, premiered in Louisville, Ky.*: catalog.afi.com/Catalog/MovieDetails/5046.

103   *"My Favorite Wife" at the Capitol Theatre, "a man has one wife too many"*: "Entertainment," *BH*, Jul. 6, 1940, 7.

103   *TDP's description in his draft registration*: TDP, WWII Reg. Card, Oct.
        16, 1940, Serial No. 591, Order No. 239, side 2, Local Board No. 1, Cam-
        eron Co., Tex., Fold3.com, Selective Service Reg. Cards, World War II:
        Multiple Registrations, database online; *personal information he gave in
        the registration*: ibid., side 1.

103   *TCB's first-marriage sons' registration*: DFCB, WWII Reg. Card, Jun. 30,
        1942, Serial No. N367, Order No. V-12211, Local Board No. 5, David-
        son Co., Tenn.; TCB Jr., WWII Reg. Card, Mar. 18, 1946, Serial No.
        W229-A, Order No. 13332-A, Local Board No. 6, Davidson Co., Tenn.;
        RCCB, WWII Reg. Card, Jun. 27, 1946, Serial No. W-504-AA, Order
        No. 13609-AA, Local Board No. 6, Davidson Co., Tenn., each from
        Fold3.com, Selective Service Reg. Cards, WWII: Multiple Registrations,
        database online.

103   *W. St. Francis house foreclosure*: "Deed Records," *BH*, Mar. 29, 1941, 15
        ("J.L. Palmer, Rec'r to T.D. Palmer").

104   *TDP bought house in the West Brownsville Addition*: Cameron Co., Tex.,
        Official Records, Warranty Deed No. 4136, Deed Records, Vol. 302,
        492-493 (recorded Mar. 24, 1941); Deed of Trust, Deed of Trust Records,
        Vol. 145, 33-36 (recorded Mar. 28, 1941); *purchase date in mid-November
        1940*: "Deed Records," *BH*, Mar. 29, 1941, 15.

104   *Palmers sold the house to Otto Manske Dec. 5, 1940*: Cameron Co., Tex.,
        Official Records, Warranty Deed No. 2446, Deed Records, Vol. 302,
        307-308 (recorded Feb. 19, 1941).

104   *FCTC as executor and trustee*: Order and Judgment, In the Matter of the
        Last Will and Testament of George B. Edwards, Deceased (Jan. 6, 1930),
        Logan Co., Ky., Order Bk. Z, 26-28.

104   *statutory guardian, filed suit in Logan Co., Ky., to have rights declared*:
        McCuddy Case 1, FCTC Petition-in-Equity under Declaratory Judg-
        ment Law (dated and filed Jun. 12, 1939); *BEM's total share of GBE's
        bequest and his residuary estate was $44,100.81*: ibid., Judgment (May 21,
        1941), 4, 9; *named defendants*: ibid., Petition-in-Equity under Declar-
        atory Judgment Law; *"sued as an unknown defendant," "in fact dead"*:
        ibid., 16; *BEM "is dead … November 1938"*: ibid., Judgment, 3.

105   *RFM claimed BEM's share of specific bequest*: ibid., Amended Answer and
        Cross-Petition of R.F. McCuddy, Individually (filed Feb. 5, 1941), 1.

105   *judge rejected RFM's claim*: ibid., Judgment, 6; *also rejected RFM's claim
        to BEM's share of residuary estate*: ibid., Judgment, 7.

105   *BMP added to the house deed*: Cameron Co., Tex., Official Records,
        Warranty Deed No. 2445, Deed Records, Vol. 302, 307-308 (recorded
        Feb. 19, 1941); Warranty Deed No. 9313, Deed Records, Vol. 304, 616-617
        (recorded Jul. 25, 1941); "Court Records," *BH*, Jul. 7, 1941, 7.

105   *last child born*: MEP, Oct. 25, 1941, 1700, Ancestry.com, Tex. Birth
        Index, database online.

105   *NYL lost appeal in state court*: Buntin Case 1, Court of Appeals Opin-
        ion (filed May 24, 1941); *filed appeal with state Supreme Court*: ibid.,
        Tenn. Supreme Court, NYL Pl.-in-Error, Petition for Certiorari and

Supersedeas, Assignments of Error, Brief and Argument (filed Jun. 14, 1941).

105   *"paramour," "stronger … justifies," "lewd relations," "disgraceful liaison"*: *NYL v. NTC*, 159 S.W. 2d 81, 84 (Tenn. 1942).

105   *NYL paid NTC $59,438.40 on Mar. 10, 1942*: Buntin Case 2, NYL Original Bill (filed Nov. 5, 1953), para. IV, 3.

106   *"many friends … anxious," "on their own terms"*: "This is Tom Palmer," advertisement, Pipkin-Manske Motors, *BH*, Jul. 14, 1941, 7.

106   *"good family car"*: "We Have Told Our Salesmen," advertisement, Pipkin-Manske Motors, *BH*, Jul. 8, 1941, 7.

106   *TDP and his boss attended trade meeting*: "Valley Ford Dealers are in San Antonio," *BH*, Jan. 7, 1941, 2.

106   *Pipkin-Manske Motors photo*: "Orange Trading Sticks Featured in Brownsville," *BH*, May 1, 1941, 15.

106   *moved to Red Tough's as parts man*: "Buntin Used to Work," *BH*, Nov. 27, 1953, 2.

106   *WWII shut down auto production*: Sarah Sundin, "Make It Do—Metal Shortages in World War II," entry posted Mar. 30, 2022, sarahsundin.com/make-it-do-metal-shortages-in-world-war-ii/.

106   *Manske's interview about the war's impact on his business*: "Manske Outlines Survival Plan for Motorists," *BH*, Aug. 3, 1942, 16.

106   *"Palmer's Service Station," Tom's own auto shop*: advertisement, *BH*, Nov. 18, 1942, 9.

106   *"make your … farther," Model A Ford coupe*: "For Sale," advertisement, Palmer's Service Station, *BH*, Dec. 4, 1942, 15.

107   *NYL re-entered the Tex. market, paid $440,000*: "Insurance Firm Hikes State Funds," *BH*, Sept. 5, 1947, 6.

12.   A Different New Life

108   *"Mr. Palmer" unable to find car in Matamoros*: "Local Man Reports Auto is 'Missing'," *BH*, Jan. 9, 1944, 2.

108   *"in the case of Thomas David Palmer of Brownsville"*: "Accident Hearing Set at Matamoros," *BH*, Jun. 12, 1944, 9.

108   *TDP broke his hip*: "Buntin Used to Work," *BH*, Nov. 27, 1953, 2; *shorter left leg*: John Seigenthaler, "BUNTIN AND BETTY MCCUDDY, 6 CHILDREN FOUND IN TEXAS," *Tenn.*, Nov. 26, 1953, 4.

108   *$116.45 DUI fine*: "$100 Fines Ordered in Two DWI Cases," *BH*, Sept. 17, 1947, 1.

108   *"very fine," TDP's reputation for drinking*: JS reporter's notes, Mrs. Lula George, Box 146, Folder 10, JS-VU; *people were sympathetic*: ibid.

109   *TDP confided to friend that Palmer was not his name*: "Buntin Used to Work," *BH*, Nov. 27, 1953, 2.

109   *OCD Sr.*: "The Dancy Story," *VMS*, Jan. 12, 1971, 2.

109   *OCD Jr. law education*: "Oscar C. Dancy, Jr. Passes Bar Exam," *BH*, Jan. 15, 1930, 11; *first job*: "Oscar Dancy, Jr. Now Firm Member," *BH*, Mar. 29, 1931, 28.

109   *OCD Jr. and wife in Orange*: "Orange News," *PAN*, Nov. 13, 1936, 16.

109 *activities, work in Orange*: "O. Dancy, Jr. Commissioned Navy Officer," *OL*, Apr. 21, 1943, 1.

110 *90 million acres*: J. Morgan Varner and John S. Kush, "Remnant Old-Growth Longleaf Pine (*Pinus palustris Mill.*) Savannas and Forests of the Southeastern USA: Status and Threats," *Natural Areas Journal* 24(2) (2004): 141.

110 *400 billion board feet*: Thomas C. Croker Jr., "Longleaf, The Longleaf Pine Story," *Journal of Forest History* 23(1) (1979): 34.

110 *Lutcher and Moore's 1877 Crescent and Star Mill, capacity of 100,000 board feet per day*: Gus LaFosse, "Timber! The history of the Lutcher Moore Lumber Company, 1877," *Rec.*, Apr. 13, 2011, 1B-2B, therecordlive.com/story/2011/04/13/news/timber-lutcher-moore-lumber-company-1877/8828.html.

110 *13,000 acres of forest left*: Varner and Kush, "Remnant Old-Growth Longleaf Pine," 143.

110 *"cut out and get out" period of four decades*: Dr. Charles Stagg, "The Long View of Landscape Changes," *1940: Last Year Home, Stories of the Heritage Families of Camp Polk and Peason Ridge*, Stacy Basham Wagner and Leslie Barras, ed. (Leesville, La.: U.S. Army, Joint Readiness Training Center and Fork Polk [now Fort Johnson] and Heritage Family Association, 2014), Pt. 1, 20.

110 *Mrs. Lutcher bought three stained-glass windows at the 1893 World Expo in Chicago, bought more*: lambstudios.com/stained-glass-panels/; *her Presbyterian church*: "Interesting Views of Orange," *HP*, Aug. 10, 1924, 35.

110 *opalescent glass dome*: Carol M. Highsmith, photographer, "The stained-glass dome, by the acclaimed J&R Lamb Studios, inside the First Presbyterian Church in Orange, Tex., is the only opalescent glass dome in the U.S." (2014), loc.gov/item/2014630800/.

110 *Carrier hired, "special refrigerating plant … summer time"*: Bruce L. Flaniken, P.E., "First Presbyterian Church Orange, Tex. Air Conditioned 1908-1912?? Or Earlier??," *The Hot Air Recorder*, American Society of Heating, Refrigerating and Air-Conditioning Engineers, Houston Chapter (Apr. 2016), 2, 6; *increased summer attendance "fifty or sixty percent"*: ibid., 11.

110 *"wonderful," "dead," "many Buicks as Fords," on to Galveston*: First Presbyterian Church of Orange, Tex., postcard signed Apr. 12, 1920, Univ. of North Tex. Libraries, The Portal to Tex. History, crediting the Heritage House Museum, https://texashistory.unt.edu/ark:/67531/metapth36689/.

110 *Martin Dies Jr. bio*: "Ex-Rep. Martin Dies, 71, is Dead; Led Un-American Activities Unit," *NYT*, Nov. 15, 1972, 1.

111 *with Garner and Rayburn's help "received federal contracts … submarine chasers"*: Hicks and Co., "Navy Park Historic District [Tex.]," National Register of Historic Places Nomination Form (Washington, D.C.: U.S. Dept. of the Interior, National Park Service, 1999), Section 8: 22; *later expanded federal contracts*: ibid.; *WWII population boom*: ibid.; *federal*

construction of Navy Park and Riverside: ibid., 8:24; *Tilley School constructed circa 1942-1944*: ibid.

111   *35,000 post-war population in 1947*: *Worley's Orange (Orange Co., Tex.) City Directory 1948* (hereafter "*Orange City Dir. year*") (Dallas: John F. Worley Dir. Co., 1948), 12.

111   *"nice well built … large porch"*: "For Sale," *BH*, Mar. 3, 1947, 7.

111   *Palmers in Brownsville until summer 1948*: *Brownsville City Dir. 1948*, 256.

111   *sold the W. St. Francis house in July 1948*: Cameron Co., Tex., Official Records, Warranty Deed #13050, Vol. 447, 185-187 (recorded Jul. 28, 1948).

111   *DPP's school accomplishments and activities*: "191 Students on Honor Roll," *BH*, Mar. 12, 1942, 3; "JH Honor Roll Students Listed," *BH*, Oct. 24, 1947, 4; "Tickets on Sale for 'Fite Nite' Friday," *BH*, Apr. 28, 1947, 5.

111   *Bettie Dancy, EAP, JP farewell party, fishing trip*: Marilyn Littlefield, "Teen Topics," *BH*, Aug. 1, 1948, 16.

111   *Dancys, JP, EAP left for Orange*: ibid.; "Three Girls Given Party," *BH*, Jul. 25, 1948, 13.

112   *Riverside outside Orange city limits, not built to code, flooded*: Mike Louviere, "Riverside, it was what it was," *OL*, Jul. 22, 2012, orange-leader.com/2012/07/22/and-now-you-know-riverside-it-was-what-it-was/; "Riverside was a City in a City," *OL*, Jun. 22, 2018, orangeleader.com/2018/06/22/and-now-you-know-riverside-was-a-city-in-a-city/.

112   *Navy Park materials of home construction*: Hicks and Co., "Navy Park Historic District [Tex.]," Section 8:24.

112   *1001 Orange Ave. deed and lien*: Orange Co., Tex., Official Records, Vol. 108, 92-93 (recorded Aug. 16, 1948) and Vol. 109, 141-142 (recording date not given), respectively.

113   *BMP secured Orange Co. courthouse court reporting position*: Gene Graham, "Texas Neighbors Rally to Side of Tom and Betty," *Tenn.*, Nov.27, 1953, 21; *TDP's jobs in Orange 1948-1952*: ibid.; *jobs in Beaumont*: ibid.; *had a run … children"*: ibid.

113   *neighbor child felt bad for the Palmer children, odd that they did not have extended family*: Sandra Sample Cain interview with the author (Mar. 13, 2015).

114   *"day and night" work, BMP nominated for, turned down, businesswomen's club*: Graham, "Texas Neighbors Rally," *Tenn.*, Nov. 27, 1953, 21; *TDP a "hustler and a good salesman"*: ibid.

114   *1950 census*: U.S. Bureau of the Census, Seventeenth Census of the U.S.: 1950— Population Schedule, Orange, Orange Co., Tex., Enum. Dist. No. 41-11, Sheet No. 43 (enumerated Apr. 14, 1950), lines 2-9.

114   *EAP, JP, DPP yearbook photos*: Stark High School, *The Orange Peel 1949*; *EAP school activities, yearbook photos*: ibid. *1950*, 33, 124, 141; *JP school activities, yearbook photos*: ibid., 47; *EAP, JP photo for the Horizon Club*: ibid., 148; *DPP 1950 yearbook photo*: ibid., 83.

114   *DPP in Spanish Club*: ibid. *1952*, 155, Ancestry.com.

114   *MRP 1950 yearbook photo*: ibid. *1950*, 98.

114   *WDP yearbook photos*: ibid. *1955*, 205 (seventh grade); ibid. *1956*, unpaginated (eighth grade); ibid. *1957*, unpaginated (ninth grade); ibid. *1959* (eleventh grade), 64, each from Ancestry.com.

114   *WDP in Chapel Club, "develop … worshipful programs"*: ibid. *1956*, unpaginated; *Rod and Reel Club, library assistant*: ibid. *1957*, unpaginated, each from Ancestry.com.

114   *BMP took court reporting position in Jefferson Co. courthouse*: "Socialite Missing 22 Years is Found," *KN*, Nov. 27, 1953, 10.

115   *"good money"*: ibid.; *"probably more than he did"*: ibid.; *night work "way up into the early morning hours"*: ibid.

115   *Palmer family still at 1001 Orange Ave., Tom as salesman*: *Orange City Dir. 1953*, 214.

115   *TDP moved from Montgomery Ward to Lack's*: ibid. *1954*, 292.

115   *BMP's photo was taken in the courthouse*: John Seigenthaler, "Mrs. Buntin to Visit Son," *Tenn.*, Nov. 27, 1953, 1.

115   *scare at work when encountering first cousin GED*: "Cousin Fails to Recognize Betty," *NDL*, Dec. 4, 1953, 1.

115   *GED with a Beaumont law firm*: *Beaumont (Jefferson Co., Tex.) City Directory 1950* (Dallas: Morrison & Fourmy Directory Co., 1950), 194.

115   *did not recognize his cousin BEM*: "Cousin Fails to Recognize Betty," *NDL*, Dec. 4, 1953, 1.

13.   Unraveling

117   *BF's tip, 1952, "I've got something on Buntin"*: JS reporter's notes, Box 146, Folder 10, JS-VU; "Slim Tip Set Off Fruitful Search for Missing Man," *BE*, Nov. 27, 1953, 1.

117   *lawyer told lawyer … told Chatfield*: "First Real Clues to Pair Were Found Only in Past Six Months," *LMA*, Nov. 28, 1953, 10.

117   *cost of search exceeded $100,000 by 1953*: "Finding of Pair Tough Job, Reportorial Achievement," *Tenn.*, Nov. 26, 1953, 1.

117   *Marine saw TCB in Colón several times*: Buntin Case 1, NYL Motion for New Trial, (Jun. 25, 1940), Ex. A, ZBL aff. (Jun. 17, 1940), Transcript, 2:619-620.

118   *JJM spotted TCB in the Bolivar Hotel in Lima, TCB left quickly*: ibid., JJM test. (Jun. 11, 1940), 2:460-461.

118   *NYL paid JJM to look for TCB in South America*: ibid., 2:468; *$500*: "Defense Contends Buntin Seen in Peru After Disappearing Here," *Tenn.*, Jun. 13, 1940, 13.

118   *ZBL character assassination*: Buntin Case 1, Hearing on NYL's Motion for New Trial (Jul. 6, 1940), JOB and RWB test., 2:630 and 2:645-647, respectively.

118   *JJM's motive challenged*: ibid., JJM test., 2:488.

118   *three Peruvian workers deposed*: ibid., depos. of Nicasio Chavez, Samuel Diaz, Aurelio Chauco (each taken Jan. 19, 1940), submitted into evidence (Jun. 11, 1940), 2:499, 2:500, 2:501.

118   *not a "higher type" of witness*: *NYL v. NTC*, 159 S.W. 2d 81, 85, 87 (Tenn. 1942).

118   *Brownsville international airport in the 1930s and 1940s*: ACCA, *Aircraft Year Book, 1930* (New York: ACCA, 1929), 218; U.S. Dept. of Commerce, Bureau of Air Commerce, Airway Bulletin No. 2, *Descriptions of Airports and Landing Fields in the U.S.* (Washington, D.C.: Government Printing Office, 1938), 187.

118   *TDP flew to Mexico City*: "Plane Passengers," *BH*, Mar. 18, 1934, 2.

118   *TDP flight from Mexico to Brownsville*: Thomas D. Palmer, passenger, "Entry Declaration of Aircraft Commander," Tampico, Mexico, to Brownsville, Tex. (airport of entry), Pan Am Aircraft MC59410 (U.S. Treasury Dept., Customs Form 7507, Apr. 30, 1946), line 14, Ancestry.com, U.S., Border Crossings from Mexico to U.S., 1895-1964, database online.

118   *flights from Brownsville to Mexico City and Guatemala City*: ACCA, *Aircraft Year Book 1930*, 516.

119   *John Sebastian Glenn, forensic accountant started the tip*: John Fetterman, "Insurance Prober Located Buntin," *Tenn.*, Nov. 28, 1953, 3.

119   *devout Catholic suffered a stroke, lived for a week*: "John Glenn Rites to be Saturday," *NB*, Jul. 3, 1952, 13; "Glenn," obituary, *Tenn.*, Jul. 5, 1952, 13.

119   *"Wall Street of the South"*: Blythe Semmer, "Nashville Financial Historic District [Tenn.]," National Register of Historic Places Nomination Form (Washington, D.C.: U.S. Dept. of the Interior, National Park Service, 2002), Sections 7:12, 8:11.

119   *"almost nothing to go on but hope"*: "Slim Tip Set Off Fruitful Search," *BE*, Nov. 27, 1953, 1.

119   *BF died that fall of a heart attack*: "William Penn Finney Dies in Washington," *Tenn.*, Nov. 18, 1952, 23.

119   *Walter Hall, Dickinson, Tex., dead-end stories about TCB*: JS reporter's notes, Box 146, Folder 10, JS-VU.

120   *Augustine Celeya, Brownsville, Tex.*: ibid.; *southeast Tex. contacts, Lutcher Stark, "money man," and J. Cullen Browning*: ibid.

120   *"tallied" with TDP's description*: "Buntin Used to Work," *BH*, Nov. 27, 1953, 2.

120   *Murray and Beyea found important clue in Brownsville*: JS reporter's notes, Box 146, Folder 10, JS-VU; *insurance co. procedures for documenting a found person*: ibid.

120   *Murray spotted man with tell-tale ear around May 3*: "'Dead' for 22 Years," *Life*, Dec. 7, 1953, 44.

120   *Palmers admitted their identity at their house around June 3*: "First Real Clues to Pair," *LMA*, Nov. 28, 1953,10; *NYL's discovery on June 3*: Buntin Case 2, NYL Original Bill, para. VII, 4.

120   *Alexander called in, recognized TCB on June 12*: "Inspector Tells of Long Hunt for Buntin," *CLC*, Nov. 27, 1953, 1; *"verified without question"on June 12*: Buntin Case 2, NYL Original Bill, para. VII, 4.

121   *JCE met with LMP, LBH on Jun. 22, 1953*: Buntin Case 2, Circuit Court on remand, NYL Response (filed Aug. 27, 1957), 16 (Transcript, 27).

121   *LMP now president of bank*: "Phillips Named Head of Broadway Bank," *Tenn.*, Jan. 14, 1948, 6.

121   *BMB and LMP married*: "Marriage Licenses," *Tenn.*, Dec. 30, 1943, 16; "Society, Mrs. Betty Buntin Weds Major Louie M. Phillips," *Tenn.*, Jan. 2, 1944, 25.

121   "*further examination … old wounds,*" "*no good,*" "*best to leave … further discussion*": Buntin Case 2, NYL Response, Ex. A, LBH letter to JCE (Jul. 10, 1953), Transcript, 33.

121   *BMP denied photos were of TCB*: ibid.; see also, Seigenthaler and Graham, "Buntin's Family Rejected 1st News," *Tenn.*, Nov. 29, 1953, 1.

121   *NYL secured injunction Nov. 5, 1953*: "BUNTIN ALIVE, SUIT DECLARES," *Tenn.*, Nov. 6, 1953, morning edition, 1.

121   "*most extraordinary,*" "*unprecedented*": "Buntin Identity Held Admitted," *Tenn.*, Nov. 8, 1953, morning edition, 14-A.

122   "*integrity and honesty,*" "*excellent character*": Federal Bureau of Investigation, Report of Douglass E. Wendel, Miami Field Office, File No. MM 161-17, "John Lawrence Seigenthaler, Jr." (Dec. 27, 1960), 1, vault.fbi.gov/john-siegenthaler [sic]/john-siegenthaler [sic]-part-01-of-01/view/.

122   *JS's initial beat*: see, e.g., John Seigenthaler, "Bandit Gets $225 in Store Holdup," *Tenn.*, May 13, 1950, 1; "Convict Killed in Prison Fight," *Tenn.*, Oct. 4, 1951, 1; "GI Bandit Nabbed After Gun Battle," *Tenn.*, Nov. 16, 1951, 1.

122   *chancellor wanted to see JS in late summer 1953*: JS interview with the author (May 25, 2011).

123   *Shriver could not recall "much" of bill of complaint*: "BUNTIN ALIVE," *Tenn.*, Nov. 6, 1953, morning edition, 15.

123   "*unglued*": JS interview (May 25, 2011).

123   *NYL's general counsel confirmed*: "Buntin Identity Held Admitted," *Tenn.*, Nov. 8, 1953, morning edition, 1; "*we have talked to Mr. Buntin,*" "*knows the petition has been filed*": ibid., 1, 14-A; "*he might vanish again*": ibid., 14-A.

123   *not "very well acquainted with the suit," TCB "might be in Texas"*: ibid., 15.

123   *TCB in pirate costume photo and formal photo*: ibid., 1, 15.

123   "*I'm just like … shown*": "Father of Legally Dead Daughter Overjoyed Today," *BA*, Nov. 27, 1953, 1.

123   *ECB, MBM knew only what they read in the newspaper*: "BUNTIN ALIVE," *Tenn.*, Nov. 6, 1953, morning edition, 15; *RCC thought "very unlikely … found," "too well known"*: ibid.

123   "*liveliest … papers*": "Exit Evans, Enter Evans," *Time*, Jul. 18, 1955, The Press Section.

124   *SE background*: Hugh Davis Graham, "Desegregation in Nashville; The Dynamics of Compliance," *Tenn. Historical Quarterly* 25, no. 2 (Summer 1966): 140.

124   "*Palmer aka Buntin*": JS interview (May 25, 2011); "*on high,*" "*firing offense*": ibid.

124   "*track the trackers*": John Seigenthaler, "It's Buntin—Long Trail Ends," *Tenn.*, Nov. 27, 1953, 21.

124   *BK bio, "can of oil"*: "Bill Kittrell Dies at Home in Dallas," 1966, Tex. Press Clipping Bureau, texaspressclipping.com/about_us/.

124   *"Stetson, string ties, and boots"*: JS interview (May 25, 2011).

124   *one of the best storytellers she ever knew*: Transcript, Claudia "Lady Bird" Johnson Oral History Interview XVIII (1980) by Michael L. Gillette, 56, LBJL-UTA.

124   *Spiral Sight Saver Stenographer's Note Book, Coil Craft No. 682 Stenographer Note Book*: Box 146, Folders 9 and 10, JS-VU.

125   *JS found, interviewed NYL investigators*: Seigenthaler, "It's Buntin," Tenn., Nov. 27, 1953, 21.

125   *Tex. contacts*: JS reporter's notes, Box 146, Folder 10, JS-VU.

125   *"hush, hush"*: JS interview (May 25, 2011).

125   *map on the wall*: ibid.; *1953 Mobilgas map of the southwestern U.S. taped to wall*: map, Box 146, Folder 11, JS-VU.

125   *money spent worried Harwell, not SE*: JS interview (May 25, 2011).

126   *went to Harlingen, "curmudgeon," "wetbacks"*: ibid.; *planned to return to Nashville, disappointed in himself*: ibid.; *"I have one hint, look for a citrus city"*: ibid.

126   *Fetterman had circled places on the map*: map, Box 146, Folder 11, JS-VU.

126   *"Orange, there's an Orange, Texas!"*: JS interview (May 25, 2011).

126   *Dolph maps*: Beaumont, Port Arthur, and Orange maps, Box 146, Folder 11, JS-VU.

126   *used Hugh Wellington Vester's name, friend from high school*: JS interview (May 25, 2011); *"Vester" ran out of the building to a theater where BK picked him up*: ibid.

128   *Beaumont contacts:* JS reporter's notes, Box 146, Folder 10, JS-VU.

128   *"beat"*: JS interview (May 25, 2011); *JH "ticked off," upcoming wedding anniversary*: ibid.; *JH continued to complain at dinner*: ibid.

128   *"every man ... identification," "face for one thing," "clothing ... tie is labeled," "his shoes have numbers," "laundry marks on his clothes"*: Buntin Case 1, PAJ test., 2:308-309.

128   *gave JH "hell," "it's him!"*: JS interview (May 25, 2011).

129   *followed the man to Orange and to a house on Orange Avenue*: ibid.; *JH was "all in"*: ibid.

129   *wore "Texas blue dungarees" to church, drove around all day*: Seigenthaler, "It's Buntin," Nov. 27, 1953, 21.

129   *the stakeout, "down on their luck," walked past them, children walked out the front*: JS interview (May 25, 2011).

129   *Orange directory listing, "TUxedo 8-3616"*: Southwestern Bell Telephone Co., Orange, Tex., Telephone Directory (1952), 35, BCAH-UTA.

130   *"clearly in love," holding hands*: JS interview (May 25, 2011); *"leave early or you'll be locked in," everyone stayed*: ibid.

14.   Exposed

131   *"Dark period," Judicial opinions"*: Albert H. Morehead and Geoffrey Mott-Smith, ed., *Albert H. Morehead's Crossword Puzzles, Series 1* (New

York: William Morrow & Co., 1952), Puzzle No. 44 (The Puzzles and The Answers).

132   *real reindeer*: "Santa Claus and His Reindeer to be in Orange Saturday," *OL*, Nov. 24, 1953, 1.

132   *JPH's first child*: William David Herring, Oct. 28, 1953, 1767, Ancestry. com, Tex. Birth Index, database online.

133   *"Betty Palmer, Court Reporter"*: Seigenthaler and Graham, "Buntin's Family Rejected 1st News," *Tenn.*, Nov. 29, 1953, 4-A.

133   *JS encountered BMP, "of course you're right," "someone here … in Nashville"*: JS interview (May 25, 2011); *went to coffeehouse, JS couldn't find JH, TDP asked JS to drive them home*: ibid.; *car ride back to Orange*: ibid.; *no questions from TDP regarding Nashville*: ibid.

133   *JS thought BMP interviewed him*: JS interview (May 25, 2011).

133   *BMP asked JS if RFM, WRM were alive, not MDM*: "Socialite and Secretary, Missing 22 Years, Found," *CJ*, Nov. 27, 1953, 22.

133   *kind to each other, deeply affectionate*: John Seigenthaler, "Mrs. Buntin to Visit Son," *Tenn.*, Nov. 27, 1953, 20.

133   *the obvious question, JS thought BEM was pregnant*: JS interview (May 25, 2011); JS reporter's notes, Box 146, Folder 9, JS-VU.

133   *"We were in love … what we did"*: Seigenthaler, "BUNTIN AND BETTY MCCUDDY," *Tenn.*, Nov. 26, 1953, 4.

133   *"we are two people … change our lives"*: "Socialite and Secretary," *CJ*, Nov. 27, 1953, 22.

134   *"We won't come out"*: JS interview (May 25, 2011).

134   *offered compensation*: *The Tennessean* form, Box 146, Folder 11, JS-VU.

135   *they refused*: "Texas: Visitors in Limbo," *Time*, Dec. 7, 1953, https://time. com/archive/6825760/texas-visitors-in-limbo/.

135   *concerned for children, pregnant daughter EAP*: Seigenthaler, "BUNTIN AND BETTY MCCUDDY," *Tenn.*, Nov. 26, 1953, 4.

135   *late into the night*: Seigenthaler, "Mrs. Buntin to Visit Son," *Tenn.*, Nov. 27, 1953, 1.

135   *SE called AP about "blockbuster" story, then called NYL's president on Thanksgiving*: JS interview (May 25, 2011); *PAJ "scared out of his wits," learned of reporter's trail from JS's mother*: ibid.

135   *TDP in his robe*: "Couple Declared Dead Found Married in Texas," *BDN*, Nov. 27, 1953, 2.

135   *"official confirmation," highway patrolman felt intrusive*: "'Legally Dead' Pair, Missing for 22 Years, Located in Orange," *OL*, Nov. 26, 1953, 1; *"What will this do to us in Orange?"*: ibid.

137   *"sympathetic hearts," "Orangeites"*: "City's Heart Goes Out to Palmer Family," *OL*, Nov. 26, 1953, 1.

137   *"boosted" his admiration, "more than ever"*: "Physician Says Uproar Was Not Cause of Daughter Losing Baby," *CST*, Nov. 29, 1953, 1; "Palmers Rally and Decide to Continue Present Life," *BA*, Nov. 29, 1953, 1.

137   *JPH had no comment*: "Couple's Other Daughter Quiet," *SR*, Nov. 29, 1953, 26.

137   *"silent and miserable"*: "Couple Plans to Continue Life as if it Never Had Been Interrupted," *PCDN*, Nov. 27, 1953, 1; *"I've never seen … before," drew smiles*: ibid.

137   *"Buntin," "no"*: "Couple Missing 22 Years Lived in Brownsville," *VMS*, Nov. 27, 1953, 1.

137   *"socialite"*: "Missing Socialite, Secretary Found as Man and Wife After 22 Years," *Miss.*, Nov. 27, 1953, 1; *"couple declared dead," "married in Texas"*: "Couple Declared Dead Found Married in Texas," *BDN*, Nov. 27, 1953, 2.

137   *"runaways," "playboy," "pretty secretary"*: "Runaways Have Difficult Story to Tell Children," *Age*, Nov. 28, 1953, 5.

137   *"legally dead but living"*: "Legally Dead, but Living," *SH*, Jul. 4, 1954, 2.

137   *Spanish-language coverage*: see, e.g., "Aparecieron Despues 22 Años, Un Financiero y Su Bella Secretaria," *Sol*, Dec. 4, 1953, 1.

137   *"lived 22 years in secrecy"*: "'Legally Dead' Couple Reveal How They Vanished 22 Years Ago," *Province*, Nov. 27, 1953, 3; *"love idyll," "old secret"*: "Grandchild's Death Darkens Tom's, Betty's Love Idyll," *ER*, Nov. 28, 1953, 2.

137   *"eloped"*: "Runaway Pair Raise Complex Legal Problems," *LAT*, Nov. 28, 1953, 2; "woman back from 'the dead'": *"Woman Back from 'The Dead',"* *Mercury*, Dec. 5, 1953, 5.

139   *"dead" man, "grand uncle," "in the kitty," "be able … be happy"*: "Came Back from 'Dead' to Claim Fortune," *ST*, Dec. 5, 1954, 17.

139   *photos of four oldest Palmer children*: "4 of 6 'Palmer' Children," photo caption, *Tenn.*, Nov. 27, 1953, 1.

139   *Thanksgiving weekend television coverage*: "NBC Television Cameraman Gets Pictures Here to Use in Missing Couple Story," *BE*, Nov. 27, 1953, 1.

139   *"had … their inning," "weather … except our life … will maintain"*: "Couple Plans to Continue Life," *PCDN*, Nov. 27, 1953, 1.

139   *"no," "pleasantly," "was the talk … give offense," insight into TDP*: Seigenthaler, "Mrs. Buntin to Visit Son," *Tenn.*, Nov. 27, 1953, 20.

139   *refused to answer questions about marriage*: "Socialite and Secretary," *CJ*, Nov. 27, 1953, 22; *NYL's suit claimed the Palmers were married*: Buntin Case 2, NYL Original Bill, 4.

139   *probable common law marriage*: see, e.g., Eugene Dietz, "Insurance Firm Wants $31,000 Left," *Tenn.*, Nov. 27, 1958, 20.

139   "'Dead' for 22 Years," *Life*, Dec. 7, 1953, 44.

139   *"dark, quiet girl"*: "Texas: Visitors in Limbo," *Time*, Dec. 7, 1953, https://time.com/archive/6825760/texas-visitors-in-limbo/.

140   *"tall … young man," "moods … exhilaration," "moods … depression"; "seemed to be … lighted skyrocket"*: ibid.

140   *"playboy"*: "Find Playboy who Vanished with Gal in '31," *NYDN*, Nov. 27, 1953, 3; "Father of Legally Dead Daughter Overjoyed Today," *BA*, Nov. 27, 1953, 1.

140   *"heiress"*: "Palmers Hope to Rebury," *OL*, Nov. 27, 1953, 1.

140   *"true love," "life of pampering … two feet"*: R.C. Snoddy, letter to the

editor, "Reader Opinions on 'Buntin Story' are Pro and Con," *Tenn.*, Dec. 6, 1953, 24; *capable and upright*: "AJL," letter to the editor, ibid.; *washing all … drain*: "Mrs. J." letter to the editor, ibid.

140   *neighbors and friends rallied*: "Quiet Orange Couple Want to Think Things Out Before Talking," *BE*, Nov. 27, 1953, 1.

140   *supportive calls, telephone taken off the hook*: "Mr. and Mrs. Palmer," *VMS*, Nov. 28, 1953, 1.

140   *"What will people think?"*: "Couple Plans to Continue Life," *PCDN*, Nov. 27, 1953, 2; *"put on … as usual"*: ibid.

140   *"highly respected citizens," "outstanding"*: Graham, "Texas Neighbors Rally," *Tenn.*, Nov. 27, 1953, 1.

140   *"many," no one critical*: "Couple Plans to Continue Life," *PCDN*, Nov. 27, 1953, 2.

141   *mayor vouched for BMP*: "City's Heart Goes Out," *OL*, Nov. 26, 1953, 1, 5.

141   *"woman of fine integrity," "very efficient reporter"*: Seigenthaler, "Mrs. Buntin to Visit Son," *Tenn.*, Nov. 27, 1953, 20.

141   *GED astonished*: "Cousin Fails to Recognize Betty," *NDL*, Dec. 4, 1953, 1.

141   *"wonderful … character," "ability and honesty"*: Seigenthaler, "Mrs. Buntin to Visit Son," *Tenn.*, Nov. 27, 1953, 20.

141   *"Texas is made … to Texas?"*: "Citizen of Orange," letter to the editor, "Reader Opinions on 'Buntin Story'," *Tenn.*, Dec. 6, 1953, 24.

141   *"broken-down fortunes"*: Röbert, *Nashville and Her Trade for 1870*, 32.

141   *BMBP cannot be found for comment*: "No Comment on Buntin," *Tenn.*, Nov. 26, 1953, 4.

141   *SE called RCC, some of TCB's family supported him, Rachel Wilmot sent*: JS interview (May 25, 2011); *tall, attractive*: ibid.

141   *screen test as Scarlett O'Hara*: "Obituary, Rachel Armstrong, 1950s TV French Chef, Model, Actress," *PBP*, Feb. 5, 2001, 22.

141   *wore black in Orange, kept faced veiled*: JS reporter's notes, Box 146, Folder 10, JS-VU; *no embrace, affectionate pat*: ibid.

141   *RFM fretted*: Seigenthaler, "BUNTIN AND BETTY MCCUDDY," *Tenn.*, Nov. 26, 1953, 5.

141   *second wife sure BMP would get in touch*: "Kentuckian is Happy Daughter Found," *CJ*, Nov. 27, 1953, 22.

142   *BMP visited "Mr. Mac," "as sweet and pretty as ever"*: John Seigenthaler, "Betty Comes Home for Russellville Visit, *Tenn.*, Dec. 13, 1953, 1.

142   *"Mrs. Betty McCuddy Buntin-Palmer," "still beautiful"*: "Former Betty McCuddy Says 'Russellville Still Beautiful!'," *NDL*, Dec. 18, 1953, 1.

142   *stepmother said no travel to Nashville*: Seigenthaler, "Betty Comes Home," *Tenn.*, Dec. 13, 1953, 1.

142   *visited with JCE, "wonderful, really wonderful"*: "Former Betty McCuddy Says," *AN*, Dec. 16, 1953, 1; *"expressed a hope," "get acquainted"*: ibid.; *nephew at Duke University*: ibid.

142   *ECB asked TCB if he is her son, "yes"*: Seigenthaler, "Mrs. Buntin to Visit Son," *Tenn.*, Nov. 27, 1953, 1; *"happy," "somewhat formal," ECB to visit Tex.*: ibid.

142 *Noel Hotel reservation under "Tom Buntin," stayed with his mother*: "Tom Buntin Visits with Mother Here," *Tenn.*, Apr. 9, 1954, 1.

143 *ECB, TCB photo*: ibid., 1, 12; *"Tom Buntin"*: ibid., 12; *"Do you recognize this man?," "just … that's all," "old times"*: ibid.; *unnamed attorneys' advice*: ibid.

143 *"settle down … or before"*: letters to *The Tennessean* and JS, Box 118, Folder 3, JS-VU.

144 *"misery … 10 or more persons," "rat," "the lowest stinker," "snooper," "slanderer," "special Hell," "curse," "thoroughly … thing"*: ibid.

Part Four - After

15. Fortunes, Revisited

147 *"resume … life," "headline readers"*: Ralph Ramos, "Report from Ramos," *OL*, Nov. 29, 1953, 1.

147 *Palmers said they would change nothing*: "Couple Plans to Continue Life," *PCDN*, Nov. 27, 1953, 1.

147 *"let sleeping dogs lie"*: "Insurance Man Knew Couple in Tennessee," *FWST*, Nov. 28, 1953, 2.

147 *"flood of interest," "tidal wave … overnight"*: Ralph Ramos, "Tragedy Pulls Curtain of Privacy Around Besieged Orange Family," *OL*, Nov. 29, 1953, 6.

147 *coast to coast*: see, e.g., "Second Grandchild Born Dead Thus Adding to Misery of Texas Couple," *DM*, Nov. 28, 1953, 14; "Physician Says," *CST*, Nov. 29, 1953, 1.

147 *"very rare"*: "There's No Blame," *Tenn.*, Nov. 29, 1953, morning edition, 4-A; *cause for stillborn baby, baby's service and burial, father on his way back from Korea*: Ramos, "Tragedy Pulls Curtain of Privacy," *OL*, Nov. 29, 1953, 6.

148 *"fraudulently obtained" to mislead*: Buntin Case 2, NYL Original Bill, 5.

148 *extrinsic fraud as a reason to overturn Buntin Case 1, rejected in lower court*: ibid., Chancellor's Opinion (filed Jul. 2, 1954), 3 (Transcript to the Tenn. Supreme Court, 45).

148 *legally dead TCB could sit in courtroom*: ibid., Tenn. Supreme Court, NYL Assignments of Error, Brief and Argument (filed Jan. 19, 1955), 21.

148 *TCB, an insurance man, should not be allowed to fool an insurance company and the courts*: ibid., NYL Brief Filed on Behalf of Appellant in Answer to Brief Filed on Behalf of Appellees (filed Mar. 8, 1956), 11.

148 *intrinsic fraud*: Circuit Court, BNB Demurrer (filed Dec. 14, 1953), Transcript, 20; ibid., BNB Brief and Arguments (filed Feb. 9, 1956), Transcript, 68-69.

148 *Tenn. Supreme Court Buntin Case 2 decision*: *NYL v. NTC*, 292 S.W. 2d 749 (Tenn. 1956).

148 *"gross fraud upon the Court"*: ibid. at 752 (emphasis in original); *"after-discovered fraud"*: ibid. at 754 (emphasis in original).

148-149 *"Our Courts, this very Court," "imposed … defrauded"*: ibid. at 754 (emphasis in original).

149   *"protect the rights of those that are defrauded"*: ibid. at 755 (emphasis in original).

149   *"the great forum of conscience," "equity delights in doing justice"*: ibid. at 759 (emphasis in original).

149   *"sizeable estate"*: "Former Betty McCuddy Says," *NDL*, Dec. 18, 1953, 1.

149   *reporter contacted CFBT official during his Thanksgiving dinner*: McCuddy Case 2, LLD depo. (Nov. 19, 1957), 7; *"any interest … will trust"*: ibid.

149   *BMP claimed her inheritance rights*: ibid., CFBT Supp. Complaint for Further Relief, Based Upon Declaratory Judgment (Aug. 30, 1957), 5.

149   *"doubts … is living"*: ibid., Order (entered Apr. 25, 1957), Logan Co., Ky., Order Bk. 77, 480.

149-150   *"most pleasant family relationships exist," "trouble, annoyance and expense"*: ibid., Compromise Agreement (Aug. 22, 1957), 3.

150   *$35,000 payment, divided legal fees*: ibid., 3, 5; *Palmer children endorsed the Compromise Agreement*: ibid., Approval (Aug. 23, 1957); *approval clause*: ibid., Compromise Agreement, 6; *trustee filed for declaratory judgment, sought "advice," approval of Compromise Agreement*: ibid., CFBT Supp. Complaint; ibid., LLD depo.,10; *Entry of Appearance, terms*: ibid., Entry of Appearance (filed Sept. 2, 1957); *judge approved the Compromise Agreement*: ibid., Supp. Judgment (Nov. 30, 1957), Logan Co., Ky., Order Bk. 77, 555.

16. Evergreen Cemetery

151   *DFC family mausoleum section in Mt. Olivet Cemetery*: Rozanne E. Folk, President, Historic Mount Olivet Preservation Consortium, "Mount Olivet Cemetery [Tenn.]," National Register of Historic Places Nomination Form (Washington, D.C.: U.S. Dept. of the Interior, National Park Service, 2005), Section 7:2.

152   *"carried the burden" of the family*: Seigenthaler, "Mrs. Buntin to Visit Son," *Tenn.*, Nov. 27, 1953, 20.

152   *TCB incapable of earning a living*: McCuddy Case 1, LBH depo., 20.

152   *"neither … vicissitudes of life"*: Buntin Case 1, Court of Appeals, NTC Def.-in-Error Reply Brief and Argument, 158.

152   *"dissatisfied … character"*: ibid., Tenn. Supreme Court, NYL Pl.-in-Error Pet. for Certiorari, 60.

152   *"libertine and a degenerate"*: ibid., Court of Appeals, NYL Pl.-in-Error Reply Brief (filed May 9, 1941), 15.

152   *picked beans for seventy-five cents*: "Buntin Used to Work," *BH*, Nov. 27, 1953, 1.

152   *smart, "hustler," family man*: Seigenthaler, "Mrs. Buntin to Visit Son," *Tenn.*, Nov. 27, 1953, 20.

153   *TDP left Lack's, joined Lee and Co.*: *Orange City Dir. 1958*, 271; ibid. *1959*, 212.

153   *Palmers moved to 294 Berkshire Lane in Beaumont*: "T.D. Palmer of 'Missing' Case Dies in Hospital," *BE*, Oct. 4, 1966, 1; *TDP joined E.E.E. Hutchinson real estate firm*: ibid.; *retired in 1964*: ibid.

153   *TCB will:* Last Will and Testament of Thomas Craighead Buntin,
        Feb. 17, 1964, Case No. 31224, In the Matter of the Estate of Thomas
        Craighead Buntin, sometimes also known as Thomas David Palmer,
        Deceased, In the County Court of Jefferson Co., Tex., Probate Division;
        "presently married to and residing with": TCB will, para. I.; *six Palmer
        children as alternate beneficiaries, in equal shares*: ibid., para. IV.;*"made no
        provision," "each … station in life"*: ibid., para. V.

153   *TCB/TDP died Oct. 3, 1966, cause of death*: TDP, Certificate of Death,
        File No. 67566, Nov. 15, 1966, Ancestry.com, Tex., U.S., Death Certifi-
        cates, 1903-1982, database online.

153   *services, obituary, cancer society memorials*: "T.D. Palmer of 'Missing'
        Case Dies in Hospital," *BE*, Oct. 4, 1966, 1, 5.

154   *"declared legally dead," "socialite," "playboy"*: "Funeral is Today for Man
        Declared Long Legally Dead," *PAN*, Oct. 4, 1966, 20.

154   *"missing man" obituary in NYT*: "Thomas D. Palmer Dies at 64; 'Miss-
        ing' Man had 2 Identities," *NYT*, Oct. 5, 1966, 47.

154   *BEM/BMP died Nov. 26, 1972, cause of death*: BMP, Certificate of Death,
        File No. 85378, Nov. 29, 1972; *her will*: Last Will and Testament of Betty
        McCuddy Palmer, Jan. 10, 1969, Case No. 34179, The Estate of Betty
        McCuddy Palmer, Deceased, In the County Court of Jefferson Co.,
        Tex.; *obituary*: "Mrs. Betty M. Palmer," *BJ*, Nov. 27, 1972, 2A, THL-BT.

154   *RFM died in 1963*: "R.F. M'Cuddy, 85, Former President of Bank,
        Expires," *AN*, Feb. 6, 1963, 1.

154   *"one of … history"*: "Tennessean Praised by Top News Officials," *Tenn.*,
        Dec. 6, 1953, 8.

154   *JS won the 1953 National Headliner Award*: "Tennessean's Seigenthaler
        Receives Headliner Award," *Tenn.*, Jun. 20, 1954, 1; *"journalistic merit"*:
        headlinerawards.org.

154   *"Tom Buntin" congratulatory telegram to JS, "personal pride"*: Western
        Union Telegram, Jun. 3, 1963, Box 146, Folder 15, JS-VU.

154   *JS bio, death*: "John Seigenthaler, 1927-2014," *Tenn.*, July 12, 2014,
        1A-6A.

154   *Kensington house sold to LMP's fraternity around 1947*: *Nashville City Dir.
        1947*, 1127; "Mrs. Betty Buntin Weds Major Louie M. Phillips," *Tenn.*,
        Jan. 2, 1944, 25.

154   *SAE damaged house:* "SAE alumni cause $12K in damages at frat
        house," Lori Mitchell, Reporter, WKRN-TV, Nashville, Oct. 31,
        2011; Barry Petchesky, "This is what Happens when Old Drunk
        Alumni Trash and Poop a Vanderbilt Frat House on Homecoming
        to the Tune of $12,000," entry posted Oct. 28, 2011, deadspin.com/
        this-is-what-happens-when-old-drunk-alumni-trash-and-po-5854399/.

154   *current valuation of Kensington house*: Metropolitan Nashville and
        Davidson Co., Assessor of Property, 2500 Kensington Place, General
        Property Information, www.padctn.org.

154-155 *fate of the Palmer's "citrus city" (Orange, Tex.) house*: author's personal
        knowledge.

www.ingramcontent.com/pod-product-compliance
Lightning Source LLC
Chambersburg PA
CBHW031023160726
47991CB00005B/1851